100 most beautiful cathedrals
of the world

100 most beautiful cathedrals of the world

A journey through five continents

Foreword

Dear Reader,

Who can put names to the Christian churches scattered across five different continents, or is familiar with the treasures enshrined within them? As its title promises, this book includes photographs
and background histories of 100 most beautiful cathedrals. We should make it clear at this point,
however, that there is no specific list as such of the world's 'Top 100' masterpieces of Christian
architecture. The cathedrals which have weathered the past 1,500 years, either as perfectly intact
originals or as rebuilt or restored edifices, are all unique.

Who can say which deserves the greater tribute? The skill of those who built the Gothic cathedrals
or the artistry of the Romanesque stonemasons? Which is rated more highly: the technical perfection
evident in the mighty domes of Renaissance cathedrals or the sumptuousness of Baroque architecture? Are the enduring symbols of religious Classicism more significant than the unexpected sense of
atmosphere encountered in 20th-century churches, where contemporary architects have pushed
back the frontiers of what is technically possible and, in so doing, realized the visionary?

There is no conclusive answer to any of these questions, so our choice is inevitably somewhat subjective. We have, however, made every effort to include the most celebrated churches from every epoch. In the first instance, we were governed by the set of criteria traditionally laid down by art historians. These great churches are more than just striking examples of artistic magnificence, however; they also forcefully represent the power of the church. More important still, they have frequently come to symbolize a people's sense of national identity, for whom the church has become a spiritual stronghold of opposition against temporal rule.

It is no coincidence that Simon Bolívar chose the square in front of the cathedral in Bogotá to exhort his fellow South Americans to join the wars of liberation against the colonial powers. Nor is it mere chance that the church in Czestochowa has become a Polish national shrine, or that the weekly prayer sessions in Leipzig's church of St. Nicholas in 1989 signaled the start of a movement to overthrow the GDR government.

There is just one final point to bear in mind. We have called our book *100 Most Beautiful Cathedrals of the World*, yet the term 'cathedral', technically speaking, is reserved for a church which is the seat of a bishop. Nowadays, however, it is frequently used more loosely in conjunction with a church as an indication of its importance. In order to reflect contemporary usage, we have used the term 'cathedral' in this broader sense of the word.

The Editor

Contents

ASIA

AFRICA

AMERICA

AUSTRALIA

Left: Never yet completed: La Sagrada Familia, the masterpiece of Antoni Gaudi PAGE 32

Center: Interior view of Amiens cathedral PAGE 42

Right: The cathedral of Santa Maria del Fiore in Florence, with its world-famous cupola PAGE 16

7

The heart of catholicism

The basilica di San Pietro in **ROME** is the papal church – the dome was designed by Michelangelo

View over the mighty dome of St. Peter's to St. Peter's Square with its colonnades (main picture)

Simon was a fisherman from Bethsaida on the Sea of Galilee. He was called to Jesus, who made him leader of the disciples and named him Cephas or Peter, meaning 'rock'. After the Crucifixion, Peter began his conversion work. His travels took him across Greece to Rome where, together with Paul the Apostle, he founded the first Christian community. He was martyred during the reign of Emperor Nero. His burial took place in a simple cemetery.

The conversion of Rome's Emperor Constantine to Christianity was the signal for the first church to be built on this site. Consecrated in 326, it consisted of a flat-roofed basilica which assumed the shape of a cross with the later addition of a transept. It became a model for sacred architecture throughout large parts of early medieval Europe. As Peter's spiritual successor, a Roman Bishop was the Bishop of all Bishops and therefore Pope. After the fall of the Roman

Empire, Rome suffered several centuries of decline. The Popes ruled like secular princes over this church state, which eventually came to encompass all of central Italy. The question of the Holy Father's person did not always remain undisputed. There were often rival popes and, for a time, there was even a rival French papal seat to Rome, situated in Avignon.

In 1506, Pope Julius II, Giuliano della Rovere, a man with a keen interest in art and a strong desire to leave his mark, issued the final order for the old church of San Pietro to be destroyed and replaced with a new and bigger edifice. The architects of the new church were Donato Bramante, Michelangelo Buonarotti, and Carlo Maderno. The project envisaged a central building shaped in the form of a Greek cross with five cupo-

model for the construction of countless other sacred buildings.

It was Gian Lorenzo Bernini, however, another Baroque architect as well as painter, sculptor, and stage designer, who created the baldachin, a monumental bronze canopy above the papal altar and the high altar itself with the figures of the Four Apostles carrying the throne of St. Peter, known as the Cathedra. Even more important, the colonnades encircling St. Peter's Square, that vast open area in which the faithful gather in their tens of thousands on important days of the Christian calendar, are also Bernini's work.

Cool, majestic beauty

The square and the cathedral form the heart of the Vatican, that conglomeration of palaces, churches, administrative buildings, museums, and gardens which remain under papal jurisdiction following the dissolution of the Church State in 1870 and formation of a unified Kingdom of Italy.

The so-called Vatican Grottos, a kind of lower level of the church, were created during construction work under Bramante when the floor was raised by 11.5ft (3.5m). Here lie numerous tombs of popes, carved reliefs, and fragments of a mosaic by Giotto di Bandino. This is just one of the many works of art to be found in the cathedral, the most famous of which is Michelangelo's Pietà.

The cathedral houses a remarkable number of other sculptures. There is at least one, if not more, at almost every pillar: figures of the apostles, saints, and popes.

St. Peter's in the Vatican leaves the visitor with an impression of cool, majestic beauty. It was, however, Michelangelo the poet who wrote: "Beauty fades when it is looked upon." Who knows whether he was referring to the cathedral?

ITALY
Rome •
Tyrrhenian Sea
Mediterranean Sea

GETTING THERE:
Flights to Rome-Fiumincino international airport or by express rail service

WHEN TO GO:
Spring or late summer/fall, as mid-summer can be very hot

OPENING TIMES:
Open daily 7:00 A.M. - 7:00 P.M. (6:00 P.M. in winter)

SPECIAL INTEREST:
The Vatican Grottos containing the tombs of various popes

Michelangelo's Pietà, the cathedral's most important art treasure, stands in a side chapel (above, right)

The high altar is situated beneath the central dome on the site of St. Peter's tomb (below, right)

las, the aesthetic inspiration for this derived from the Pantheon in Rome and Santa Maria del Fiore, the cathedral church of Florence.

In the beginning was Bramante

Bramante was an artist who had found favour under the Sforzas in Milan and had also designed the plans for enlarging the Vatican palace. He only directed the building work in its early stages. After a period when work progressed in fits and starts, Michelangelo eventually took charge of the project in 1547 and it was he who designed the mighty ribbed dome, rising above the high altar and built on the site of St. Peter's grave. Archaeological excavations after 1940 showed that the remains of a skeleton found there could indeed be those of Peter the Apostle.

The enormous costs incurred by its construction were met by the whole of Catholic Christianity through the purchase of letters of indulgence. This trade drew the protest of a certain German Augustinian monk called Martin Luther. There is an extremely poignant connection between the building of triumphal St. Peter's and the victory of the Reformation in Europe.

The Baroque artist, Carlo Maderno, found himself having to re-design the plans yet again and abandon Bramante's ground-plan. He added a long nave, reintroducing the design of the Latin cross. The new St. Peter's was consecrated in 1624. It measures an impressive 692ft (211m) in length and 433ft (132m) in height to the top of its cross, making it the largest church in the world and the

Milan's mighty cathedral

Santa Maria Nascente reflects the power of the Lombards. The church dates back to the fourth century

The 1951 film *Miracolo a Milano* by director Vittorio de Sica, regarded as one of the most outstanding achievements of Italian Neo-Realism, is set in the immediate post-war period and centers around Milan cathedral. Not only is the cathedral the background to the plot but it is also a symbol of the miracle referred to in the film's title. A good fairy frees some poor homeless wretches from their confinement in a truck and takes them to heaven. Their discovery of oil in the heart of Milan had aroused the criminal greed of the landowner. This kind of brush with 'big business' was symptomatic of post-war Italy. Lombardy still remains a region of intense economic activity and wealth and Milan is, of course, the capital of Lombardy.

The first settlers in this northern part of the Po Valley were probably Celts and, by the time of the Roman Empire, the town had already acquired considerable economic power. Later on, it was attacked and laid waste by various invading forces until the Late Middle Ages, when it began to flourish again under the protection of local nobility, namely the Della Torre, Visconti, and Sforza families. It became a commercial and financial center, attracting to it many important artists, the most famous of whom was Leonardo da Vinci; it was here that he created one of his most magnificent works, his fresco painting *The Last Supper*.

Piazza del Duomo, a natural meeting place

The fresco can be seen in the refectory of the old Dominican monastery of Santa Maria delle Grazie on the Corso Magenta and not, as you might expect, in Milan's most famous sacred building, the cathedral, which is famous in its own right. It dominates the heart of the Old Town, overlooking the vast Piazza del Duomo which provides a natural meeting place for all. Pensioners, street people, and lovers, not to mention pigeons, congregate there in the evenings. Leading out of the Piazza, directly opposite the cathedral, is the Galleria Vittorio Emanuele II, reputedly the most prestigious street in Europe, bristling with exclusive restaurants and shops; it leads to the Piazza della Scala, home of the country's most famous Opera House.

Size, bustle, and art are what most visitors associate with Milan and this is equally true of the cathedral itself. The sheer size of it is extraordinary. It is 518ft (158m) in length and 217ft (66m) wide. It is estimated that it

could easily accommodate 40,000 people. Its gigantic proportions are similarly reflected by other statistics; for example, it is adorned by altogether 3000 statues and took almost 600 years to build, since many of its features, such as the majority of windows, were not installed until the nineteenth century. The last finishing touches were added relatively recently.

A narrow staircase leads down from the main façade below the level of the Piazza to the archaeological remains of the church of San Giovanni alle Fonti, which dates back to the early fourth century and is thought to be the oldest octagonal baptistery in Christendom. There is much to suggest that it represents the earliest origins of the present-day Duomo, Santa Maria Nascente.

Italy's second largest church

Its actual construction began at the behest of Gian Galeazzo Visconti, the city's ruling aristocrat at that time. The foundation stone was laid in 1385/86. His aim was to construct the biggest cathedral in the world, an aim in which he initially succeeded until the reconstruction of St. Peter's basilica in Rome got underway. Nevertheless, Milan cathedral remains the second largest church in Italy.

No one knows the name of its architect. The building is clearly Gothic in style, a fact which even those who otherwise dispute the existence of a uniquely Italian style of Gothic find difficult to deny. Its geographical and cultural proximity to other places in Europe, where this style was emerging, may well have been a contributing factor in this respect. The nave has five side aisles, while the transept has three. Altogether 52 soaring columns rise to a ribbed vault, while outside the side constructions are supported by 40 buttresses. Milan cathedral clearly bears out Gothic architecture's fascination with the vertical, as is clearly illustrated by the numerous pinnacles which decorate the gables and crown the façade.

The cathedral's imposing interior can be largely traced back to the sixteenth century, when Milan's archbishop was the significant figure of Carlo Barromeo. He commissioned his favorite architect, Pellegrino Tibaldi, to carry out extensive construction work. The archbishop was devoted to charity and demonstrated selfless commitment during a major outbreak of the plague. He was later canonized and his remains laid to rest in one of the cathedral's octagonal chapels, named in his honor.

GETTING THERE:
Direct international flights to Milan's Malpensa airport. Good rail and road links from all directions

WHEN TO GO:
Spring and late summer/fall

OPENING TIMES:
The cathedral is usually open all day

SPECIAL INTEREST:
The wall tomb of Gian Giacomo Medici in one of the side chapels and the world-famous 11th-century bible cover in the cathedral treasury

The Piazza del Duomo is a focal point for local residents and tourists until late into the night. In the center is the main portal of the cathedral (main picture)

One of the building's more unusual architectural features is that you can walk out onto the roof above the nave (below, left)

The main façade boasts a magnificent doorway crafted in bronze. The picture (below, right) shows a section of it, depicting a group of figures

The cathedral of the Doges

San Marco in **VENICE** has taken many elements from the Eastern Church

All the splendor and riches of Venice can be seen in this view of the interior of St. Mark's with its five domes, built mainly in 1043-73 (main picture)

The main façade is also reminiscent of Byzantine models with its decorated, round arches (above, right)

View of the domes from the campanile. They were completed around 1260 and give the church its distinctive appearance (below, left)

Crucifixion scene from the Pala d'Oro, the screen of the high altar. The pictures show scenes from the life of Christ. They are made from sheets of gold and silver, inlaid with pearls and precious stones (below, right)

St. Mark, the author of the Gospel that bears his name, was one of Jesus' disciples. The Last Supper took place in his parents' house in Jerusalem and the early Christians also gathered there after Christ's death. He went on missionary journeys with St. Paul the Apostle, served St. Peter as an interpreter, and founded the Christian community in Alexandria. He died around the year 67, the victim of a murderous attack.

His followers concealed his body. Eight hundred years later, it was acquired by Venetian merchants, who brought it to their home city where it was buried in a newly built church. The Basilica di San Marco became the city's principal church, St. Mark became its patron saint, and his symbol, the winged lion, appeared on its coat of arms.

Originally the place to which the people from the coast retreated as they fled from Germanic invaders, the settlement soon became a flourishing trading power with its own harbor. Organized on republican principles and with an elected leader, the Doge, at its head, the city controlled the sea-routes in the eastern Mediterranean. It had intensive contacts with Byzantium and also with Islamic countries through commerce, warfare, and culture. The distinctive way the Venetians portray themselves, particularly in art and architecture, goes back to this time. The architecture was also influenced by the city's unusual geographical situation. Venice is built on an archipelago of 118 islands, with 180 canals flowing between them, and 450 bridges. No other city landscape is quite like it.

The cathedral, together with St. Mark's Square and the Doges' Palace, forms the city center, emphasized by the campanile San Marco, the 325 ft (99 m) high bell tower. Although there has been a bell tower on that spot since the twelfth century, its present incarnation is still relatively new as the tower fell down in 1902 and had to be rebuilt. At its feet is the Loggetta, a small, marble hall designed by Jacopo Sansovino.

The legendary library

This sculptor and architect of the Venetian High Renaissance hailed from Florence. He brought with him all the artistic experience available in the city of the Medici, and he had a lasting influence on the architecture of the entire city of Venice. Numerous palaces, churches, and public buildings were constructed according to his plans, including St. Mark's library, next door to the cathedral, which is considered to be his most beautiful and important work. It stands in the Piazzetta San Marco, a bank of earth by the harbor basin separated from the larger piazza by the Campanile.

The cathedral, which was both the Doges' chapel and the state church, dominates St. Mark's Square by the sheer brilliance of its exterior. It is not the building that was commissioned by Doge Giustiniano Partecipazio in the ninth century but its successor, commissioned by Doge Domenico Contarini. Work on it began in the

middle of the eleventh century. The Basilica di San Marco is a centrally built church with a total of five cupolas, which was somewhat unusual for Catholic central Europe at that time.

Inspiration from Constantinople

The ground plan is in the shape of a Greek cross. The architecture follows the structure of Byzantine churches in other ways, too, being directly modelled on the church of the Holy Apostles in Constantinople.

The Venetians were not Greek Orthodox but Roman Catholic, however, so their choice of Byzantine models was more the result of their evident fondness for extravagance and exoticism.

They could afford it and it was what they wanted, and they were also in constant professional contact with the regions concerned. The four famous bronze horses above the middle door of the cathedral bear witness to this in their own way. They are late Hellenistic works, captured by the Venetians after the conquest of Constantinople in the fourth crusade and brought to Venice in 1204. Since then

they have been galloping after the mosaics on the cathedral façade, pagan icons confronting their later imitations.

The bronze middle doors also come from Byzantium, further spoils of war. The interior of the cathedral is shrouded in semi-darkness, yet it gleams and shines as the many mosaics are all gilded. During the Christian Middle Ages, the ancient technique of mosaic as practised in both Greco-Roman antiquity and Islam was a Byzantine speciality.

This was the inspiration for St. Mark's cathedral, which has 5071 square yards (4240 square meters) of mosaics recounting biblical stories, from the expulsion from Paradise to the miracle of Pentecost, as well as the life of St. Mark and the transfer of his bones to Venice.

In the Byzantine spirit

The golden mosaics in the church of San Vitale in **RAVENNA** are a legacy of the early Christians

Ravenna
ITALY

Mediterranean Sea

GETTING THERE:
Nearest airports Bologna and Rimini. Direct motorway links from all directions

OPENING TIMES:
Usually 9:00 A.M. – 7:00 P.M. daily. April-August, September-March 9:00 A.M. - 6:00 P.M.

SPECIAL INTEREST:
As well as the mosaics of ecclesiastical and worldly figures, there are remarkable representations of animals in the mosaics

View of the central dome with its mosaics (main picture)

San Vitale at dusk (below, left)

The Empress Theodora with her crown. At her side, two courtiers (below, right)

A "silent, thousand-year-old city of churches and ruins" was how the author Hermann Hesse described Ravenna when he arrived in the former capital of the West Roman Empire at the beginning of the twentieth century. And what is it like now? After a long period in oblivion, the 'Byzantium of the West' has once again become a bustling city, with espresso machines hissing in the glittering bars of the Via Cavour and shops selling 'alta moda' (high fashion) and fine design.

The change came about after the World War II, when new industries were established and, more significantly, tourists discovered the legendary glory of the 'eternal Ravenna' with its precious mosaics and Byzantine style buildings and, in particular, the church of San Vitale. Twelve hundred years ago, an admirer wrote that no building in Italy could stand comparison with it – a fine testimony to the days of this city's greatest glory.

Ravenna, which today lies more than four and a half miles (seven kilometers) from the sea, was once on the coast; Augustus had a military harbor for 250 ships built here. In 402, the Emperor Honorius took up residence in the city and made it the capital of the West Roman Empire until it was taken over in 476 by the invading Germanic tribes under their powerful leader Odoacer, along with the rest of the Empire. He also made Ravenna his residence but it was soon besieged and overrun by Theodoric, king of the Goths, who had been sent by Byzantium – a brutal act, which ultimately ushered in a period of great glory. As the seat of the Byzantine exarchs, especially during the reign of the emperor Justinian I (527-565), Ravenna was adorned with Christian churches and thus the art of the West blended with that of the Orient.

When Bishop Ecclesius began building San Vitale in 525, he must certainly have been inspired by the round churches he had seen on a visit to Byzantium. The money – 26,000 gold pieces – was probably provided by a rich banker, hoping by this means to secure for himself a better place in heaven. In 547, the mosaic-lined church was consecrated and placed under the protection of the martyr St. Vitalis of Milan.

Matroneum for the women

San Vitale is an octagonal central-plan building with flat-roofed galleries and a dome. The church is built entirely of bricks, which are particularly long and flat in shape. The central dome is encircled by two ambulatories, built one above the other, the upper one forming the matroneum. In ancient Christian basilicas, this was where the women took part in the service.

On entering the inner sanctum, you are overcome by a strangely solemn mood, as although the two galleries are shrouded in a mysterious twilight the central hall is absolutely flooded with light.

The very architecture seems to direct your gaze to the mosaics, which are concentrated in the depths of the

presbyterium and in the apse. Two different schools of artists can be clearly distinguished here. In the presbyterium, a group of artists following the Romano-Hellenistic tradition is recognizable, while the works in the apse reveal the influence of the Byzantine school. There is more movement in the way the figures in the mosaics in the presbyterium are portrayed whereas in the apse, with the exception of the figure of Christ, they stand in stiff, motionless ranks.

Theodora with her courtiers

In the presbyterium, the decoration on the left wall shows episodes from the life of Abraham, including the imminent sacrifice of his son Isaac which is particularly impressive because it is so true to life. The episodes from the story of Abel and Melchisedech, which can be seen on the right hand side of the presbyterium, are very similar in style. In the concha of the apse, we can see the Savior enthroned, flanked by two archangels, Bishop Ecclesius and

St. Vitalis. While this image shows the Court of Heaven, however, below it on the left we can see the Emperor Justinian with his earthly retinue and, on the right, the Empress Theodora, surrounded by ladies-in-waiting and courtiers. The striking thing about these mosaics is that only the Imperial couple and their most intimate circle are given individual features; the other figures are depicted in a stiff, stereotyped manner.

In comparison with the golden splendor of the mosaics, one or two works of art to the right of the apse pale into insignificance. There is a special charm in the fact that, next to the fragments of Bishop Ecclesius' sarcophagus, a small marble box is also preserved, a memento of the financier Argentarius, whose money made the dazzling mosaics possible in the first place.

The spirit of the Renaissance

Santa Maria del Fiore in **FLORENCE** – a new chapter in the history of architecture

Florence
ITALY

Mediterranean
Sea

GETTING THERE:
Flights to Florence international airport. Good rail and motorway links from all directions

OPENING TIMES:
Daily until further notice, except for restricted admission to tourists during services. Steps lead up into the dome which is open Mon-Fri 8:30 A.M. – 7:00 P.M., Sat until 5:40 P.M. Closed Sundays

SPECIAL INTEREST:
Beneath the dome are the remains of a 4th/5th-century, Christian church

This illustration from 1447 shows the cathedral as it would have looked at the time (margin, above)

This photograph, from the campanile, scarcely does justice to the ingenuity of the Dome's design (main picture)

The sheer size of the cathedral can be seen in the photograph on the right (center). The main façade was not added until the nineteenth century

The Last Judgment **fresco lining the dome's ceiling was begun in 1572 by Giorgio Vasari. It was completed after his death by Federico Zuccari (above, right)**

View of the interior of the dome and the choir (below, right)

Attracting around six million tourists each year, Florence ranks with Rome and Venice as one of Italy's most visited cities. As in the case of its two rivals, it is primarily the country's political and cultural heritage that draws the swarms of visitors. Florence started life as an insignificant Celtic-Roman settlement, but grew steadily in importance during the Late Middle Ages, eventually becoming a major economic power on the Italian Peninsula, second only to Venice.

Its economic strength was rooted in banking, textile manufacturing, and wood processing. One of the great merchant families, the Medici, exercised almost total control over the Republican-style local government, even managing to elevate individual members to various European thrones, particularly in France.

Florence is regarded as the true birthplace of Italian language and literature, producing writers such as Dante, Petrarch, and Boccaccio. The city became the focal point of Renaissance art, architecture, and philosophy. For six years, until 1871, Florence was also the kingdom's capital city after Italy's unification, in the wake of the Risorgimento movement.

The adjoining campanile

The name 'Florence', 'Firenze' in Italian, is derived from the Latin 'florentia', meaning 'one that blooms'. The word 'flower' ('fiore') also features in the name of the largest of Florence's magnificent churches, Santa Maria del Fiore. This is the bishop's church, the cathedral; its dome rises above the roofs of the Old Town, alongside its adjoining campanile. This bell tower is the work of Giotto di Bondone, who is credited with being an early exponent of Renaissance and perspective painting. Like most of his fellow painters, he also worked as an architect.

Santa Maria del Fiore's bell-tower is clad in different colors of marble. This technique can be seen in other northern Italian cities, for example Genoa and Siena, where the pattern is predominantly striped, whereas in Florence the decorative pattern of the marble is much more multi-colored. The cathedral itself echoes the style of this polychrome effect, even though its façade was not added until a much later date, after 1875.

Architect Arnolfo di Cambio got the initial construction work underway about five hundred years earlier in 1296. Later on, Francesco Talenti designed a huge basilica with a

transept in the style of Italian Gothic. Santa Maria del Fiore measures 525ft (160m) in length, making it the third longest Italian cathedral after St. Peter's in Rome and Siena cathedral.

The austerity and sobriety of the cathedral's interior makes a powerful impression. A set of steps leads below ground to the excavated remains of an earlier building, the Santa Reparata, built at the turn of the fourth and fifth centuries. At the heart of Santa Maria del Fiore is the tower crossing and its domed ceiling, lined with a fresco of the Last Judgment.

Vasari's ceiling fresco

Its creator was Giorgio Vasari, one of the major group of artists dominating the Florence Renaissance scene. He was both painter and sculptor. Not only did he design the Uffizi gallery, among other buildings, but he was also a writer. His book entitled *Le vite de' più eccellenti Pittori, Scultorie e Architettori*, published in 1550, is the first ever substantive study of Italian Renaissance art. It covers everyone: Cimabue and Giotto, Donatello and Michelangelo, not to mention Vasari himself, all of them Florentines and all of them involved in the creation of Santa Maria del Fiore and its associated buildings.

The same is also true of painter and architect Filippo Brunelleschi. He was the original protagonist of perspective painting and it was he who designed the dome of Santa Maria del Fiore. He was commissioned with its design in 1419/20 and was assiduous in his preparations for the project. He travelled to Rome where he conducted detailed studies. On his return, he submitted his designs and work began. He supervised the work until its completion in 1436. Its design constituted a departure from all the previous principles of medieval cathedral tower construction. Brunelleschi's octagonal dome, consisting of two concentric shells linked together, was unusual and innovative in every respect. It is regarded as the first real piece of Renaissance architecture and one of the most important and most beautiful into the bargain.

Donatello's sculptures

Right in front of the main façade of Santa Maria del Fiore is the Romanesque baptistery of St. Giovanni. It is considerably older than the cathedral itself and dates from as early as 1128, its design echoing the baptism chapels of early Christianity. This too makes a

feature of various colors of marble, while the bronze doors were created by a member of the Pisano family, Andrea, as well as Lorenzo Ghiberti, a rival of Brunelleschi.

On display in the cathedral museum are the originals of pieces which originally formed part of the building but which have now been substituted by copies: sculptures by

Donatello from the base of the bell tower, works by Andrea Pisano, and terracottas by Luca della Robbia, who developed and perfected the old techniques of terracotta production to new heights of artistic achievement. He, too, numbers among the great sculptors of the early Renaissance period. That he was allowed to use themes derived from classical antiquity in his 'singers' gallery', in what was after all a Christian cathedral, reflects the spirit of progressive tolerance and cultural curiosity which prevailed at this time. "Florence was my lyre…did she not sound sweet?" asks one of the Medici family in a work by Thomas Mann. The answer to this must be that she indeed sounded very sweet, and continues to do so today.

The glory of Tuscany

The cathedral of Santa Maria Assunta in SIENA is a masterpiece by Pisano

GETTING THERE:
Via Florence. Continue by rail, or by car about 38 miles (60km) south along the SS 2

OPENING TIMES:
Usually 9:00 A.M. - 7:00 P.M. daily, 6:00 P.M. in the winter months

WHEN TO GO:
July, for the festival, otherwise May/June and Sept/Oct when there are fewer tourists

SPECIAL INTEREST:
The marketplace with the famous festival of the 'Palio delle Contrade' in July

The cathedral complex towers majestically over the Old Town of Siena. The square tower, which is recognizable from a long way off, rises to a height of 335ft (102m) (main picture)

View of the nave with its marble columns and mosaics (below, right)

The façade surrounding the main door still has its magnificent decorative statues (below, left)

Wagner's last opera, *Parsifal*, with its eponymous knightly hero, is set mainly in the castle housing the Holy Grail, the chalice that held the blood of Christ. In his stage directions and sets for the first performance, Wagner refers to a real building – which is neither a castle nor on the border between the Celtic and Germanic lands – Santa Maria Assunta in Siena in Tuscany. Wagner had visited this cathedral on one of his trips to Italy and been deeply impressed by the interior.

It is, in fact, one of the most beautiful churches in a country which is not short of architectural gems. Like other churches that were planned to be particularly large and ambitious, it has remained unfinished. This very incompleteness, however, makes it a true delight. It is aesthetically quite extraordinary, displaying an extravagant wealth of materials and detail. Its fragmentary nature has the effect of deliberate refinement.

The impression of superabundance also arises from the fact that the cathedral is not a single architectural construction but the center of a collection of many parts, buildings, and spaces piled on top of one another. Connected to the transept is the unfinished New cathedral, which nowadays contains an extensive museum. In front of it, there is a square named after Jacopo della Quercia, one of the artists who worked here. On the northern side of the cathedral stands the archbishop's palace and opposite the main façade there is a hospital, the Ospedale S. Maria della Scala. The little Piazza S. Giovanni with its Gothic baptistery constitutes the entrance to the cathedral area.

On the highest hill

The Duomo di Santa Maria Assunta stands on the highest point in Siena. The city, which was probably one of Caesar's military camps, was the seat of the bishops as long ago as the fourth century. Like other settlements in Tuscany, it was built around a hilltop. An independent republic in the twelfth century, it achieved prosperity and political power as the headquarters of rich bankers who owed their existence to the silver mines of Montieri. The older of the two present-day universities in Siena was founded as long ago as 1240. The precious Old Town of Siena is considered the most beautiful anywhere in Tuscany.

Santa Maria Assunta is built in the Italian Gothic style, which is quite distinct from the French. The walls are not pierced, its lines do not thrust

heavenwards; instead it looks back in many ways to antiquity. In Siena, the materials are used to create an effect of surprise; for instance, alternating bands of different colored marbles – red, black, and white – have been used on the façades.

This is the work of Giovanni Pisano who, like his father Nicola, is considered one of the great architects of the thirteenth/fourteenth centuries. He was a contemporary of Cimabue and Giotto, the painters whose work marked the end of Gothic art and the beginning of the Renaissance. This change of style can also be discerned in the Pisanos' architecture. The campanile, which stands on a square base, is also encrusted with dark and light marble. The higher you climb, the more arches there are in the arcades, creating an impression of great elegance.

Inlaid floors

The polychrome effects continue inside the cathedral, with the alternation of black and white on the walls. Fifty-six pictorial representations of scenes from antiquity and the Bible, in marble intarsia and sgrafitti, are to be seen on the floor. The work took almost two hundred years.

Santa Maria Assunta is designed as a three-nave cathedral with a triple transept, based on the usual cruciform ground plan. The crossing is covered by a huge dome, which gives it the feel of a central-plan building, and it was precisely here in the crossing, under the light from the dome, that Wagner got the idea for his Castle of the Grail. Italian buildings of this kind are probably modeled on the ancient Roman pantheon. Imitations of the pantheon are a particularly emphatic way of referring back to antiquity, and Siena is a very early example of this, the architectural designs of Brunelleschi and those of Michelangelo coming later.

The exterior of Santa Maria Assunta was completed around 1264. Eighty years later, the decision was taken to extend the cathedral, in order to make it the biggest church in Italy. Work began but, in 1348, plague broke out, putting an end to the proceedings. The building remains incomplete, but its importance is undiminished.

Home of the Franciscans

The remains of St. Francis of **ASSISI** rest in the monastery church of San Francesco

GETTING THERE:
Assisi is roughly equidistant from the airports of Rome, Florence, and Rimini. Onward travel by car on motorways and main roads

OPENING TIMES:
Usually 7:00 A.M. - 7:00 P.M. daily

SPECIAL INTEREST:
The frescoes in the Upper and Lower churches

The huge monastery complex stands on a hill overlooking a broad valley (main picture)

From the colonnades, the visitor has an impressive view over the land at the foot of the hills (below, left)

Around 1295/1300, Giotto di Bondone painted the *Apparition of St. Francis at the Chapter of Arles*. The fresco decorates the south wall of the nave of the Upper church (below, center)

Interior of the Upper church (below, right)

They called him 'poverello', the poor one, yet after his death they built him one of the most magnificent and richly decorated churches in the world. Francis of Assisi, the son of a wealthy cloth merchant, was born in Umbria in 1181. Despite an apparently glittering future, he renounced all worldly goods and, in 1209, with the Pope's blessing, he founded an order of mendicant friars, which quickly attracted a following. Besides missionary work, the order's chief aims were poverty and the care of the sick and the oppressed.

After missionary journeys through southern France and Egypt, Francis returned to Assisi. He did without a church of his own and lived in houses and simple lodgings made available to the order by charitable citizens. In the garden of San Damiano, when almost blind, he wrote the *Hymn to the Sun*, one of the earliest poems in Italian. When he died on 3 October 1226, lying naked on the stone floor, he owned nothing.

Lower church and Upper church

Why then does such a basilica exist? Why was it decorated by the best painters of the time? Just two years after his death and one day after his canonization on 17 July 1128, work began on a church, which was not planned to be either a monastery church or a collegiate church but simply a burial place. Francis himself had selected the 'Hill of Hell', the place where local criminals were executed, as his last resting-place, because it kept alive the memory of the suffering of Christ on Golgotha. His body was transferred to the newly built church in 1230.

Architecturally, the church is considered one of the wonders of the medieval world, because there are two absolutely magnificent churches built one above the other on this site, an idea which has been attributed to Brother Elia da Cortona, the saint's favorite. In the Lower church (1228-1230), the Romanesque style and influence of early Christian mausoleums are clearly recognizable in the nave, the crossing, and the dome with its strong supporting ribs, while the Upper church (1230-1253), a hall church with a single nave, is influenced by Gothic and, in particular, the Sainte-Chapelle in Paris.

In both churches there are outstanding frescoes by Cimabue,

Giotto, Pietro Lorenzetti, and Simone Martini. They are the most important set of paintings of the thirteenth and fourteenth centuries in Italy, and are reckoned to be the most extensive area of wall-painting anywhere. The frescoes by Giotto in the Upper Church, painted between 1296 and 1304 when he was only 25, caused a great sensation at the time. In 28 paintings, the artist tells the legend of St. Francis in a quite revolutionary way. In these pictures, he does more than just paint with a new vividness; the faces of his figures have individualized features and the landscape bears directly on the particular episode from the saint's life. Unesco has placed these paintings on the World Cultural Heritage list.

Frescoes destroyed

1997 was a year that will never be forgotten in Assisi, as on 26 September two severe earthquakes shook the province of Umbria and the Marche region. Part of the Upper church collapsed, four people were found dead under the ruins, and 2152 square feet (200 square meters) of frescoes were destroyed. Despite the distress in the

area, where over 50,000 had been made homeless, world attention focused on the church and its frescoes. In a unique restoration operation, some 200,000 absolutely minute particles were sifted from the rubble and finally put back together with the help of computer animation, after years of ceaseless toiling on the 'biggest jigsaw in the world'. The Upper church was ready for reopening just in time for the Holy Year of 2000. The Lower church – which is also painted – with its chapels and the tomb of St. Francis – had escaped the earthquake largely undamaged.

For centuries, St. Francis' coffin was thought to have been lost, until it was rediscovered in 1818 in a walled-up crypt beneath the Lower church along with a third church, thus completing the miracle of San Francesco. Today, the simple stone coffin containing the body of St. Francis is on display in the Lower church, which has once again become a place of pilgrimage for millions of visitors from all over the world.

Norman-Arabic art

With its cloisters and mosaics, the cathedral of **MONREALE** on Sicily is one of the most famous Norman monuments

ITALY

Tyrrhenian Sea
Mediterranean Sea
Palermo

GETTING THERE:
Flights to Palermo airport. Frequent ferry crossings from the Italian mainland. Monreale is about 9 miles (15km) away from Palermo by bus or taxi

OPENING TIMES:
Usually open all day

SPECIAL INTEREST:
The apse with its mosaic of Christ

In the words of French writer Guy de Maupassant, it is impossible not to fall in love with these cloisters, this peaceful haven, a secluded enclosure which inspires a person to profound thought while walking slowly round the arcades. He was referring to the world-famous cloisters of the "wonderful monastery of Monreale," built to a square groundplan measuring 154ft by 154ft (47m by 47m), its 228 pillars enclosing a delightful garden. No two pillars are exactly alike, but vary in motif and decorative ornamentation. The cloisters have been preserved in almost pristine condition and, together with the cathedral, constitute a unique masterpiece of Norman-Arabic architecture.

Legend has it that the Virgin Mary appeared to the Norman king, William II (1154-1190), in a dream, instructing him to build a church and monastery in her honor. This dream dovetailed perfectly with the political situation prevailing at the time since William, the third ruler, to succeed to the Sicilian throne, had just seen his power diminished when the archbishopric of Palermo was established.

By founding a new diocese and building Monreale, comprising a castle, cathedral, bishop's palace, and cloisters in 1174, he hoped to redress the balance in no uncertain terms. He presented the monastery to the Cluniazensians, thus ensuring the support of the powerful Benedictine Order. All that remains of this magnificent complex of buildings today are the cathedral and cloisters – not to mention a hillside town of 27,000 inhabitants, who, it is said, feel a closer affinity to the Normans than to the Italians.

How Sicily became a kingdom

Phoenicians, Greeks, Carthaginians, and Romans, not to mention Byzantines and Arabs, had all left their mark on the island before the Norman king, Roger I, succeeded in vanquishing the heathen Saracens in the name of the Pope. Under his son, Roger II, all Norman territories were gathered into one single, centralized kingdom, Sicily, with Palermo as its capital.

During the reign of Roger II, as well as under his successors William I and William II, a great many buildings were constructed, reaching a peak in the building of Monreale. This splendid collection of buildings became a magnificent showpiece of Arab-Norman art and is now regarded as the most significant legacy of this particular type of architecture, so characteristic of southern Italy. Despite some deviations from the original style, resulting from later additions to the cathedral, the clearly structured façade with its two defensive towers represents the epitome of Norman architecture, while the almost lyrical wall decorations are essentially Arabic in style.

The original decorations can still be seen in the three east apses, where the medieval custom of decorating the church walls with fabrics and carpets on high feast days was cleverly translated into stone. Decorative arcades, rosettes, and friezes in mosaic form are interlaced with incrustations of black and white lava rock and the yellowish stone of Monte Pellegrino with such delicate artistry that the walls look as if they are hung with tapestries.

Domed ceiling depicts Biblical episodes

The cathedral, which measures 335ft (102m) in length and 131ft (40m) across, is a cruciform basilica, consisting of a central nave and two aisles in traditional Latin design. The actual nucleus of the building, however, is the square of the choir. The shafts of light flooding in also converge on this area, highlighting the choir as the focal point of the building. All this helps to create the impression of a Byzantine-style construction built around a central core.

Islamic influence is also evident in the central nave, the transept, and apse, which cover a total surface area of 7584 square yards (6340 square meters) and are decorated with magnificent mosaics set against a gold background. These wall mosaics are the work of local Byzantine artists who, between 1179 and 1182, created these unique Biblical scenes, illustrating episodes from the Old and New Testaments. Stylistically speaking, they represent a transition from the rather rigid style of Byzantine mosaic work to a more pictorial art form which is set against a background of gold.

Despite the splendor of the central nave and transepts, it is the apse which is the main focus of attention. The mosaics here are regarded as the most magnificent of their kind anywhere in Sicily. Set in gold, they depict the heavenly hierarchy: above the saints is the Virgin Mary, flanked by archangels and apostles.

Looming over them is the powerfully authoritative figure of Christ Pantocrator, lord of the world, measuring 44.5ft (13.3m) in height and 23ft (7m) in width. In his left hand, he is holding an open book with the words: "I am the light. He who follows me will not walk through darkness."

View along the central nave to the apse, showing the decorated beams spanning the ceiling (main picture)

Monreale's cloisters are considered a pinnacle of achievement of Arabic-Norman art (above)

View of the mighty cathedral and cloistered arcades, with its long nave and bell tower, from the inner courtyard (below)

The Greek Agía Sophía

THESSALONIKI in Greek Macedonia played an important part in the early years of Christianity

•Thessaloniki
Aegean Sea

GREECE

Mediterranean Sea

GETTING THERE:
Via Thessaloniki international airport. Rail and motorway connections from Athens and central Europe. Ferry connection from Piraeus

OPENING TIMES:
Usually 8:30 A.M. – 1:00 P.M. and 3:30 P.M. – 7:30 P.M.

SPECIAL INTEREST:
The 8th/9th-century mosaics

The ascension of Christ from the great 9th-century mosaic in the dome (main picture)

Detail from the mosaic of the Madonna with the angels (below, right)

The main doorway of Agía Sophía with its flattened dome in the center of the building (below, left)

Thessaloniki is one of the biggest cities in Greece and lies at the center of the Greek province of Macedonia. In the fourth century BC, this area was the starting-point for the creation of an empire, when Philip of Macedon conquered the rest of Greece. His son, Alexander the Great, went on to create an empire that covered the entire eastern Mediterranean region.

It soon crumbled after Alexander's death. Macedonia became first a Roman province, next a Byzantine possession, then southern Slavic tribes moved in and, after the Ottoman conquest of the Balkans, it was to remain under Turkish rule for almost five hundred years. Today, a small part of Macedonia belongs to Bulgaria, the south forms part of the republic of Greece, and what was once Yugoslavian Macedonia has become an independent state.

Greek Macedonia was home to one of the earliest Christian communities in Europe. St. Paul the Apostle visited it twice, and also maintained a correspondence with its members: "But since we belong to the day, let us be self-controlled, putting on faith and love as a breastplate and the hope of salvation as a helmet." Thus he wrote in connection with a warning against drunkenness and the consequent somnolence.

The quotation comes from the first of the two epistles to the Thessalonians, Thessalonica (as it used to be known) being his destination. The dates of his visits are known: 49/50 and 59. The city, still a relatively recent foundation at the time, had

become the capital of the Roman province of Macedonia. Thessalonica was situated on one of the main trade routes of the Roman Empire, the Via Egnetia, from the Adriatic to the city of Byzantium, later Constantinople and now Istanbul.

The community, which had been distinguished by Paul's visits and letters, became the starting point for the missionary activity in the Balkans which gave us the Slavonic church alphabet, among other things. The Slavic Apostles St. Cyril (or Kyrillos) and St. Methodius were clerics from Thessalonica.

The Ottomans were tolerant

In the sixth century, under the Byzantine emperor Justinian, the city grew to become the second biggest in the whole of the eastern Roman Empire. Many new churches were built. It was besieged by the Avares and the Goths, and successfully captured in battle and plundered by the Saracens. Normans, Venetians, and crusaders followed. When the Ottomans took over, the occupying powers – as in other parts of their empire – proved to be fairly tolerant in matters of religion. Christians were able to practise their faith although, as they made up just a quarter of the inhabitants, they were in a minority.

There were many more Turks, and almost half the inhabitants were Jews. We are told in the Acts of the Apostles: "…there was a Jewish synagogue. As was his custom, Paul went into the synagogue, and on three Sabbath days he reasoned with them from the Scriptures…." From this it is evident

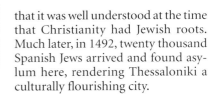

that it was well understood at the time that Christianity had Jewish roots. Much later, in 1492, twenty thousand Spanish Jews arrived and found asylum here, rendering Thessaloniki a culturally flourishing city.

Three-nave church with a dome

In 1917, the fifth year after its return to Greece, a huge fire broke out in the Old Town. It raged for three days, destroying ten thousand buildings. The city had to be completely rebuilt. Any ancient and medieval monuments still standing, such as the two best known churches in the city, St. Sophia and St. Dimitrios, are survivors of this disaster.

Agía Sophía is a three-nave, domed, cruciform church on an almost square ground plan, built in the eighth century on the site of an older church. The overall impression it gives is of a massive, self-contained, Orthodox, metropolitan cathedral.

There are several galleries ranked one above the other, visible from the outside by their rows of windows. The building is modeled on the imposing Hagia Sophia in Istanbul, but here in Thessaloniki, of course, the dome is visibly more flattened. What makes it different, at least from St. Dimitrios church, which had to be completely rebuilt after 1917, is that a greater proportion of the ancient building has been preserved.

This means, above all, the mosaics. They are considered the most beautiful in the whole of Thessaloniki. They decorate the walls and expand into grandiose pictorial compositions in the interior of the dome. They were created after the end of the iconographic controversy that shook the Byzantine church in the eighth century. A council tried to oppose the worship of icons in the eastern Roman Empire, which resulted in the wilful destruction of countless works

of art. Byzantine art with its special aesthetic qualities came close to disappearing altogether.

Fortunately, things did not go quite that far, and some particularly perfect examples can be seen in Agía Sophía. On a golden background, the twelve apostles and Mary, the mother of Christ, with two angels at her side, form a circle. Four other angels are bearing Christ up to heaven, enthroned on a rainbow and surrounded by an aureola. All this is in the spirit of St. Paul, who wrote to the Thessalonians: "But the Lord is faithful, and he will strengthen and protect you from the evil one."

A miracle of Byzantine architecture

Hagia Sophia in **ISTANBUL** was once the religious focus of the Byzantine Empire

Black Sea
Istanbul
TURKEY
Mediterranean Sea

GETTING THERE:
Flights to Istanbul international airport

OPENING TIMES:
Usually 9:30 A.M. – 6:30 P.M.

SPECIAL INTEREST:
The 9th-century, Christian art treasures

Christ depicted on a Byzantine mosaic (below)

Hagia Sophia in Istanbul was once the greatest church in Christendom. That was a long time ago, in the days when Istanbul was still known as Constantinople, though even this was not the city's original name. Previously known as Byzantium, it was a colony established on the shores of the Sea of Bosporus in BC 660. Thanks to its ideal location, it developed into a thriving port and affluent commercial center. It was destroyed by the Persians and rebuilt by the Spartans; Alexander the Great conquered it, as did Imperial Rome. Constantine the Great made it his seat of government and, since he was the first Roman emperor to embrace the Christian faith, his new capital city, henceforth known as Constantinople, became a religious focal point.

The name 'Byzantium' henceforth referred to the empire ruled from Constantinople. History usually teaches us that the Old Roman Empire was vanquished by emergent Germanic tribes during the fifth century. This was certainly true of the western Mediterranean region. Byzantium, however, continued to exist for another thousand years. It saw itself as successor to the Roman Empire and remained an undisputed major power, extremely advanced in terms of culture and civilization, and far superior to western Europe. If people remain unaware of such historical facts, it is because the victorious Turkish invasion and conquest of Constantinople in 1453 dramatically severed all connections with this period of history.

Imperial coronation church

Sophia bore witness to all these historical changes. It was the main coronation church of the Byzantine Empire and the bishop's cathedral of the patriarch of Constantinople. The original building plans date back to the time of Constantine the Great, whose sons commissioned the building. The first building was constructed on the site of a ruined temple to Apollo and completed in 360. The second ecumenical counsel was held there in 381. The building was attacked by arsonists, the damage repaired in 415, and the church reconsecrated. During the so-called Nika Revolt of January 532, a national insurrection against the Emperor crushed by General Belisar, Hagia Sophia was once again destroyed.

The reigning emperor Justinian consequently set about completely rebuilding the church, appointing Isidoros of Miletus and Anthemios of Tralles as principal architects. Thousands of workers were brought in and building materials were gathered from ancient temples, with marble supplied by monuments in Athens, Delphi, and Ephesus. The building took less than six years to complete and, by Christmas 537, the new church had been formally opened by Patriarch Menas.

The Greek name of Hagia Sophia means 'divine wisdom', a title which can either be interpreted in general terms or seen as an attribute of Christ's spirituality. It could also be connected with St. Sophia of Rome, who was martyred during the Christian persecutions under Diocletian, a direct predecessor of the Christian emperor Constantine. The legends surrounding St. Sophia refer to her Latin name of Sapientia and she is depicted with a palm and a book. There is no way of knowing whether the name refers to this specific holy figure and/or the abstract concept of Christ's divine wisdom.

Plundered by knights

Although the bulk of Justinian's Hagia Sophia remained intact, it did suffer some serious setbacks in the years that followed. In 558, an earthquake caused the collapse of the great dome, which had to be reconstructed. Another earthquake in 986 likewise caused considerable damage. In 1206, during the fourth crusade, which was not so much waged with the aim of freeing Jerusalem as capturing the wealthy city of Constantinople, Hagia Sophia was sacked by Christian knights from Roman Catholic western Europe, who looted its precious treasures. The church still retained its power, however, employing around 600 people including 80 priests, 150 deacons, 40 deaconesses, 60 subdeacons, 160 readers, 25 singers, and 75 doormen.

Major changes followed Sultan Mehmet's occupation of Constantinople. Hagia Sophia was converted into a Turkish mosque. The interior, Christian furnishings disappeared and were replaced by Islamic decoration. Four minarets were also added. It remained so for the next 400 years, during which the Ottoman Empire expanded and came to dominate the Levant and virtually the whole Balkan region before eventually declining in power. The revolution of Kemal Ataturk transformed Turkey into a secular state and, in 1934, Hagia Sophia was converted into a museum.

It is a combination of a basilica and central building. The rectangular nave is surmounted by a great dome and two smaller half-domes on either side, as well as other conch vaults. Around the north and south sides of the church are two-story galleries. The walls are punctuated by its many windows and the shallow dome, measuring 108ft (33m) across and rising to a height of 184ft (56m), is supported by an upper gallery of windows, giving the impression that it floats on air. It is its sense of space that makes this cathedral so special. The Christian art treasures, incrustations, and mosaics, many of which date from the ninth century, have been uncovered, depicting Biblical figures and eastern Roman church leaders. They number among the greatest works of Byzantine art treasures in the world.

View of the interior of Hagia Sophia with its encircling galleries (main picture)

Hagia Sophia was converted into a mosque under the Ottomans and acquired four minarets (below)

27

ATLANTIC OCEAN

• Santiago de
  Compostela

SPAIN

Mediterranean
Sea

GETTING THERE:
Flights to Labacolla
airport 8 miles (13km)
outside the town. Good
rail and bus links

OPENING TIMES:
Open daily through
the year

WHEN TO GO:
April to October

SPECIAL INTEREST:
The cathedral's 16th-
century cloister

The sumptuously
ornate façade of St.
James' cathedral rises
above the town like a
mountain peak
(above, right)

This view of the high
altar epitomizes the
splendor of Spanish
Catholicism
(above, left)

Pilgrims mark the end
of their pilgrimage by
laying hands on one of
the pillars (below,
left margin)

The Pórtico de la
Gloria, decorated with
sculptures by Maestro
Mateo (below, center)

The world's largest
incense burner needs
the combined strength
of eight men to set it in
motion (below, right)

The patron saint of Spaniards

The cathedral of SANTIAGO DE COMPOSTELA – a place of pilgrimage through the ages

Cockleshells (or pilgrims' scallops) were often used in the Middle Ages as drinking vessels, especially by pilgrims (hence their name) making their way to Compostela. They wore them wedged in their hats as a sign that they were pilgrims heading for Santiago de Compostela in northern Spain.

James, a fisherman on the Sea of Galilee and brother of John the Baptist, was one of Jesus' twelve disciples, who later became one of the first Christian martyrs: He was executed in 41 on the orders of Herod Agrippa I. During the seventh century, monks brought his remains to the Iberian Peninsula where they rested in the Estremadura region until the Moorish invasion when they were removed to north-west Spain. Veneration of the saint began during Frankish times: James (Santiago in Spanish) became the patron saint of the Iberian Peninsula.

Santiago de Compostela is the capital of Galicia, a poor province with heavy rainfall, unlike the rest of Spain. The dialect spoken here is closer to Portuguese than Castilian Spanish. Moorish rule was more short-lived here than elsewhere and the great respect the Islamic conquerors had for the tomb of St. James preserved its sanctity.

By the eleventh century, the flood of pilgrims to Santiago de Compostela had become so great that this shrine was regarded as the most popular of all pilgrim destinations, even ahead of Rome and Jerusalem. The faithful came from all over Europe and even from the Caucasus. Established pilgrim routes were associated with particular hospices that were listed and categorized in relevant itineraries, the oldest travel guides in the history of civilization.

In the heart of the Old Town

Pilgrims still make their way to the town, particularly on St. James' Day, 25 July. They find it a friendly place with numerous churches and a delightful, old center, at the heart of which is the Plaza del Obradoiro. On the east side of this square stands the majestic cathedral with its twin-towered, Baroque façade, lavishly decorated with statues, pinnacles, pilasters, and other decorations, designed by the architect Fernando Casas y Novoa between 1738 and 1750. Above the central section in a niche is a first statue of St. James.

A sweeping flight of steps leads up to the main entrance. Beneath these steps lies the Catedral Vieja (Old cathedral), an imposing vault dating from the eleventh/twelfth centuries, the oldest existing part of the building. Entrance to the cathedral is through the Pórtico de la Gloria, once the façade, now part of a porch. It is decorated with numerous carvings, the original colors of which are no longer discernible; these represent one of the largest and most exceptional collections of Romanesque sculpture anywhere in Europe. They were created between 1166 and 1188 by Maestro Mateo.

The tympanum depicts Christ surrounded by the Four Apostles. Beside them stand two angels swinging incense burners and eight holding the various instruments of the Passion. In the center is a pillar, representing the roots of the tree of Jesse. The stone is worn away, as it is traditional for pilgrims completing their pilgrimage to the cathedral to place their hands on or kiss the stone. Another statue of St. James sits on top of the column, looking down with tranquil gaze.

Pure Early Romanesque

The interior of the cathedral is built of granite, in pure Early Romanesque style. The galleried basilica with its transept has numerous chapels leading off it, the most important of which is the magnificent Capilla Mayor, a sumptuously decorated construction located above the shrine of St. James.

The high altar is a mass of Baroque figures, fashioned in silver, alabaster, and jasper. In the center is a third statue of the saint, this time in wood. It dates from the thirteenth century. Around 1700, it was adorned with all kinds of jewelry made from precious metals and studded with gemstones. Either side of the high altar, a narrow staircase leads up behind the altar, which pilgrims can climb to kiss the saint's robe. Only then is the pilgrimage successfully completed.

Beneath the altar is a crypt containing the sepulchre of St. James and his disciples, St. Theodore and St. Athanasius.

The other doors giving access to the cathedral are the Puerta de la Azabachería, completed in 1769 and located on the north side, and the Puerta Santa on the eastern side, a product of the Baroque period, complete with figures of the apostles and church fathers, dating from the twelfth century. The Puerta Santa is only opened in years when 25 July falls on a Sunday. The south-facing Puerta de las Platerías is the oldest surviving doorway.

Beneath the dome above the crossing hang the supports for the Botafumeiro ('smoking barrel'), the thurible or censer which is reputedly the largest in existence; it well deserves its literal name, being over 6.5ft (2m) in height. It makes its appearance on religious festivals, and requires the combined weight of at least eight strong men to be set in place and swung.

The burial place of El Cid

The cathedral of **BURGOS** dates from the Gothic period with fifteenth century decorations

ATLANTIC OCEAN

Burgos

SPAIN

Mediterranean Sea

GETTING THERE:
By motorway from Barcelona. Flights from Madrid. Good rail links

OPENING TIMES:
Usually from 9:30 A.M. - 1:30 P.M. and from 4:00 P.M. - 7:00 P.M.

SPECIAL INTEREST:
Treasures in the chapels

The cathedral is situated right in the heart of the Old Town (main picture)

The tower above the apse is one of the finest examples of Spanish stonemasonry (below, left)

The tombs of Contestable and his wife (below, right)

In 1636, *El Cid*, a tragicomedy by Pierre Corneille, was premiered in Paris. The piece was a triumph, sealed Corneille's reputation as a writer, and has long been regarded as a masterpiece in the annals of French classical literature. It tells a story of love, intrigue, and chivalry in a Spanish nobleman's house. Corneille borrowed the theme from Spanish literature. Since the Late Middle Ages, the legendary figure of El Cid has been the hero of countless poems, the first of which was *Cantar de mío Cid*, the oldest literary monument in the Spanish language.

The eponymous hero, a clever and courageous knight, strives successfully to free his country from foreign Islamic rule and return it to Christianity. The word 'Cid', however, is actually Arabic in origin, meaning 'lord', and the historical truth of it is that El Cid fought on both the Spanish and the Moorish sides, as a veteran campaigner who hired himself out at his own discretion. That he has become a folk and national hero has more to do with wishful thinking and mythology than historical fact.

Once the capital city

El Cid, whose real name was Rodrigo Díaz de Vivar, was a nobleman from the Burgos region. He now lies buried in the city's cathedral. Burgos has enjoyed capital city status several times during the course of its history: in the eleventh and twelfth centuries, it was capital of the United Kingdom of Castile and Léon and later, during the Spanish Civil War, became the seat of government of General Franco's fascists.

The cathedral is situated at the foot of the hill on the left bank of the Río Arlánzon and is reputedly one of the most beautiful examples of sacred Spanish Gothic architecture. Because of its comparatively early construction and the European origins of its architects, it bears strong similarities with cathedrals in France, the acknowledged birthplace of Gothic architecture. In Spain's more southerly regions, buildings of this kind bear the hallmarks of Moorish influence, evidence of which can also be seen in Burgos.

The Capilla de Contestable at the eastern end of the cathedral, for example, is richly endowed with the lace-like filigree ornamentation typical of Late Spanish Gothic. This style, known as 'estílo platéresco', echoes the intricacy of Islamic wrought iron work.

Pure Plateresque

Let us, for the moment, turn our attention from the interior to the exterior. At first glance, the Santa María cathedral appears to have all the usual characteristics of European Gothic: saintly statues at the portals, a twin-towered façade facing west (with estrellón), a rose window. The original, marble white sandstone has long since faded to a leaden gray. The towers were built by a foreigner, Juan de Colonia. Others who took part in the construction include Gil de Siloé from Flanders and Philippe Vigarny of Burgundy.

The ground plan of the cathedral is in the manner of a basilica with a central nave and an aisle either side. Around the periphery are numerous chapels, as well as a cloister and chapter-house. The tombs of El Cid and his wife Jimena were not installed here until 1921, when they were finally laid to rest beneath the cimborio, the dome over the crossing, remarkable for the pure Plateresque style of its decoration: the delicate lattice-work of the eight-pronged star is complemented and framed by an extremely ornate surround. It was created in 1568 by Juan de Vallejo, following the collapse of the original cupola.

In the north transept, between the Capilla de la Natividad and the Capilla de Santa Ana, is a T-shaped golden staircase, the Escalera Dorada. It derives its name from its gilded banisters and leads up to the Puerta de la Coronería, 26ft (8m) above. It is one of the pieces by Diego de Siloé.

The choir and Capilla Mayor are separated from the rest of the interior by a high metal grille. The choir stalls with their lavish carvings are prima-

rily the work of Philippe Vigarny of Burgundy, known in Spain as Felipe de Borgoña. In the center of the choir is the tomb of Bishop Mauricio, co-founder of the Catedral de Santa Maria, who died in 1240. The cathedral's foundation stone was laid by King Fernando II of Léon. The union with neighboring Castile was already fragile, leading to many more wars between the two regions.

Construction work lasted around three hundred years. All the Plateresque work originates from the fifteenth century, when this particular style reached its zenith, and it is inter-

esting to note that even the foreign artists involved in its construction adopted or were obliged to adopt this uniquely Spanish style of architecture. That they came to Burgos in the first place was thanks to Bishop Alonso de Cartagena, a man with a keen interest in the aesthetic, who did much to promote the cathedral's construction.

The fly-catcher

The high altar is situated in the Capilla Mayor, a lavishly gilded chapel dating from 1580 and the work of Rodrigo and Martín de la Haya. There is a unique collection of singular treasures in the Catedral de Santa Maria. At the center of the choir is an enamel and copper effigy of Bishop Mauricio; the figure of Christ in the Capilla del Santísimo Cristo is apparently made from a piece of buffalo hide; and in the Capilla de Santa Tecla with its ornate Rococo décor is a Romanesque font, together with a manikin which opens and closes its mouth with clockwork precision as the hour strikes. The general populace has been somewhat lacking in respect for this mechanical wonder, giving it the nickname 'papamosca', meaning 'fly-catcher'.

Antoni Gaudí's vision

La Sagrada Familia – the perpetual building site in **BARCELONA**

Antoni Gaudí y Cornet, born in 1852 in Reus near Tarragona, studied in the Catalonian capital Barcelona, where he later set up as an architect and was to spend the rest of his life. His first major commission was a residential building, the Casa Vicens. It caused something of a sensation, and delighted the industrialist Eusebi Güell, who commissioned extravagant projects from the young architect such as the Palau and Parc Güell, a grand residence and park in the Modernist style of the times.

New departure for architecture

The aesthetic principle Gaudí subscribed to was Art Nouveau, a movement that had started in Great Britain and quickly spread throughout Europe, bringing the eclectic historicism of the late nineteenth century to an end and replacing it with a new, unified, formal language. It made use of decorative flower motifs and flowing lines. The new style took over painting and the applied arts in Catalonia too, as Antoni Gaudí conveyed his interpretation of Art Nouveau both through the Güell commissions and his other projects in Barcelona. In 1887, he designed a residence for the bishop of Astorga, near León, in the form of a castle with a highly unconventional mixture of Gothic and Art Nouveau. By that time, he was already engaged on his fourth year of work on the building of the visionary Templo de la Sagrada Familia (Temple of the Holy Family).

The church stands on the Carrer de Sardenya and is still a building site today. Whether the project will ever be finished remains uncertain. Originally a Neo-Gothic building was planned for the site, of the kind devised in hundreds in the departing nineteenth century. A year after building work commenced, Antoni Gaudí was entrusted with the task of continuing it. He changed the original plans and designed a huge church to match the size and pretensions of cathedrals of the High Middle Ages.

As in the Bishop's Palace in Astorga, Gothic and Art Nouveau were combined together. The ground plan is a five-nave basilica with a transept and an apse. As the nave ended up relatively short and all kinds of extras were built on, the impression is now more that of a central plan church – an impression supported by the planned dome, which is supposed to reach a height of 525ft (160m). For the time being, towers dominate the scene. Eight of them have been completed, 377ft (115m) high; four stand to the east and are part of the Portal de Nacimiento (Nativity Façade). Their outlines are reminiscent of High Gothic bell towers with spires, but closer inspection reveals that there is no division between the bases of the towers and the roof, with the contours of the spires slightly curved.

Twelve pointed towers are planned in all. They are intended to symbolize the twelve apostles. Among the borrowings from Gothic are decorations that originate from the plant forms of Art Nouveau. One further portal has since been completed, the Passion Façade. Its design is in stark contrast to the filigree Nativity Façade.

With no corners or edges

The pointed Gothic arches above the rose window are also flattened and curved. In the buildings he designed for Güell, Gaudi already showed an aversion to all straight lines, corners, and edges, and eliminated them wherever possible. The buildings of the Austrian artist Friedensreich Hundertwasser, which follow similar principles, clearly emulate Gaudí's Catalonian Modernism.

As far as the engineering is concerned, Antoni Gaudí invented a new technique for distributing load to replace the buttresses and flying buttresses so typical of Gothic architecture. He demonstrated it by means of a model that has become famous, using sandbags and string. In addition, he considered it important that the building work should be done mainly by hand in the manner of the medieval cathedral builders. This slowed down the project and made it very much more expensive. Gaudí spent a total of 43 years on it. When he died in 1926, less than half of it had been completed. Work continues, but nowadays controlled machinery is also being used, which certainly improves progress, but not only does it go against the artist's intentions, it has also resulted in a certain uniformity and sterility in the quality of the finish. Inside, there is an altar and beneath it a crypt, in which the Catalan architect Antoni Gaudí y Cornet lies buried.

GETTING THERE:
International airline connections via El Prat airport, about 7 miles (12km) from the city

OPENING TIMES:
Usually 9:00 A.M. - 6:00 P.M. Sep-Mar. Apr-Aug 9:00 A.M. - 8:00 P.M.

SPECIAL INTEREST:
The filigree west façade with scenes of the birth of Christ. The view of Barcelona from the bell tower and the colorful mosaics on the other towers

Romanesque architecture by the Tormes

The oldest part of **SALAMANCA** cathedral dates back to the twelfth century

GETTING THERE:
International airline connections to Madrid. From there, by good country roads, or from the north by motorway. Also easily reached by train

OPENING TIMES:
Usually Tues-Sat 10:00 A.M. - 2:00 P.M. and 4:00 P.M. - 7:00 P.M.; Mon 4:00 P.M. - 7:00 P.M.; Sun 10:00 A.M. - 2:00 P.M.

WHEN TO GO:
May/June and September/October

SPECIAL INTEREST:
The high altar in the old cathedral with its 53 paintings

View over the Tormes to the cathedral with its two domed towers (main picture)

The choir of the old cathedral with the 12th-century central dome and the golden cock (below, left)

The side aisle with its buttresses was not neglected when the cathedral was being given its splendid decoration (below, center)

Closer to heaven: looking up at the vault of the great dome (below, right)

The prose work *El Lazarillo de Tormes* was first published in 1553. Its hero is a rogue, or picaroon (from the Spanish 'picarón'), a stock character that started a whole European literary genre which continues to this day. The river Tormes flows through the city of Salamanca in western Spain, so it is assumed that it was also the home of the unknown author of the first picaresque novel.

The city was a center of classical education. Its university, founded in 1218, is one of the oldest in the world. Fray Luis de León, the 'Spanish Erasmus', studied here, and another of its students was Miguel de Cervantes, the author of *Don Quixote*. The old university buildings are still standing. They are justly famous for the main façade in the Plateresque style – Spanish Late Gothic with Islamic-Moorish overtones.

Golden-yellow stone

The university buildings were constructed in the golden-yellow stone from Villamayor, as were the two cathedrals which face on to the Plaza Mayor, the main meeting place of Salamanca. The north portal of the Catedral Nueva (New cathedral) is also pure Plateresque and is very similar to the façade of the university, its immediate neighbour.

The two churches are so close to one another that they could be mistaken for a single building, with the Catedral Vieja (Old cathedral) seeming like a chapel of the new. The latter was built between 1513 and 1733, its architecture being part Late Gothic and part Baroque. The Catedral Vieja

was built between 1100 and 1200, by an unknown architect.

It is pure Romanesque, a style with a specific history of its own in Spain that has resulted in a distinctive aesthetic character.

Continuation of late antiquity

In those regions that were once part of the Roman Empire, Romanesque implies a direct continuation of late antiquity. Ground plans, forms, and ornaments were taken from Roman originals as, regardless of whether or not they had been adapted to Christianity, they were readily available as patterns. Iberia was also a Roman colony at one time but, following its invasion by Germanic tribes, the Moorish-Islamic conquerors ushered in a completely different culture with a distinct aesthetic canon. The centuries of Moorish rule produced an Iberian pastiche of styles, the most famous of which was the 'estilo plateresco'. The religious services, which were tolerated by the Moors, had their own special liturgy known as Isidorian or Mozarabic, and this had further aesthetic consequences.

The Christian reconquest of Iberia started in the north and spread southwards. The Moors were driven out of Galicia, León, Asturias, and Castille around 1100. This was the heyday of the Romanesque in Europe and Iberian architects now began to build in this style, although they did not look to antiquity for their patterns so much as towards Italy and France. There were lines of communication along the pilgrimage route to Santiago de Compostela and through communities of settlers in the country. Occasionally, a kind of symbiosis with the Mozarabic tendencies ensued. For example, columns ranged in rows one above the other, such as are found in the Catedral Vieja of Salamanca, were a particular feature of the Spanish Romanesque.

Moorish influence

The most beautiful view of the cathedral is from the old bridge over the Tormes, which was once part of a Roman street.

The Catedral de Santa María de la Sede can be approached through the Puerta de Acre, a gate in the right hand aisle of the new cathedral. The Catedral Vieja is a vaulted basilica, with arches that clearly come to a

point, something that may be seen as a nod in the direction of Moorish architecture. The nave is a fairly simple, very stately, and extremely atmospheric construction. The capitals of the pillars are richly ornamented with animal heads and bodies, and human forms.

A vast retable is displayed in the apse, an altarpiece with 53 scenes from the life of Christ and his mother, Mary. Together with the fresco on the ceiling depicting the Last Judgment, it is the work of Nicolás Florentino, dating from the mid-fifteenth century. The centerpiece of the retable is a statue of the Virgen de la Vega (Holy Virgin). It dates from the Romanesque period and was covered in bronze and precious stones.

The most impressive part of the cathedral is the tower above the crossing. This kind of domed construction represents yet another special feature of the Spanish Romanesque, with the one in Salamanca probably being the most impressive of all. On the spire of the cupola stands a cockerel, leading to the name 'Cock Tower'. The Spanish – 'la torre del gallo' – sounds rather more impressive.

From minaret to tower

Traces of Islam can still be seen in the cathedral of **SEVILLE** – Columbus is buried here

The box-like shape of the cathedral gives the impression of a medieval hall church, seen here from the south side. Windows, galleries, pilasters, and finials make the façade less stark (main picture)

The view up the pillars to the nave ceiling reaches to 184ft (56m) (above, right)

Quien no ha visto Sevilla, no ha visto maravilla, says a Spanish proverb – he who has not seen Seville, has not seen a miracle. This city in the south of Spain stands at the mouth of the river Guadalquivir, from whose harbor the ships of the explorers Christopher Columbus and Ferdinand Magellan once set sail. It is well known to art-lovers because of the painters Velázquez and Murillo and through the operas of Mozart, Rossini, and Bizet that are set here. It was probably founded by the Phoenicians and was an important port in Caesar's time. It became the capital under the Vandals and the Visigoths, and remained an important urban center during Moorish rule.

In 1248, Seville was the penultimate bastion of Islam to be taken by Ferdinand III of Castille in the course of the re-conquest, and he chose it as his residence. The Moors had now been driven out of almost the whole of Spain, including Andalusia; only Granada held out until 1492, coincidentally the year in which Columbus set off on his momentous expedition.

There is still much in Seville to remind us of its long Islamic past, especially in its architecture. The city symbol, the cathedral tower known as the 'Giralda', had once been the minaret of the principal mosque, erected at the end of the twelfth century. It was first rededicated as a church by the victorious Christians and finally demolished in order to build a cathedral on the site. Work began in 1402 and the building was consecrated in 1506.

Staying with the Giralda for the moment – incidentally, the name means 'weather vane' – the tower is 305ft (93m) high and tapers to a point. The bell chamber at the top was added by the Christians. The

great ring of 24 bells is to be found in the gallery below, together with a wooden house called the Matraca which contains rattles. These are used instead of the bells during Holy Week and make a macabre, spine-chilling noise, in keeping with the somber mood of this religious occasion.

Mad architects
Seville cathedral is one of the great churches of the Christian world. This applies to its physical size as well as its cultural importance as a monument of Late Gothic architecture in Spain. The ground plan shows a five-nave church with side chapels which means that the apse and transept do not extend beyond the outer walls, thus creating a massive, almost box-like, building. It is 384ft (117m) long and 249ft (76m) wide.

The aisles are almost as high as the 131ft (40m)-high nave, producing an effect similar to the Late Gothic hall churches of central Europe. The architects of the church wanted to create a building that, in their own words, would make people think they were mad. A Fleming and two Frenchmen were involved, and probably a German as well, Master Simon of Cologne, who had already distinguished himself by his work on Burgos cathedral. The cupola is assumed to be his work.

Islamic portals
It was not only the minaret that was taken over from the Islamic building that previously stood there. The foundation walls were also retained, which had a substantial influence on the shape of the building. Some of the portals originate from the mosque. For instance, the Puerta del Perdón (Gate of Pardon) in the north, leading directly into the Patio de los Naranjos (Courtyard of the Orange Trees) is a survival from the Islamic period. The octagonal fountain in the middle of the courtyard was part of a Midhà, an Islamic ritual bath.

The Great Door, the Puerta Mayor, leads out to the west. It stands between the Puerta del Bautismo (Gate of the Baptism) and the Puerta del Nacimiento (Gate of the Birth), both of which are richly ornamented with statuary. Other doors lead to the south and east.

Inside, the light enters through four-part lancet windows with very rich tracery. Under the crossing are the choir and the Capilla Mayor (Great Chapel). The retable or altarpiece is a huge piece of Gothic carving, which took several master stonemasons working together 80 years to complete. In the center is the statue of the Holy Virgin Mary, after whom the cathedral is named. It is made of silver and surrounded by 45 carvings recounting her life and that of her son, Jesus Christ.

In the Sacristía de los Cálices (Chalice Sacristy) there are paintings by Goya and Murillo. The Chapter House is also richly decorated. The cathedral houses a number of important tombs, including those of kings such as Pedro el Cruel (Peter the Cruel), who died in 1369. Columbus is buried in the south transept.

ATLANTIC OCEAN

SPAIN

Seville · Mediterranean Sea

GETTING THERE:
San Pablo airport, 3 miles (5km) from the city center. Fast rail connections from Madrid

WHEN TO GO:
May/June/October

OPENING TIMES:
La Giralda and the cathedral, usually Mon-Sat 10:30 A.M. – 5:00 P.M., Sun 2:00 P.M. – 6:00 P.M.

SPECIAL INTEREST:
The greatest retable (altarpiece) of the Christian world. Impressive view over the city from the Giralda tower

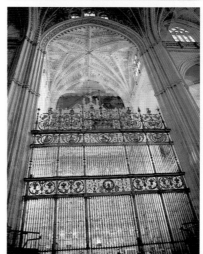

Columbus was originally buried in Havana. When Cuba became independent in 1892, his body was returned to Seville, from where he had set out. His tomb is in the cathedral (above)

All the splendor of Spanish craftsmanship can be seen in this view of one of the aisles (below)

Lisbon's oldest basilica

The cathedral Sé Patriarchal is in the heart of **LISBON**

GETTING THERE:
Flights to Lisbon's international airport. Direct rail links from Madrid and France. Good motorway links from Madrid and Galicia

OPENING TIMES:
Usually 7:00 A.M. - 5:00 P.M. No admission to tourists during services

SPECIAL INTEREST:
The 14th-century cloisters, the treasury, and adjoining chapels

One of the burial chapels near the choir with the tombs of Pacheco, a military leader, and his wife (below, left)

St. Anthony of Padua, Augustinian canon and later a member of the Franciscan Order, traveled to Morocco and France as a preacher, eventually ending his days as a hermit in central Italy. He was beatified less than a year after his death, the shortest canonization procedure in ecclesiastical history.

He was born Fernando Martin de Bulhom, the son of a Portuguese nobleman. He took his vows as a priest in Coimbra. The church of Santo António da Sé, in the heart of Lisbon's Old Town, now stands on the site of the house where he was born, near the cathedral.

St. Anthony's biography also reveals much about historical events taking place in 13th-century Portugal during his lifetime. His travels to North Africa as a missionary followed in the wake of the Moors' gradual withdrawal from the Iberian Peninsula. This was largely a result of the crusades, with Italy as their logistical focal point.

Portugal succeeded in accomplishing its Reconquista sooner than its Spanish neighbor. Being a seafaring nation, it cast an ambitious eye across the Atlantic and, for a while, successfully rivalled Spain in terms of its colonial conquests in Africa, Asia, and Latin America. The riches acquired there and brought back to the motherland were not solely of a material nature but included other benefits such as a fund of knowledge, not to mention scientific and artistic inspiration and stimuli.

Anglo-Saxon influence

The origins of Sé Patriarchal date from a much earlier time. Not only is it Lisbon's principal church, but also its oldest. The original church on this site was turned into a mosque under Moorish rule. After the Reconquista, when Alfonso I successfully recaptured Lisbon in 1147, the mosque was torn down to make way for a new Christian church, untainted by any foreign religion. Construction work began in 1150.

For once, the name of the architect is known, a seldom enough occurrence during the High Middle Ages. He was Roberto, *magister operis* (master of the works). His most significant architectural achievement was the Sé Velha, the old cathedral in Coimbra, which is very similar in design. Both churches share the same Norman-style, west façade in common. This element of Anglo-Saxon influence should be no surprise since the ties between Portugal and England are historical ones, which have endured to this day. Even the cathedral's first bishop was English: Gilbert.

Tombs in the choir

Sé Patriarchal was rebuilt during the fourteenth century at the instigation of King Dom Alfonso IV, in what was the increasingly popular style of Late Gothic.

The most significant art works from this period are the magnificent wrought-iron portal in front of one of the chapels and the choir section. A devastating earthquake, which struck Lisbon in 1775, also inflicted severe damage on the cathedral, which has since been repaired. Since 1990, archaeological excavations have been in progress around the site, uncovering Roman and Phoenician remains which give a fascinating glimpse of the history of the area.

Sé Patriarchal consists of three aisles, conforming by and large to the design of a Romanesque basilica. To the left of the cathedral entrance is the font where the infant Bulhom was baptized. The choir contains the tombs of Dom Alfonso IV and his wife Brites; King Alfonso was also known as 'the Brave', although he is most renowned for having ordered the murder of his son's wife. She was a member of the Castilian royal family and King Alfonso feared that the marriage would be detrimental to Portugal. One of his most loyal followers, Lopo Fernandes Pacheco, is also buried here in his own chapel.

The cathedral contains a number of other chapels. The first one, immediately adjacent to the main entrance, contains a nativity scene carved by a Baroque artist, Joaquim Machado de Castro. It is made from terracotta,

illustrating the popularity of this material in Portugal and Lisbon where it is commonly used as an artistic and aesthetic medium. Similarly, colored tiles called 'azulejos' are frequently used to decorate Portuguese houses, both inside and out, in the poorer districts as well as in more affluent residential areas.

Relics of St. Vincent

One of the other chapels is dedicated to St. Vincent and once contained his remains. The silver casket containing these is now housed in the sacristy behind the aisle on the right. Vincent of Saragossa was an archdeacon, who lived towards the end of the third century and was famous for his great oratorial skills.

He was arrested and executed during the persecution of Christians under Emperor Diocletian. Legend has it that ravens kept a vigil over his

remains, which were eventually thrown into the sea and washed ashore in southern Portugal at the spot now known as Cabo de São Vicente. He is often depicted in pictures with a ship, and is also the patron saint of wine-growers and viticulturists. It is small wonder that Portugal, a seafaring and wine-growing nation, has a special fondness for this particular saint.

Off the ambulatory around the choir in Sé Patriarchal is a door leading into the cloisters. These date from the fourteenth century and consist of an upper and lower gallery. The main façade of the cathedral, which almost resembles a twin-towered fortress, was completed in 1380.

Below the cathedral is the Alfama district of the Old Town, with its narrow little streets winding down the hill, its picturesque houses, and well-worn cobblestones. Noble families

once lived in this area, but nowadays ordinary folk reside here in the shadow of the squat towers of Sé Patriarchal which rise stiffly and imperiously above the town.

The cathedral Sé Patriarchal with its two, Late Romanesque towers is situated in the Old Town (above)

The casket containing 16th-century relics (below)

In the Manueline style

The monastery of St. Jerónimos in **BELÉM** is a monument to the splendor of Portuguese decorative art

ATLANTIC OCEAN

PORTUGAL
•Lisbon

Mediterranean
Sea

GETTING THERE:
Flights to Lisbon's international airport. By rail from Madrid and France. By car via motorway routes from Madrid or along the coast

OPENING TIMES:
Usually Tues-Sun 10:00 A.M. – 5:00 P.M., although opening times can change at short notice

SPECIAL INTEREST:
The cloisters of 1517 and 1522

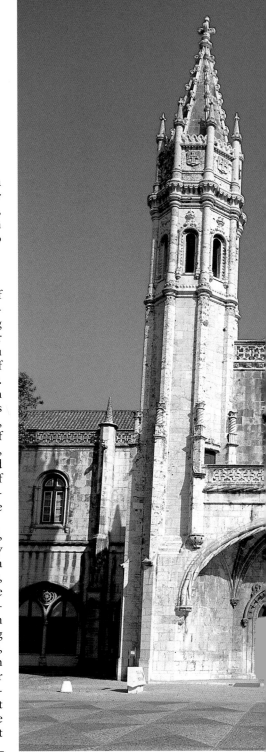

Situated on the right bank of the Tejo river estuary, just southwest of Lisbon, lies Belém. The name is an abbreviation of Bethlehem, the birthplace of Jesus Christ, and is in itself an indication of the town's strongly religious character. At the heart of Belém is a large monastery named after Hieronymus, or St. Jerome, so-called father of the church, who lived towards the end of the fourth century and is chiefly renowned for his definitive Latin translation of the Bible, the Vulgate. He spent much of his life in Bethlehem, where he was in charge of several monasteries.

The Hieronymites' monastery in Lisbon dates back to Henry the Navigator. Born in 1394, the third son of King John I of Portugal, Henry had a keen interest in all things nautical. He revolutionized navigational practices and was the instigator of numerous innovations in ship-building techniques. It was on his initiative that the 'caravela' was developed, an improved version of the Hanseatic cog, and later used for voyages of discovery. His aim was to find a sea route to Asia which would bypass the need to trade with the Arab middlemen. Had it not been for Henry the Navigator, the voyages of Christopher Columbus might never have taken place.

Thanks to Henry's efforts, Portugal became an important seafaring nation and colonial power. Its possessions stretched from Africa to China and South America. Colonial influences and three centuries of Islamic rule under the Caliphate of Córdoba combined to produce a particular style of architectural ornamentation, known as the Manueline style, in honor of King Dom Manuel, who reigned 1495-1521.

Trees as supporting pillars

The Manueline style is an offshoot of Late Gothic architecture. The supporting pillars and overhead vaulting put one in mind of trees and their branching foliage. Everywhere you look, there are richly carved motifs of fish, coral, and exotic plants in stone. Circular windows are framed with images of nautical symbols, such as anchors, navigational instruments, and coiled ropes. Other examples of this style can be seen in Batalha, Setúbal, and Tomar. The best and most lavish example of this style of architectural ornamentation indigenous to Portugal can be seen at the monastery of St. Jerome in Belém.

It was built on the site of a chapel, in which sailors would gather to pray before their ships set sail. Vasco da Gama, the famous seafaring explorer, is also said to have worshipped here before setting off in 1497 on his successful circumnavigation of Africa. In memory of this great voyage, King Manuel I had a monastery built, modeled on the mausoleum in Batalha. Building work began under Matheus Fernandes, and was continued by João de Castilho, the most notable architect of the Manueline period. The entire complex was built

between 1517 and 1551, under the supervision of João de Castilho. At the heart of the monastery is the church of Santa Maria. Sculptures in the church's interior are the work of Nicolau Chatranez, a Frenchman.

The tomb of Vasco da Gama

The church of Santa Maria has a nave and two aisles and measures 302ft (92m) in length and 74ft (22.6m) across, rising to a height of 82ft (25m). The octagonal pillars are decorated with ornate reliefs.

In the transept and apse are the tombs of King Manuel I, his successors, and numerous relatives: a total of seven kings, seven queens, and nineteen infants of the House of Aviz, in other words, the dynasty which began with King John I, Henry the Navigator's father.

It is not only members of the royal family who were laid to rest in the church. The Hieronymites' monas-

tery is to Portugal what the Panthéon in Paris is to France. Beneath the organ platform in the church of Santa Maria are the tombs of Vasco da Gama and Luís Vaz de Camões, Portugal's greatest poet, who died of the plague in 1580. He had led an extremely colorful life, full of love affairs and fist fights. He traveled as far as Macao in China and Moçambique in Africa. His greatest epic poem entitled *Os Lusídaes* was composed during his travels and exalts Vasco da Gama's voyage of exploration. It is somehow fitting that the explorer and his literary chronicler are buried in the same church.

On the northern side of the monastery is the cloister created by João de Castilho. It is a double-galleried construction with elaborately ornate Manueline decoration. It comprises a stone lion fountain, dedicated to St. Jerome. He is usually portrayed removing a thorn from a lion's paw.

This is entirely allegorical, with the lion symbolizing the true doctrine and the thorn representing the flaw in it. Hieronymus was not only a translator and abbot, but also a passionate opponent of any deviations from accepted theological teachings.

The main portal of St. Jerónimos monastery in Belém with its two towers (above, left)

The central nave and high altar in the church of Santa Maria (above, right)

Vasco da Gama rests in his sarcophagus at the foot of pillars decorated in the Manueline style (below, left)

The complex variety of typical Manueline ornamentation is also evident in the ceiling vaulting (below, right)

A high point of French Gothic

AMIENS cathedral is famous for its precious statues and reliefs

After the Revolution, the historic province of Picardy in the north of France was divided into the three départements of Aisne, Oise, and Somme. The name of the region recalls a weapon, the pike, and the soldiers who carried it, as in the days of the French kings they mostly came from this part of the country.

Picardy has borders with Champagne, the Paris basin, and the Channel coast, and Flanders is not far away. The air smells of damp and mist. The capital of the former province and administrative center of the present-day département of Somme is Amiens. The city, which stands on the middle reaches of the river Somme, is home to all kinds of industries and has a university named after Jules Verne, the pioneer science fiction writer, who met his death in Amiens.

The unmistakable heart of the city is the cathedral of Notre-Dame, the biggest Gothic church in France, with twice the capacity of Notre-Dame de Paris. This is not the only superlative that this cathedral can boast. With its astonishing total of 3600 sculptures, most of which are to be found on the west front, it can claim another first place among the medieval churches in France and the rest of Europe.

Beginning with the west front

In the thirteenth century, when the cathedral was built, Amiens was a prosperous town. Its origins go back a long way. The area was originally settled by Celtic tribes, who were conquered by Caesar during the Gallic Wars. The Romans named this province Ambianum. An important thoroughfare passed close to Amiens, which became a Christian bishopric in the fifth century.

Before the present cathedral, there were several wooden churches which finally gave way to a Romanesque cathedral. This burned down in 1218 and work began on the rebuilding. The bishop responsible was Evrard de Fouilloy, and we also know the name of his architect, Robert de Luzarches, who was succeeded in 1225 by Thomas de Cormont and his son Regnault.

Contrary to custom, they began by building the west front and the nave, and these were also the first parts to be finished. Some previously existing buildings had to be moved to make room for the extensions, including the church of St. Firmin and the hospital for the poor. Work was interrupted between 1240 and 1258 for lack of money. Later, the choir was built and the first windows put in. King Louis IX of France, known as St. Louis, visited the cathedral when he came to Amiens in order to settle a dispute between Henry III of England and his barons. The decision has entered the history books as the Mise of Amiens.

Relics of St. Firmin

By 1269, the major part of the work was finished. The short building time had the effect of ensuring the greatest possible stylistic unity. In 1279, the relics of St. Firmin were ceremonially transferred to the new church in the presence of the kings of France and England. Firmin was the first bishop of Amiens and suffered a martyr's death in the days of the emperor Diocletian. He is now the patron saint of the city.

After 1290, the chapels were begun. The south tower was erected in 1366 and the north tower in 1375. Ten years later, King Charles IV of France, known as Charles the Mad, married Isabella of Bavaria in the cathedral. Meanwhile, the Hundred Years' War was raging between England and France, in which Picardy was constantly caught up, but minor work continued inside the cathedral, including the installation of the superb organ. Like other medieval buildings, Amiens entered a twilight period during the Renaissance and Baroque eras. It was not until the nineteenth century that Eugène Emmanuel Viollet-le-Duc, the founder of the movement for the preservation of historical monuments in France, drew attention to the building and initiated the most essential restoration work, which is still continuing. Tourists visiting Amiens today come as a rule to see the impressive cathedral.

It is a three-nave basilica, with a five-nave choir and a Lady chapel built out to the east. The two non-matching towers are low and do not quite reach to the height of the roof turret. The buttresses appear unusually protuberant. Apart from its rich sculptural decoration, the west front also has a large rose window.

Inside, the visitor is impressed by the cleverly ornamented floor with its famous octagonal labyrinth, in which lines of black and red marble lead to a central stone. There, you can see images of the three architects and the man who first commissioned them, with white doves fluttering between them. An inscription dating from the Middle Ages tells the story of the building of the church.

The sculptures take the form of saints and gargoyles in the shape of animals and demons. Both towers have galleries with stone statues of kings. All the sculptures were once painted. Time and weathering have washed most of the paint away. It has been preserved in only a few places, for instance on the relief telling the story of St. Firmin and especially on the gilded virgin on the central pillar of the south portal of the transept – a magnificent statue of the Madonna with angels hovering round her.

GETTING THERE:
Good road and rail connections from Paris, or via Lille airport

OPENING TIMES:
Usually 8:30 A.M. - 6:45 P.M. daily. In winter, 8:30 A.M. - 12:00 A.M. and 2:00 P.M. - 5:00 P.M.

SPECIAL INTEREST:
The choir stalls with 110 carved stalls and 4000 Biblical scenes

Exterior of Amiens cathedral. The main façade with its two low towers is particularly beautiful (main picture)

With its tall pillars and impressive vaulted ceiling, Amiens became the model for cathedral building west of the Rhine. View of the vaulting in the transept (below)

The smile of Reims

Notre-Dame was the model for cathedral buildings on the French side of the Rhine

In the Palais du Tau, the former palace of the bishops of Reims, is a 9th-century jewel protected by thick, bulletproof glass. It is an oval gold pendant, set with precious stones of various sizes. This jewel was once owned by Charles, King of the Franks and Holy Roman Emperor, otherwise known as Charlemagne – Carolus Magnus in Latin. He wore this pendant as an amulet. There is a certain historical logic to the fact that it is now in Reims, as in Charlemagne's time the city was truly the center of France, more important than Aix-la-Chapelle or Paris. It remained so for some time, due to the annual trade fairs which drew merchants from all over Europe.

Scene of royal coronations

The cathedral of Notre-Dame (Our Lady) is the seat of the bishops of Reims. It was the scene of the crowning of Frankish and French kings, starting with Charlemagne's father Pépin (or Pippin) and ending with Charles X in 1825. The reason for this was that the Frankish leader Clovis, the Merovingian conqueror of Late Roman Gaul, was baptized in Reims, on the very spot where the cathedral now stands.

The coronation ritual was of more than ceremonial significance in at least one case. After her victory at Orleans during the Hundred Years' War between England and France, Joan of Arc, the shepherdess from Lorraine, was told by heavenly voices that Charles VII should be crowned king. In commemoration of this, there is a small, bronze, equestrian statue of her outside the Palais de Justice.

At the time Joan carried out her ceremony, the cathedral was already in its present form. As with all great medieval cathedrals, there had been churches on the site before it. The oldest, dating back to the fifth century, was probably commissioned by the newly-baptized Clovis. After a great fire in 1211, Jean d'Orbais, one of the first master builders of the time whose name we know, began work on a Gothic cathedral which, with its four successors, was largely completed by 1294. Only the towers took longer. The last to be finished was the crossing tower, erected in 1485.

This means that the 454ft (138.5m)-long cathedral with its two truncated towers is a building of great stylistic unity. Because it stands so close to the lands that would later come to be called Germany, it became a model for cathedral builders on the German side of the Rhine as well. This was probably because the workers were not tied to any one country and moved freely from one building site to the next, taking with them the knowledge and experience they had acquired elsewhere.

In the mysterious light

Notre-Dame de Reims is a three-nave basilica with a transept and a chevet, or ring of chapels, around the choir. The huge nave, with its slender bundle pillars running up into pointed arches, creates an atmosphere of mystery, partly because of the way the light is broken up and filtered through the stained glass windows. The glass dates from many different centuries. The great rose window above the main door is entirely thirteenth century.

The last work of importance is that of Marc Chagall, the 20th-century artist from Vitebsk in White Russia, who in old age developed a fondness for Biblical themes and provided church window designs for Metz and Mainz as well as Reims.

The cathedral of Notre-Dame de Reims is most famous in the history of art for its exterior. It boasts an extraordinary richness of statuary, and the artistic standard of the carving is very high. You can see Jesus Christ the Savior at the various stages of his life, and there are saints, the Virgin Mary, French kings, and several Old Testament characters including a brilliantly executed figure of King Solomon.

The cathedral of the angels

Above all, there are angels; countless angels, leaning on pillars, kneeling under canopies, and, most famous of all, the one on the left door, known as 'le Sourire de Reims', or 'the Smile of Reims'.

In this case, it is not the original, but a replica. Reims, the capital of the Champagne region, has been an arena of conflict at least since the days of the Celtic tribe of the Remi. Romans, Huns, and Franks passed through or settled here, hordes of soldiers devastated the area during the Hundred Years' War, and finally the German armies of two world wars marched over it in the twentieth century. Between 1914 and 1918, the territory of Champagne and nearby mountain region of the Ardennes were bitterly fought over. Reims suffered severe damage. The cathedral of Notre-Dame was burned to ruins. It has since been fully restored and every modern-day attention has been paid to detail in the preservation of historical monuments.

Apart from the crowning of kings and the chaos of war, Champagne's reputation is based on a drink. The land is the source of the sparkling wine that bears its name, whose precious grapes ripen in or near Reims. On fine days, you can see pensioners sitting on the benches in the Place du Cardinal Luçon in front of the cathedral, with piccolo bottles of a champagne that fetches high prices in the luxury food stores of the world. There they sit, quietly drinking, daydreaming, and smiling, with the angels on the cathedral smiling in return.

Sublime setting

Notre-Dame, the most famous church in **PARIS**, was built on an island in the Seine

GETTING THERE:
International rail and air links. By Métro to Cité. Accessible by river, disembarking at Notre-Dame quay

OPENING TIMES:
Usually open from 8:00 A.M. – 6:45 P.M. daily

SPECIAL INTEREST:
The rose windows in the west and south façades

"**A**ll harmonious parts of one magnificent whole, superimposed in five gigantic stories, unfold before the eye in one untroubled mass," wrote Victor Hugo, whilst conceding that it was "hard not to regret, not to feel indignation at the numberless degradations and mutilations which time and men have wrought simultaneously on this venerable monument."

These words stem from *Notre-Dame de Paris*, which was published in 1831 and, more than just a novel, was also a treatise on the scarred beauty of the cathedral that was once

the palace of the archbishop of Paris.

At the time of writing, the building was in poor repair, a circumstance that seemed to worry no one but Hugo. It was his novel that sparked a reawakening of public awareness, resulting in the commissioning of two architects, Lassus and Violett-le-Duc, to undertake its restoration.

Historical background

Notre-Dame de Paris is situated on the Ile de la Cité, an island in the Seine which is the oldest inhabited part of the city and was first occupied by

Celts and Romans. Bishop Maurice de Sully initiated the cathedral's construction in 1145, its foundation stone being laid in 1163 by Pope Alexander III himself. The choir was dedicated in 1182 and, by 1250, the west front and twin towers were completed. This was the period of early Gothic architecture; according to Hugo's novel, French crusaders brought back the pointed arch design from the Orient, although historically speaking this is not entirely accurate.

Notre-Dame is a multi-storied, galleried basilica, built to a Gothic

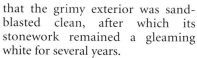

ground-plan. There are altogether 37 side chapels, originating in the thirteenth and fourteenth centuries, as did half of the choir stalls. Stone slabs in the floor commemorate the graves of numerous bishops. The treasury contains monstrances, written texts, and reliquaries, the most important being the Crown of Thorns and a piece of the True Cross. Both are on display to the public on Good Friday.

The comparative gloom of the cathedral's interior is heavy with incense. Only a small proportion of the original stained glass windows has survived intact, for example those in the crossing. Most of them were removed in the eighteenth century by order of the court. Their restoration was not fully completed until after World War II.

The cathedral's façade features three asymmetrical portals, above which rise two 226ft (69m)-high,

square-topped towers. The original plans clearly envisaged these being crowned with steeples. The fact that they were never built has endowed the cathedral with its unique and unmistakable silhouette.

A product of centuries

Notre-Dame, like most other cathedrals throughout Europe, has centuries of influence engraved in its stonework. Ambition and individual tastes, not to mention general apathy, have all played a part in creating the church we see today. Master builder Jean de Chelles, creator of the North Portal in 1250, was succeeded ten years later by Pierre de Montreuil, who created the east-facing Red Portal. Then came Soufflot, the Baroque artist, followed by Lassus, Viollet-le-Duc, and, finally, André Malraux, writer and Minister of Culture under De Gaulles. It was at his instigation

that the grimy exterior was sand-blasted clean, after which its stonework remained a gleaming white for several years.

Hugo, who lamented the disappearance of the original elaborate statuary, would have been pleased that this has since been restored – though not necessarily in its authentic form, since the figures of the apostles, for example, now include one whose face is modeled on Viollet-le-Duc. The majority of sculptures are originals or at least copies of the originals. The carvings depict the Last Judgment, St. Anna, various kings, prophets, and angels, and, as one would expect, numerous figures of the cathedral's namesake, Our Lady, the Virgin Mary. What the visitor cannot see is that these statues were all painted in former times.

With six-and-a-half million people visiting it every year, Paris is by far one of the world's most popular cities. A large proportion of tourists include Notre-Dame on their sight-seeing itinerary, placing it among the world's most frequented churches. Behind the ranks of coaches are burial sites, which offer an insight into the island's archaeological origins. "Time is the architect," wrote Victor Hugo in 1831, and so it has remained.

Island of culture on the site of an ancient settlement in the heart of the city: the unmistakable landmark of Notre-Dame, with its twin towers, viewed here from the river (far left)

The view from these towers, looking east across the cathedral roof towards the Seine and the eastern part of the city (right)

The interior of this most famous of Paris churches once witnessed the coronations of Henry VI and Napoleon (above, center)

A winged gargoyle perches among the sculptures of the façade (below, center)

A wealth of rose windows

CHARTRES cathedral – a model for other Gothic churches

GETTING THERE:
By car, about 62 miles (100km) south-west of Paris via motorway. Good rail and bus links

OPENING TIMES:
Usually 9:00 A.M. to 6:00 P.M. daily

SPECIAL INTEREST:
The cathedral's many colored, stained-glass windows

The small town of Chartres, situated 62.5 miles (100km) south-west of Paris, has on two occasions during its history been linked with people or events of national importance. Firstly, there is Jean Moulin, one of the leaders of the French resistance movement against Nazi occupation during World War II. He was captured by the Germans in 1943 and died during deportation. He had formerly held the position of Prefect in Chartres, hence the many memorials in his honor, reflecting the town's pride in its close association with him.

Much earlier, in 1594, Henry, King of Navarre and the first Bourbon to rule in Paris, was crowned ruler of France in Chartres cathedral, an unusual departure from tradition as this ceremony was normally performed in Reims. Henry IV, one of France's most significant rulers and author of the Edict of Nantes, wanted to re-establish religious freedom in France. He himself changed his faith four times, ultimately dying a Catholic. The location he chose for his coronation anticipated the faith he was to embrace at the end of his life. The cathedral has for a long time been a place of pilgrimage and is regarded as one of the main bastions of Catholic France.

Two thousand stone figures

This sacred building has served as a source of inspiration for numerous writers. Charles Péguy, one of France's leading Modernists, was inspired to write emotively on the subject of the cathedral.

The abundance of detail and items of special interest are simply overwhelming. There are around two thousand magnificent examples of medieval stone figures. Even at the time of their creation, the veneration they engendered was so great it extended beyond the Rhine. There are 3 large rose windows and 150 stained-glass windows dating from the thirteenth century. No other church can boast such incomparable glories.

The cathedral of Notre-Dame stands in an elevated position above the River Eure on the site of what was once a Gallo-Roman sanctuary. It was not until 300 years after the Roman invasion of Gaul that the town of Carnutum, as it was then called, experienced its first Christian bishop. The two crypts, the older one dating from the Carolingian period, are remnants of this early period of its history.

The year 1195 saw the start of construction work on the present-day cathedral, incorporating the intact remains of the early Gothic west front of its predecessor. The unknown architect of the central nave took this style of architecture further, achieving new levels of height and lightness which, together with its architectural stabilizing features, came to serve as a blueprint for many other cathedrals, not just in France but in England and Germany too.

The present-day cathedral was consecrated in 1260. The original design included plans for nine towers, but these never materialized. Notre-Dame de Chartres has only the 344ft (105m)-high Vieux Clocher and the 384ft (117m)-high Clocher Neuf. The upper part of this was not added until the sixteenth century and its filigree detail contrasts sharply with the pure Gothic style of the south tower, completed four hundred years earlier.

Place of pilgrimage

The cathedral has three portals: to the west is the Royal Portal, with another at either end of the transept. Each portal has three doorways, each of which is surrounded by several tiers of rich, sculptural ornamentation, not to mention the sculpted figures featured on the doorways themselves and on the choir screens.

It is not easy to single out individual details for special mention. The figures depict scenes from the entire Bible and the stained-glass windows follow on with this representation of Bible stories, completing or varying them or depicting stories from the lives of saints, such as Thomas à Becket, who spent several years in exile in France before returning to England, where he was murdered in his own cathedral of Canterbury. Thomas visited Chartres on several occasions.

Chartres did not entirely escape the rigours of the French Revolution. The cathedral was transformed into a Temple of Reason, its most precious relic, a veil belonging to the Virgin Mary, was removed, and a statue of the Madonna from one of the crypts was burned. Plans to destroy the cathedral altogether were not carried out, however, and half a century later the destroyed statue was replaced. The crypt is once again the place of pilgrimage that it was in the Middle Ages. Chartres cannot hope to compete with the mass allure of Lourdes in this respect, but the town is nevertheless proud of the fact that ever-increasing numbers of pilgrims, including young people, are choosing to visit it.

The impressive simplicity of the central nave reflects the aspiration to heaven characteristic of Gothic architecture (main picture)

The main façade is dominated by its non-matching spires (right)

The scene of Noah and his wife going aboard the Ark is an example of 12th /13th century, early glass-painting (above)

The most famous rose window in Europe

STRASBOURG cathedral, with its unique stained glass windows, is a miracle of Gothic architecture

❝The first time I went to the cathedral, my head was filled with what is generally recognized as good taste. From hearsay alone, I honored the harmony of masses, the purity of form, I was a sworn enemy of the intricate arbitrariness of Gothic ornamentation," wrote the German poet Johann Wolfgang von Goethe. But then: "When I approached it, what an unexpected sensation of surprise the sight aroused in me! My soul was filled with one great overall impression, which I could taste and enjoy, but was quite unable to understand or explain, because it was made up of a thousand details, all in harmony with one another."

Goethe spent some time as a student in Strasbourg. In 1771, he received the degree of Doctor of Law from the university, and had a passionate love affair with the daughter of a priest nearby. He wrote an essay about the cathedral, which has become famous. At that time, Strasbourg was still a predominantly German-speaking city. The university was German-speaking and Alsace, with the city of Strasbourg at its center, was a largely autonomous region. The radical change in becoming an integral part of the French republic came about as a result of the Revolution; the revolutionary hymn *la Marseillaise* was actually written here.

In 1793, at the height of Jacobin rule, the cathedral became a 'Temple of Reason', with 235 of its precious sculptures being destroyed. The Gothic tower was topped by a Jacobin metal cap. The reverence for culture and history expressed by Goethe did not become a virtue again until later, when the bourgeoisie had fully established itself and started to seek out its historic roots.

Architect from Germany

In his essay, Goethe mentions one of the architects of the cathedral by name: Erwin von Steinbach. He was the architect of the west front. Other names have come down to us, more than for other cathedrals of the High and Late Middle Ages: Ulrich von Ensingen, who built the north tower; Johannes Hültz, who was responsible for the tower cap; and Bernhard Nonnenmacher, who completed St. Catharine's chapel. These architects were of German origin, but they built in the Gothic style that came from France. Strasbourg cathedral unites the cultural trends and activities of the two neighbouring countries. The result is one of the great buildings of medieval Europe.

The building has a long history. Originally a Carolingian chapel stood on the site, at the time when Strasbourg was one of the great cities of the Frankish empire. The division of the empire is recorded in the Oaths of Strasbourg, one of the earliest documents to be written in French and German, rather than the usual Latin. The chapel was burned to the ground in 1007. Work on the new building began in 1015. When the cathedral was half completed, it was seriously damaged in another major fire. Altogether, the cathedral took a good four hundred years to build. Alterations and improvements continued until well into the nineteenth century.

Built as a parish church

The cathedral stands between two prestigious open spaces in the Old Town of Strasbourg: the Place de la Cathédrale to the north and the Place du Château to the south. The latter is named after the Château des Rohan, which was once the seat of office of the archbishops and takes its name from an ancient French noble family whose best known representative was Cardinal Rohan, the main participant in the 'affair of the necklace' that preceded the Revolution.

The Place de la Cathédrale is dominated by a number of impressive, late medieval noblemen's houses – notably the Maison Kammerzell with its splendid half-timbered façade, and the Cathédrale de Notre-Dame, which was first and foremost a parish church. The inhabitants of Strasbourg invested considerable sums in this building and much evidence of this remains.

It is built in the red sandstone of the Vosges. Geologically speaking, this is identical with the Black Forest sandstone used in the construction of Freiburg cathedral. There are two side aisles flanking the 334ft (103m)-long nave. Of the two towers that were originally planned, only one was finished, in 1439. It reaches to a height of 466ft (142m), and the view through the Gothic tracery of its spire is breathtaking. Chapels and sacristies open off the transept.

The cathedral is famous for the colorful rose window in the west front, which is an impressive 44ft (13.5m) in diameter, and the so-called 'imperial' windows. Then there is the splendid astronomical clock at the south end of the transept, dating from around 1550. Notable sculptures are the figures of Ecclesia and Synagoga (church and synagogue) that survived destruction by the Jacobins, the coronation of Mary, the font of 1453, and the sculpture of the Mount of Olives dating from about the same period.

Patron saint of the church

The oldest parts of the cathedral to be preserved are, as usual, the crypt and the crossing, both of which are clearly Romanesque in origin. The organ is from the famous Silbermann workshop. The most beautiful of the chapels is the Chapelle St. Laurent, dedicated to St. Lawrence. St. Lawrence is the patron saint of cooks, bakers, and brewers. Those he protects are still at work in the immediate neighborhood today – as you can tell from the aromas wafting through the streets.

GETTING THERE:
Via the international airport on the edge of the city. Good rail and motorway connections in all directions

OPENING TIMES:
Until further notice, daily 7:00 A.M. - 11:30 A.M. and 12:40 P.M. - 7:00 P.M. No admission for tourists during Mass and prayers

SPECIAL INTEREST:
The astronomical clock in the transept

The west front, illuminated at night, and the great rose window (main picture)

View of the vaults on the south side of the nave with the high stained glass windows (below, left)

Corbel on the west front. The two sculptures represent the judgment of Solomon (below, center)

Distant prospect of the cathedral (below, right)

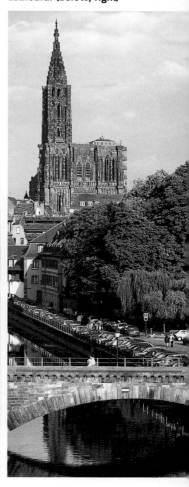

The modern temple

Le Corbusier's pilgrims' chapel in **RONCHAMP** is the most famous church to be built in the twentieth century

ATLANTIC OCEAN

Ronchamp

FRANCE

Mediterranean Sea

GETTING THERE:
Via the motorway Mulhouse-Besançon, turning off at Belfort. Ronchamp lies about 22 miles (35km) to the north

OPENING TIMES:
Currently 10:00 A.M. - 6:00 P.M. daily

SPECIAL INTEREST:
The pilgrimages on 15 August and 8 September

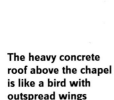

The heavy concrete roof above the chapel is like a bird with outspread wings (main picture)

The interior is spartan and unadorned. Only the light falling through the multicolored glass of the windows gives the church its particular solemnity (below)

Le Corbusier called the pilgrims' church Notre-Dame-du-Haut in Ronchamp a 'high seat', as it symbolizes both height and eminence. Admirers have since described the church as being like 'a graceful flower', 'a bird', and 'a sculpture', sitting enthroned above the soft, green countryside of Franche-Comté. It has thus become a twofold place of pilgrimage. Pilgrims come here in tens of thousands to pray to the Virgin Mary but also as admirers of the architect, who set out his manifesto in the form of this church. It is built of plain reinforced concrete, yet seems to defy all laws of gravity with the roof hovering above the building like a bird soaring into the air.

A triumphal march right from the start? By no means, as Le Corbusier had to suffer more malice, criticism, and ridicule for Notre-Dame-du-Haut than for any other of his works – not to mention the hostility of the disconcerted inhabitants.

The Swiss-born architect was, however, the spontaneous choice of the ecclesiastical authorities in 1950, when it came to building a new church on the site of a crusaders' chapel that had been destroyed by the German army. There had been a temple on the site back in heathen times and a Marian chapel had stood there since the fourth century. Le Corbusier hesitated at first, then agreed after being captivated by the atmosphere of the place. "A respectable personality" he later wrote "was present, the landscape, the four corners of the earth. They were what decided it."

Building in concrete

Le Corbusier wrote detailed comments on the progress of his designs and also on the building work, which dragged on for two years. The decision to build in concrete was partly determined by the height of the site and access problems. He also saw it, however, as a material that does not deceive or dazzle. The church was ready for consecration in 1955, and has since become one of France's major tourist attractions.

People approach the church almost reverently. As they climb the steep slope, it suddenly appears on the open hillside between the trees and bushes. Le Corbusier experienced architecture as a 'play', the staging of a production on which the curtain rises very slowly. A firmly anchored main tower, walls that are not vertical with openings of different kinds, and a floating roof lend lightness to the body of the church. The planes of the limewashed walls seem to dissolve beneath it. As if pressed down by a giant hand, the roof, which has been left in undressed concrete, slopes down to the lowest part of the chapel. Each of the four façades bears a different signature, emphasizing different perspectives. Like a grey-green sea, the woods, fields, and valleys of the countryside spread out far below; they are far, too, from the present day.

Entering the church at the north door calls to mind early Romanesque churches and mosques. The south wall of the chapel opposite commands attention, being transformed into a kind of sculpture by means of the light. The windows, like magic triangles, rectangles, and squares, are set deep in the walls and their glass, mostly colored, allows only a small amount of light to penetrate.

The silence of light

"A vessel of silence and of gentleness," wrote Le Corbusier, adding: "A wish? Yes, to succeed in expressing the feelings that are unloosed here through the language of architecture." The light sources are arranged in such a way as to emphasize the high altar. A seventeenth-century Madonna, which had stood in the previous church, was integrated into the chapel.

Concentration on the essential is also a feature of the interior layout and the high altar, pulpit, choir stall, balcony, and even the confessionals consist of simple shapes in concrete. The wooden seats and cast iron communion rail are crucial elements, enlivening the interior space. At the same time, the two sides of the chapel are distinguished by variations in spatial effect – one side is influenced by harmony, the other by the dissolution of equilibrium.

The church only holds about two hundred people, which is not enough

for a place of pilgrimage. On the two Marian festivals of 15 August and 8 September, when up to thirty thousand people flood into Ronchamp, the parvis – built for precisely this purpose – becomes a huge, open-air cathedral. Mass is then celebrated on the simple altar in the outdoor choir and the architecture, together with the trees, landscape, and sky, create a room more beautiful than any church can offer.

The suburb of Heaven

Led by Richard the Lionheart, the third crusade began in 1190 in the monastery church of **VÉZELAY**

The Romanesque cathedral of Vézelay rises like a castle above the city (main picture)

The capitals of the pillars are ornamented with figurative representations from the height of the Romanesque period. It is unique for a religious building to have so many of these grouped together (below, right)

Nuns and monks gather for prayer in the Gothic choir at the end of the nave (below, center)

Part of the west front (below, left)

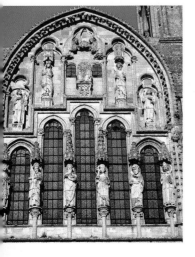

When you see the 'colline éternelle', the 'eternal hill' of Vézelay, crowned by the cathedral of Sainte Madeleine and emerging majestically from among the Burgundian vineyards, you understand why people talk of a 'suburb of Heaven'. Medieval pilgrims flocked there in such vast numbers that up to 12,000 people, including 800 monks and nuns in their flowing habits, then lived in the town, which today has only 500 inhabitants. Even in those days, people climbed the steep Rue St. Pierre, which is now lined with houses from every century and, together with the cathedral, has come under the protection of the German organization Erbe der Menschheit (Human Heritage).

A Benedictine convent and the church in St. Père sous Vézelay formed the nucleus of the town, which was founded between 858 and 864 in the valley of the Cure. After its destruction by the Normans in 887, a monastery complex was built on a more advantageous site on a hill overlooking the river, and it soon began to prosper.

Relics of St. Mary Magdalene

A crucial factor in the meteoric rise of the monastery was the cult of St. Mary Magdalene, promoted by the foundation at Cluny. Key to this were the relics of Mary Magdalene, the penitent and companion of Christ, which had somehow been acquired from Provence. Vézelay was not just a place of pilgrimage in its own right, however; it was a starting point for pilgrims from Lorraine, Germany, and Switzerland to join the route of St. James for the great pilgrimage to Santiago de Compostela.

The town attained great political importance in 1146, when Bernard of Clairvaux addressed a reputed 100,000 of the faithful in the presence of King Louis VII and called people to the second crusade. Forty-four years later, under the leadership of Philip Augustus and Richard the Lionheart, the third crusade actually started from Vézelay.

The building of the church was also determined by historical events. At the end of the eleventh century, in order to accommodate the hordes of pilgrims, the Carolingian church with the tomb of Mary Magdalene in its crypt was replaced. In 1120, however, a fire that cost over a thousand lives destroyed the new building, which was as yet incomplete. Over the course of the next 15 years, it was replaced by the present Romanesque basilica. The three-aisled vestibule was completed in 1150; the choir in the Gothic style was added later, following another fire.

Vézelay began to decline around the middle of the thirteenth century, when doubt was cast on the genuineness of the Mary Magdalene relics. Her body had been found in St. Maximine in Provence, so people no longer wanted to go on pilgrimage to Vézelay. Monastic life continued until 1537, however, when the monastery was converted into a choir school. During the Wars of Religion, Vézelay was ravaged several times by the Huguenots; in 1790, it was completely closed down.

Famous tympanum

One by one, all the monastery buildings were demolished, until only the church remained – a 'heavenly castle', whose uniqueness was rediscovered by the 'romantic' nineteenth century with its newly awakened love of the Middle Ages. On the initiative of the poet Prosper Mérimée and other art enthusiasts, work was begun on restoring the crumbling church, and the young architect Viollet-le-Duc restored its Romanesque strength and beauty. Sainte Madeleine has now been entrusted to the care of the Fraternité Monastique de Jérusalem, a modern religious community founded in Paris. Every year, more than a million visitors come to Vézelay.

Anyone climbing the steps to the great door in the west front first enters the narthex, a completely separate vestibule and church for pilgrims. Three entrances lead from here into the church itself. The middle one is surmounted by a tympanum, one of the most famous in the Romanesque style. The more than life-size figure of Christ in the mandola sits enthroned above the disciples, and a semicircular panel with the signs of the zodiac and images of the seasons gives a lively account of the everyday life of the people.

Romanesque pillar decoration

On entering the church, there is a feeling of surprise at its extreme width; in fact, vaults so wide and at the same time so high are unusual in Romanesque architecture. The nave is 39ft (12m) wide by 210ft (64m) long, with the aisles not humbly bowing before the nave but raising their heads majestically.

The Gothic choir, which stands at the end of the nave, is absolutely flooded with light, further increasing the brightness of the church. The clever way in which brown and white stones have been laid next to one another in the arches also produces a lively effect.

Apart from the tympanum, the sensational thing from the art history point of view is the rich ornamentation on the capitals of the 60 or more pillars, which with their scintillating sculptures are considered to form one of the most beautiful collections of Romanesque art.

As you descend to the crypt, you are entering straight into history, as this area was built in the Carolingian era. Here, relics of Mary Magdalene, brought from another church in Burgundy, are once again on show.

Conviction of the existence of the spirit of the 'suburb of Heaven' can also be entered into when standing on the terrace behind the cathedral. From here, there is a view for miles over northern Morvan, fields and meadows, red roofs and white cattle; a landscape over which church bells have rung out for more than a thousand years.

Gothic brick architecture

ALBI cathedral in south-western France is a reminder
of the wars waged by the Church against the Cathari

The cathedral of St.
Cécile perches above
the town and River
Tarn like a castle
(above, right)

Building work began in
1282 after the end of
the Albigensian wars. A
special feature of this
great church is its well-
preserved, decorative
wall painting (below,
right)

During the fifteenth
century, the baldachin
was added on the
south side, a magnifi-
cent covered portal
with porch (below, left)

Gothic brick architecture is normally regarded as being restricted
to northern Europe. Any region want-
ing to imitate the lofty churches of
France and southern Germany with
their vaulted ceilings reaching heav-
enward, but lacking local sandstone
quarries, had no choice but to resort
to alternative materials, in this case
bricks of fired clay.

It became clear that the suitabil-
ity of this building material was not
confined to the construction of
dwellings but could be used equally
well for the walls, towers, pillars, and
ribbed vaulting of Gothic cathedrals.
The earliest examples of this type of
construction can be seen in southern
Scandinavia; it later spread to other
areas, for example the coastal towns
of the Baltic and the Cistercian
monasteries of central Germany.

A preference for clay

Albi, situated in Gascony in south-
western France, 50 miles (80km)
north-east of Toulouse, boasts a
brick-built Gothic cathedral. Cinema
enthusiasts, familiar with the film of
The Three Musketeers by Dumas, in
which the main character, D'Artag-
nan, hails from Gascony, will know
that the contemporary building trend
at the time, not only in that particular part of southern France but in
Paris too, reflected a definite preference for the warm, reddish-brown
color of bricks, which showed to particular advantage when combined
with sandstone casings for windows
and doorways.

The brick-built Gothic cathedral
of Ste. Cécile of Albi had been standing for well over 150 years. The archbishop's church of this town situated
on the River Tarn exemplifies the
brick Gothic of southern France. One
should not compare it with the
Marienkirche in Lübeck, which
became the model for brick-built
cathedrals in the Baltic region. The
color of the bricks used here is a pale
yellow, verging on grey, which at first
glance gives the appearance of sandstone architecture.

Defensive walls

The layout of this great building is
also different from those of northern
Europe. There is no spire on the
tower, no transept, no side aisles. The
cathedral consists of a huge, 328ft
(100m)-long and 98ft (30m)-high,
rectangular edifice. There is no traditional west front. There is, however, a
bell tower, at the base of which is a
chapel dedicated to St. Claire.

Albi cathedral had very close connections with the Palais de la Berbie.

The word 'berbie' derives from the
Latin 'bisbia', meaning 'bishop'. Their
defensive walls give the cathedral and
Palais an almost fortress-like appearance, which seems quite justified,
however, considering the history of
the place and surrounding area.

During the Middle Ages, Albi
found itself at the center of an hereti-
cal movement. The Cathari believed
in the strict dualism of good and evil,
pure and impure, with evil and
impure being the work of Satan.
Ascetism was regarded as the key to
one's salvation. This doctrine was
embraced by followers throughout
Europe, not just among the nobility
but also among the general populace.
In southern France, they were known
as 'Poblicants' or the 'Albigenses'. Papal
Rome waged a crusade against them,
known as the 'Albigensian war', which
lasted from 1209 to 1229 and ended
in a terrible bloodbath for the Cathari,
who were branded as heretics.

Construction of the cathedral at
Albi began over half a century after
the end of the Albigensian war. Ste.
Cécile represents an architectural triumph of victorious Papism. The simple Manicheism of the Cathari was
replaced by the large, colorful variety
of Christian traditions surrounding
the Virgin Mary and various saints.

Frescoes restored

The cathedral's interior is very colorful. This was the customary style of all
medieval churches but, whereas in
other places colors have been allowed
to fade, painted over, or washed away,
in Albi they have undergone continual
restoration. There are numerous
chapels situated between the pillars
soaring high up into the cathedral's
roof, giving rise to symmetrical
spaces, more or less square in shape.
On the outside, each chapel is characterized by a semicircular curved pro-
jection, resembling a tower.

Ste. Cécile owes its careful preservation to the historic efforts made
during the nineteenth century. What
Viollet-le-Duc accomplished elsewhere in France was achieved in Albi
by a man called César Daly. He was
active at the time of Henri de
Toulouse-Lautrec's birth in a house
near the cathedral. This was the
Impressionist painter with the crippled legs who painted prostitutes,
can-can dancers, and scenes from the
Moulin Rouge in Paris. A museum
has now opened in the Palais de la
Berbie dedicated to his work. It is
appropriate perhaps that Cécile, from
whom the cathedral derives its name,
is the patron saint of music and also,
no doubt, of fun-loving girls.

A monument to Flanders

The Onze Lieve Vrouwe cathedral in **ANTWERP** is a monument to bourgeois wealth and Gothic glory

North Sea

English Channel

Antwerp
BELGIUM

GETTING THERE:
Good rail and motor-way connections from all directions. Flights to Antwerp or Brussels airport

OPENING TIMES:
Usually Mon-Fri 10:00 A.M. - 5:00 P.M., Sat 10:00 A.M. - 3:00 P.M., Sun and Bank Holidays 1:00 P.M. - 4:00 P.M.

SPECIAL INTEREST:
Painting by Rubens in one of the side aisles

The stonemasons' delicate filigree work on the tower is clearly visible in this aerial view of the cathedral, Market Square, and the Old Town (above, right)

View up into the domed ceiling (above, left)

***Descent from the Cross** by Peter Paul Rubens (below, right)*

Scenes from everyday life in the Onze Lieve Vrouwe cathedral. Painting by Hendrik Steenwijk, Jr. and Jan Brueghel, Sr. from around 1609 (below, left)

The devil must surely have had a hand in building a tower of such height. It rises to 404ft (123m) and its lace-like, filigree design of pointed arches is of such ephemeral delicacy that it gives the appearance of dissolving into space. In medieval Antwerp, it was said that Satan had scratched himself against the tower, leaving dirty marks behind.

And today? The cathedral of Onze Lieve Vrouwe (Our Beloved Lady), situated in the heart of the town, is still a source of wonder to the hordes of visitors who come to see it, along with the tiny houses which were built here within the church grounds. They proved a good source of income for the clergy, who would also have to bear financial responsibility for their ambitious design plans for the church (seven aisles in the long nave).

The building is one of Antwerp's miracles but, at the same time, a snapshot of its past history. For, not content with a construction of seven aisles in this so-called 'Golden' sixteenth century, Emperor Charles V was persuaded to lay the foundation stone for an additional section comprising two further aisles. He remarked on doing so that "This monument is worth a kingdom." The fact that this addition never materialized just goes to show that even kingdoms cannot always provide sufficient collateral.

170 years under construction

A small chapel once stood on the site of the cathedral, which, after various episodes of building work, eventually developed into an imposing Romanesque church. In the mid fourteenth century, work began on a Gothic cathedral, which was to take 170 years to complete. The finished result in the sixteenth century was an edifice measuring 390ft (119m) in length, with a roof covering an entire hectare in area and boasting a total of 128 glass windows. In the sixteenth century, it was seen as the epitome of Flemish Gothic, a fitting architectural monument for such an undeniably important, commercial metropolis.

The transfer of the country's commercial offices from Bruges to Antwerp, the discovery of America, and Emperor Maximilian's granting of privileges to the city, all served to boost Antwerp's importance, promoting it to its unique position as the principal commercial center in Europe. More than 1000 business and trading enterprises were based here, dealing in beer and brocade, gold and silver, linen, spices, and silk. In 1576, the city was plundered by the Spaniards, under the leadership of Field Marshal Farnese, and its trade routes blockaded. This was to mark the start of its decline.

It was a long time before cultural life began to blossom again. Its re-emergence was partly thanks to an early 17th-century painter, whose monumental work has made the cathedral of Our Lady a major attraction for art enthusiasts.

Peter Paul Rubens, already highly esteemed in Spain for his work as diplomat, settled in Antwerp as a painter, creating three huge paintings for the cathedral: *Descent from the Cross, Raising the Cross*, and, finally, *The Assumption of the Virgin.* "My talent is such," he commented, "that there has never been a project, no matter how big or complex, in which my self-confidence has not proved to be well-founded."

Salute to Rubens' paintings

These works by the 'Prince of Painting' were a splendid addition to the cathedral's furnishings. People loved these giant paintings on account of the extremely life-like quality of the figures, their vitality, and the vivid-

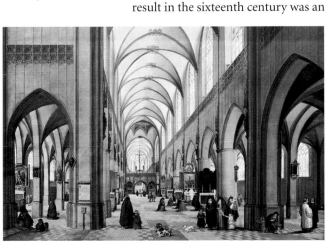

ness of their colors. Napoleon himself was so fascinated by the paintings that he had them shipped over to France after conquering the Belgian provinces. When they returned to Antwerp 20 years later, the cannons fired a welcoming tribute and all the church bells were rung.

It took the entire nineteenth century to rebuild the church's interior, which revolutionary troops had destroyed and stripped. Instead of restoring the old guild altars, however, highly ornate altars were erected in their place, dedicated to different saints and the Virgin Mary. There was still a great deal of controversy as to whether the church should continue in the Classical style or switch to neo-Gothic, which was deemed more appropriate to the rekindled interest in Catholicism.

The supporters of neo-Gothic won the day, with the result that the present-day church, with its choir stalls created around 1840, its chapels decorated with carvings of wreaths and garlands, and the altar in the chapel of the Sacrament, exhibits a cohesive style. The stained-glass windows are likewise in the neo-Gothic style and depict scenes from various episodes of the town's history. The Baroque period is also represented, however, by the magnificent pulpit, organ, and imposing crucifix.

The two world wars inflicted little damage on the church of Our Lady. During the 1960s, however, serious structural problems came to light, which entailed decades of restoration work. This has now been completed for the most part.

Anyone meandering through the forest of pillars and revelling in the magnificence of so many works of art will understand why Charles V was willing to risk his kingdom for this monument. Antwerp cathedral, Belgium's largest and loveliest church, would have been worth the sacrifice.

In the church of the Ghent altar

The winged altar was the gift of a nobleman to the cathedral of St. Bavo in **GHENT**

View across the market-place from the Belfry to the west tower of St Bavo's (main picture)

The Ghent altarpiece, painted by Jan van Eyck in collaboration with Hubert van Eyck and completed in 1432. Mary, God the Father, and John the Baptist (above); the Adoration of the Lamb (below)

In the old days, the city skyline must have made a powerful impression on people as their ships sailed into the 'Manhattan of the Middle Ages'. The towers of St. Michael's church, the belfry, and St. Bavo's cathedral rise imperiously and majestically amid the music of the carillons. No other city in Belgium has as many protected buildings as Ghent; its 400 churches, bridges, and town houses transport the visitor into a bygone age.

Secular and ecclesiastical power stand facing one another on the St. Bafsplein, with the belfry's soaring 312ft (95m) outstripping the 292ft (89m)-high west tower of the cathedral. On the opposite side, especially in the evening when it is illuminated, the façade of St. Bavo's seems to grow up into heaven, even though its origins were modest as is the case with most cathedrals.

In the tenth century there was a small church, dedicated to John the Baptist and also Sts Vedastus the Confessor and Bavo, standing near the site of the present-day cathedral. In the middle of the eleventh century, this was replaced by a cruciform Romanesque building, parts of whose impressive crypt have been preserved. At the end of the thirteenth cen-

tury, when the aisles had to be demolished because they were crumbling, the time was ripe to begin building a Gothic cathedral, which was finished in 1569. The emperor Charles V, who was born in Ghent, had also urged that this majestic church be completed. The founding of the bishopric of Ghent, with St. Bavo's as its cathedral, followed in 1561.

The elegance of the west tower

Like many cathedrals in the Low Countries, Ghent's most important church did not escape the iconoclasts, who destroyed valuable stained glass windows as well as irreplaceable treasures. In the nineteenth century, the outside was again refurbished and the buildings crowding around the church demolished, allowing the noble Gothic exterior with its elegantly ornamented west front to be seen to even better effect. A spiral staircase of 444 steps leads up to a balustrade, from where one can look out over the sea of red roofs and countryside around the Schelde estuary.

When entering the church by the main door, the enormous size of the cathedral is an immediate surprise. At 367ft (112m) long, 141ft (43m) wide, and 108ft (33m) high, it is one of the biggest churches in Belgium. In particular, the contrast between the High Gothic choir in plain, blue, Doornich stone and the colourful brick and sandstone of the nave generates an amazing excitement. The choir is the most beautiful part of the cathedral, forming a delightful link between French Gothic and Flemish Baroque.

Generous gifts

The dominant feature of the nave is the pulpit of white Italian marble and Danish oak, the work of the Ghent sculptor Laurent Delvaux in 1745. There is a marble relief on the back commemorating Bishop Triest, whose money paid for the pulpit. He contributed a huge amount to the furnishing of the cathedral, his memory being kept alive today by his splendid marble tomb in the Italian-Flemish Renaissance style which stands near the high altar.

Visiting the 25 chapels, filled with masterpieces of Netherlandish painting and sculpture, is like a stroll through the history of art. Slender and elegant, the Baroque organ – famous for its exceptional richness of sound – seems to fill the north transept like a shout of joy.

A rich nobleman presented the best known work of art in the city, the Ghent altarpiece, which is also one of the most famous paintings in Europe. Painted in 1432 by the van Eyck brothers, not only is it shrouded in mystery as far as its creation is concerned, it has also had such a momentous past that its history reads like a detective story. On more than one occasion the altarpiece was rescued at the last minute from the iconoclasts or the flames, only to be carried off by the Calvinists and subsequently recaptured by the Spanish commander Farnese who restored it to its original place.

Napoleon took individual panels to Paris, details from it adorned the Prussian royal court for a time, and fragments were also in the possession of the Brussels museum. It was not possible to put it all back together again until 1920, whereupon a spectacular church robbery in 1934 led to a panel being lost forever and having to be replaced by a replica. Fortunately, it was taken to safety in both world wars so that, after extensive restoration, the "all too precious" painting (as Albrecht Dürer described it) can inspire people again today.

Faces full of character

The Ghent altar is a winged altarpiece with a fixed central section and two movable wings. The central panel shows the Adoration of the Lamb, with God enthroned above and flanked by Mary and John the Baptist.

On the sides are maidens playing musical instruments and also Adam and Eve, both so naked and realistic that Joseph II of Austria had them put in the attic. The scenes are so vivid and the colours so brilliant they appear to have been painted only yesterday. It is possible to stand for hours before this image of the medieval world with its landscapes, flowers, and faces full of character, enjoying its magic. It does not seem to matter that it is now secured behind bulletproof glass; of much greater importance is the preservation of this masterpiece for future generations.

Gothic in Brabant

BRUSSELS cathedral was redecorated in Baroque style after the havoc wreaked by iconoclasts

An imposing flight of steps leads up to the cathedral of St. Michael and St. Gudula, making the façade, with its three portals and the 226ft (69m)-high double towers rather like those of Notre-Dame de Paris, appear even more magnificent. The steps were built in 1861, when the city – whose architecture bore the marks of the Baroque and Classical periods – was refurbished in the decades following the foundation of the kingdom of Belgium in 1830.

There was a church on the Treurenberg as long ago as the seventh century, at the place where the trade routes from Bruges to Cologne and Maubeuge in the Netherlands met. There, travelers would seek the protection of their guardian, the Archangel Michael, as well as lodging and hot food. Around 1200, a canonical church was built on the hill, but trade was so good that only 26 years later Hendrik I of Brabant began the construction of a Gothic cathedral. The building work continued for nearly 300 years.

It is the Brabant Gothic style that gives the present church its joyous lightness and an almost Moorish splendor. It is highly imaginative, precisely detailed, and finely wrought. This is largely due to the building material, which came from quarries in Flanders. The sandy Flemish limestone is easy to work, facilitating delicate tracery and rich ornamentation. Brabant Gothic is a further refinement of the classic Gothic forms and reaches perfection in the truly gigantic proportions of Brussels cathedral, which is 361ft (110m) long, 164ft (50m) wide, and 87ft (26.5 m) high.

The gift of a pulpit

The cross-rib vaulting of the nave, together with the triforium and windows, make the division of the cathedral clear. Twelve round pillars with acanthus-leaf capitals, typical of Brabant Gothic, break up the interior space. The lofty windows, dating from different periods, also have an important part to play in the majestic effect of the interior. They often depict stories of the families of the kings and dukes who ruled Brabant, including the Austrians who held sway in the sixteenth and eighteenth centuries. The oak pulpit, carved by Hendrik-Frans Verbrüggen in 1699, was presented by Maria Theresia in 1776. The French poet Victor Hugo wrote to his wife about it, saying: "it is all philosophy, all poetry."

The two towers of the cathedral are an oddity, as double towers are not, in fact, typical of Brabant Gothic.

The south tower was finished in 1451 and the north tower in 1480, with the collaboration of Jan van Ruysbroek who was also the architect and builder of Brussels town hall.

The results of destruction

Inside, despite its many art treasures, the cathedral does not seem too ornate; the turbulent history of the city has left its mark.

In 1579, during the great debate between Catholics and Calvinists, almost all the altars, statues, and paintings were destroyed by the iconoclasts. They also attacked the shrine of St. Gudula, the cathedral's second patron saint; though they scattered her bones, however, they could not destroy the myth. St. Gudula was descended from the Carolingian nobility and was born around 670.

The damage caused by the iconoclasts led to the church being completely refurbished at the end of the sixteenth century, in the Baroque style. This is most obvious from the many pictures painted in the genre but can also be seen in the chapels, like that of 'Our beloved lady of deliverance', built in the mid-seventeenth century on the orders of the Archduchess Isabella.

Rich, ecclesiastical treasures are also on display inside the chapel of the Holy Sacrament, including a thousand-year-old, Anglo-Saxon reliquary cross. The central nave is now dominated by the mighty 'swallow's nest' organ, built by Gerhard Granzing, the Barcelona-based, German organ-builder. The instrument has 4300 pipes and 63 registers and is famous for its exceptionally rich variety of sound. The coronations and funerals of the Belgian royal house take place in the cathedral.

A center for the world

The cathedral provides the perfect backdrop for great events. Pope John Paul I celebrated High Mass there during his visit to Belgium and it was the natural stage for the wedding of the heir to the Belgian throne.

In summer, the steps are a meeting place for young people from all over the world. Since Brussels became the capital of Europe, the cathedral, with its Gothic splendor and gentle carillon, has been playing yet another new role – as a center of nations.

GETTING THERE:
Via the nearby international airport. Excellent rail and motorway links from all directions

OPENING TIMES:
Usually 10:00 A.M. - 6:00 P.M. No visits during Mass on Sundays and festivals

SPECIAL INTEREST:
The treasures in the chapel of the Holy Sacrament

The two truncated towers of Sts Michael and Gudula were once the symbol of Brussels (main picture)

Solemn ceremony in the church used for coronations. Crown Prince Philippe and Princess Mathilde were married here on 4 December 1999 (below, center)

Madonna with a model of the cathedral (below, right)

The tombs of the House of Orange

Members of the Dutch royal family are laid to rest in the Nieuwe Kerk in DELFT

As you wander alongside the canals with shafts of light spilling across the water, it is impossible to ignore the feeling that Delft is indeed a city full of secrets. The same sense of mystery is evoked by the paintings of Delft painter, Johannes Vermeer, depicting silent figures, seemingly imprisoned within their houses. This atmosphere is at its most intense, however, whenever a Dutch king or queen, a prince consort, or Queen Mother is laid to rest.

With its narrow streets and little squares, its monasteries and churches, the town provides a melancholy backdrop for such funeral processions coming from Den Haag. Their final destination is always the same: Nieuwe Kerk (New Church) in Delft's market square. For the past 400 years, virtually every member of the Dutch royal family has been buried here. Forty-two of them, all laid to rest together in the same vault. After each internment, the tomb is resealed with a large stone and four copper rings. The tomb of the House of Orange is not open to the public; not even spouses of the departed are admitted to the vault afterwards. This city of dead kings is surprisingly strict in upholding medieval ritual.

The original building was a wooden church, erected to the Virgin Mary. This was replaced in 1396 by a basilica in the Late Gothic style. The church took shape during three phases of construction: first to be built were the transept, choir, and lower section of the tower; then, the nave and side sections, eventually followed in the latter half of the fifteenth century by the ambulatory. The tower was not completed until 6 September 1496, one hundred years after construction began.

An army of patron saints

While building work was still in progress, the basilica was placed under the protection of St. Ursula, who, according to legend, was martyred along with 11,000 other virgins. Despite the weighty protection one might have expected from such a large number of patron saints, the church suffered a disproportionate share of misfortune. In 1536, lightning is thought to have sparked a fire in the tower, which destroyed large parts of the town. In 1566, it became a victim of the iconoclasts, and, in 1654, the 'Delft canon explosion', in which 90,000 pounds (40,816 kilos) of gunpowder ignited in the cellars of a former monastery, reducing two-thirds of the town's buildings to rubble and at the same time severely damaging the church.

Delft was, by then, already an important center in the Netherlands by virtue of its role as the burial site for members of the House of Orange-Nassau, even though it had acquired this special status more as the result of a stroke of fortune than by design. As chance would have it, when William of Orange fell victim to a political assassination attack in 1584 during a visit to his temporary residence in Delft, the traditional royal burial site at Breda was under Spanish occupation and therefore inaccessible. The royal family therefore chose Nieuwe Kerk in Delft for the entombment and succeeding members of the House of Orange followed suit.

Protestant persecution

The history of the Netherlands, more than any other European country, is punctuated by major clashes between Catholics and Protestants. In 1555, the country passed to Charles V's fanatical son, Philip II – the 'terror of Europe' – and there followed a period of persecution on an unprecedented scale. It was not until the reign of William of Orange that part of the Netherlands managed to liberate itself from Spanish rule and the country eventually became an independent kingdom.

The Dutch people erected a unique monument in Nieuwe Kerk to the 'Father of the Netherlands' just 30 years after his death. A magnificent memorial of black, white, and gold-veined marble, created by the sculptor Hendrick de Keijser, and arguably the most beautiful Renaissance monument anywhere in Holland, was erected on the spot where the high altar once stood in the days of its Catholic past. In the center lies the white marble figure of William of Orange, with his dog keeping vigil at his feet. Refusing to eat or drink, it died a few days after its master's murder. Pilgrims flock to the mausoleum from all over The Netherlands.

The exterior of the church is equally impressive, its Gothic façade towering imperiously above the market place, crowned by a 354ft (108m)-high tower. A spiral staircase of 356 steps climbs up to three platforms, which provide a spectacular panorama across the picturesque rooftops and market place of Delft.

The Grote Markt (large market) bustles with activity until the early hours of the morning. Here, in the shadow of the monument to scientist Hugo Grotius who put Delft on the international map and is also buried in the Nieuwe Kerk, you can experience the carefree atmosphere of Delft's student life. You will also find Delft's 'gold' on display here: the pottery with its distinctive blue design for which Delft has been famous since the seventeenth century.

GETTING THERE:
Good rail services and motorway links throughout Holland. Motorway direct to Schiphol international airport

OPENING TIMES:
Until further notice, from April-Oct, Mon-Sat 9:00 A.M. - 6:00 P.M., closed Sun. From Nov-Mar, Mon-Fri 11:00 A.M. - 4:00 P.M., Sat 11:00 A.M. - 5:00 P.M.

SPECIAL INTEREST:
The tomb of William of Orange. Panoramic view of the town from the tower

The tower of Nieuwe Kerk Cathedral soars over Delft marketplace. In front of it is a statue of Hugo Grotius, the founder of modern natural law (left)

The tomb of William of Orange was already attracting large numbers of Dutch pilgrims in the seventeenth century, as illustrated by the 1651 painting by Gerard Houckgeest (right)

The most beautiful Madonna in Holland

St. Jan's cathedral in **'s-HERTOGENBOSCH** is a showpiece of Brabant Gothic – and a church where the Virgin Mary is worshipped

North Sea

NETHERLANDS

's-Hertogenbosch

GETTING THERE:
The city is easily accessible by motorway from all directions. Good rail connections also

OPENING TIMES:
Usually 8:00 A.M. - 4:30 P.M. daily. No entry to tourists during services

SPECIAL INTEREST:
The Madonna in a sea of flowers, surrounded by lighted candles

She stands in a sea of flowers, her face lit by hundreds of candles. The statue of 'Our Sweet Lady of Den Bosch' is the most impressive work of art in St. Jan's cathedral. The statue appears to have miraculous powers, and the people of this city of 120,000 inhabitants come to unburden their troubles to it.

This Gothic statue of Mary, dressed in a magnificent cloak and wearing a noble crown, was probably carved between 1280 and 1330 by an artist from the Maasland area, and it symbolizes the permanence of the cathedral. So the 'Zoete Lieve Vrouw' was smuggled out of the city during the

military activities of 1629 and did not return to 's-Hertogenbosch until 1853, where she has remained ever since.

St. Jan's cathedral with its magnificent portals and chapels is more like a mountain range than a church. Its true extent only becomes evident when you walk around it. For two hundred years it was worked on and polished, until it became the most famous example of Brabant Gothic in the Low Countries. It can be compared with the cathedral of Our Lady in Antwerp and also with the great French cathedrals, because the two styles have been merged here in a masterly way,

In order to strengthen his power in the border regions to the north, Duke Henry I of Brabant founded a settlement in 1185 at the confluence of the Dommel and the Aa, and conferred city status on it. The Duke's Wood, as the city was named – though the locals just called it Den Bosch – soon profited from its situation at the intersection of important trade routes, and this found expression in the building of a Romanesque cathedral dedicated to St. John the Evangelist.

Modest merchants

As it was one of the biggest cities in the northern Netherlands at that

General view of St. Jan's cathedral (main picture)

View along the nave, with the altar (above, left)

The Gothic Madonna with the infant Jesus in her arms and surrounded by flowers (above, right)

One of the special treasures of the church interior is the pre-Reformation font (below)

time, the citizens decided to build a new church in the Brabant Gothic style. Work began in 1380 to a design by Willem von Kessels, and the main choir, the ambulatory, and the chevet (ring of chapels) were built under his direction. Around the end of the fifteenth century, work started on the nave, but it ground to a halt after a few decades.

Being realistic merchants, the city fathers realized that the building might not turn out quite as magnificently as planned. The west front was not finished. For lack of money, they even abandoned the plans for an impressive tower and gave the old one a new top.

In the sixteenth century, Den Bosch became caught up in the Reformation. In 1566, iconoclasts ran riot in the church that had been elevated to a cathedral five years before, destroying valuable church property. Not until 1579 did the conflict come to an end with the victory of the Catholics over the Reformers. But there was one more chapter to come. In 1629, the city was conquered by the

united Netherlands forces and the cathedral was re-dedicated as a Reformed Church. Napoleon was the first to restore the church to the city's Catholic majority, after his victory over the Netherlands in 1810, and this act was later confirmed by a decree of King Willem I. In 1859, work began on repairing the church and the restoration was completed by 1984.

Masters of light

The unity of style apparent in the present-day church is due not least to the fact that the plan for a cruciform basilica with a single transept and five naves was kept to throughout the time the cathedral was being built. As in the cathedral of Our Lady in Antwerp, there are bundle pillars without capitals instead of round columns, an artistic device that makes the 92ft (28m)-high cathedral appear to reach even higher up into heaven.

Breadth and height are the two key architectural features of St. Jan's, while the almost puritan decoration attracts the eye to the works of art inside. The font, the pulpit, the choir

stalls, and the organ have all survived from the time of the Reformation. The medieval passion altar portrays the story of Christ's passion in lifelike images and depicts the eternal suffering of his mother Mary.

The worship of Mary has always had an important role in Den Bosch. Between 1479 and 1494, the chapel of the Brotherhood of Our Lady was built, and this still adorns the cathedral as a communion chapel. As well as the extremely delicate, filigree stonework and the riotous ornamentation, the eye is struck by a window, deliberately set in crooked, which allows the last rays of the day's sun to penetrate the sanctum – evidence that the Dutch were masters of light not only in painting but also in architecture.

The city councillors' church

The Marienkirche in **Lübeck** the most perfect example of brick Gothic; for centuries, it had the highest towers in the world

North Sea
Baltic Sea
Lübeck
GERMANY

GETTING THERE:
Good rail connections from Hamburg and Scandinavia. Easily reached via the A1 motorway

OPENING TIMES:
Until further notice, daily 10:00 A.M. - 6:00 P.M. No entry to tourists during services

SPECIAL INTEREST:
The Bell chapel in the church

Complete with new spires, the towers of St. Mary's loom over the Old Town of Lübeck. That the church paid for by the city councillors stands right next to the town hall is evidence of the Lübeck merchants' self-confident attitude towards the Bishop (main picture)

The nave is 262ft (80m) wide and it is 128ft (39m) up to the vaulted ceiling (below, left)

The Old Town of Lübeck was largely destroyed by the hail of bombs on 29 March 1942. St. Mary's was also struck and badly damaged (below, right)

Five meters were sufficient to establish the balance of power in medieval Lübeck, as the city councillors self-confidently built their church precisely that much higher than the bishops' cathedral. The two towers of the Marienkirche (church of St. Mary) stood 410ft (125m)-high at the time of its consecration in 1310 and, until Cologne cathedral was completed in the nineteenth century, they remained the tallest twin church towers in the world.

It was certainly not modesty that moved the city council to build a church that could compete with the magnificence of others, especially the huge cathedral in Cologne. "Pious madness" was how Arnold Wulf, the master builder of Cologne cathedral, later described both buildings. While the people of Cologne lived for centuries with an unfinished ruin, however, the Lübeckers managed to complete their 'folly' because they could count as well as dream and – even more importantly – they were able to pay.

Model for the Baltic region
The boldness revealed in the architecture of the Marienkirche was also the basis of the wealth of medieval Lübeck. From the twelfth century onwards, the merchants plied their ships across the whole Baltic region; they traded with France and Flanders and were paid handsomely for shipping salt. After the founding of the Hanseatic League, Lübeck automatically became its center and, with its seven-towered skyline, set a pattern for the entire Baltic region. St. Mary's also played a crucial part, becoming the model for 70 churches.

The Marienkirche was the third church to stand on this site. The wooden church built at the time of the city's foundation was succeeded by a Romanesque basilica. When the latter was badly damaged in a fire, a three-nave cathedral in the Gothic style – the latest trend – was favored, with an ambulatory choir, a chevet (ring of chapels), and a west front with twin towers. The achievement of St. Mary's was to translate the formality of the French cathedral style, intended for soft white stone, into native brick. Four million bricks were used in the building.

The interior is dominated by the sense of space created by the 128ft (39m)-high nave, which is flanked by the artistically carved pillars of the arcade. The fact that the church is painted may surprise those accustomed to North German Puritanism. The paintings remained hidden for centuries and only reappeared during the great fire in 1942.

Nowadays, one cannot think of St. Mary's without remembering the night of 28-29 March 1942. In revenge for the destruction of the city of Coventry and its famous cathedral, Royal Air Force bombers reduced one-fifth of Lübeck to rubble and ashes. The Marienkirche was completely burned out, the towers collapsed, and the bells crashed down into the church floor. The art treasures, of which St. Mary's had more than all the other churches in North Germany, were mostly burned. Only a few pieces were saved. Among them was a tabernacle, an altar to the Virgin of 1518, a late Gothic memorial stone carved by the sculptor Bernt Notke, and a bronze, 14th-century font.

Famous organ music
With remarkable dedication, the whole interior was renovated after World War II. The choir screen was not rebuilt, however, so there is now an unrestricted view along the great nave.

The only parts that survived the fire unscathed were the former Briefkapelle (Letter chapel), used by the public letter-writers after the Reformation, and the Herrenkapelle (Lords' chapel). The Bell chapel, in which the shattered bronze bells lie exactly where they fell, is a moving memorial. The whole of Lübeck contributed to the rebuilding of the church, including Thomas Mann, winner of the Nobel Prize for Literature and a native of Lübeck.

His grandparents' house stood in the shadow of the Marienkirche and the carillon – so he wrote – found its way into his dreams. Like his brother Heinrich, Thomas Mann left his native city, but his novel *Buddenbrooks* is a memorial to Lübeck – and to the Marienkirche.

The organ, which has now been rebuilt, has been described as a miraculous world of sonorities. Heinrich Buxtehude spent 40 years here as Director of Music and his 'Abendmusiken' concerts attracted people from far away. Johann Sebastian Bach also came here and would very much have liked to follow Buxtehude as Cantor of the Marienkirche, if he had not had to accept the hand in marriage of the Director's daughter along with the post!

A Protestant cathedral

The Baroque-style church of St. Michaelis in **HAMBURG** was designed by architect Ernst Georg Sonnin

The church of St. Michaelis rises up out of the harbor on a ship's port (or left) side as it returns home to the port of Hamburg after a long trip. The sight is enough to bring tears to the eyes of even the toughest old sea dog. Built on a stretch of Hamburg's sandy coastline, the Michel, as this church is fondly known, is the city's most famous landmark.

It is a symbol of fresh beginnings wrested from the jaws of defeat; a friend, protector, and meeting-place for the otherwise rather reserved citizens of Hamburg. No other building enjoys the same degree of fame as this youngest of the city's five principal churches, which is why it became the venue for peace celebrations to mark the end of wars. The German Kaiser was invited to the consecration ceremony as an honorary guest in 1906.

Compared with the other four churches, all more than 700 years old, St. Michaelis is relatively new. It was not until the mid-seventeenth century that the growth of the new town outside the old city walls necessitated the building of a representative church. The first church of St. Michaelis was consecrated in 1661. With a layout suggestive of a three-aisled basilica, its design concept was, right from the start, based on the idea of representation.

Reminiscent of a castle

In 1750, the church was almost completely gutted by fire after being struck by lightning. It was only the incredible donations of money that made it possible for an opulent new church to be built. Between 1751 and 1762, a Late Baroque-style building was created by the two architects Johann Leonhard Prey and Ernst Georg Sonnin It was more reminiscent of a castle than a church and is regarded today as the most important Protestant church after Dresden's Frauenkirche.

The building still lacked a tower at the time of its dedication and it was not until Ernst Georg Sonnin devised a plan for building a tower without any scaffolding that the Michel finally acquired its distinctive appearance. It rises to 433ft (132m). The Rococo-style interior was the work of Cord Möller, who created a festive ceremonial assembly hall, with the altar and pulpit as its focal point.

Southern German charm

In 1906, the building was once more gutted by fire. The people of Hamburg were so dismayed by this disaster that work began without delay to restore the church to its former glory. This time, modern building materials such as steel and concrete were used and a magnificent portal was added to the church. The Michel was severely damaged for a third time

when large sections of it were destroyed in the 1943 bombing raids, but once again it has benefited from full reconstruction.

The church radiates the sort of graceful charm that is more often encountered in southern Germany. Its portal is crowned with a bronze statue of the Archangel Michael. With its pillared arcades, two-storied galleries, and richly stuccoed ceilings, the interior is nothing like the austere, brick-built Gothic buildings usually found in northern Germany. The scale of the interior is immense, measuring 88ft (27m) in height, 233ft (71m) in length, and 167ft (51m) across. The impact is softened by a gallery in the shape of a Greek cross, subtly connecting the main nave with the transepts.

Music by Telemann and Bach

The church accommodates 3000 people. The area in the main well of the building is furnished with heavy oak pews, including the Senate pews, decorated with their coat of arms, while the gallery area is mainly used for concerts. The three organs are an indication of the important role music has always played in the church of St. Michaelis. Georg Philipp Telemann and Carl Philipp Emanuel Bach both played in the Michel and composed some of their most important pieces here.

All that remains of the Baroque furnishings is a baptismal font, fashioned from precious marble. It was commissioned by Hamburg merchants from Livorno, Italy, in 1763. An offertory box, a gift from Ernst Georg Sonnin, the architect, was rescued from the flames in spite of its enormous weight. Like the pulpit, the 66ft (20m)-high altar dating from 1910 is designed in a Neo-Baroque style, and with clearly discernible elements of Art Nouveau.

Up until the eighteenth century, the Michel, like other churches, was still in use as a burial place. Its crypt contains the tombs of Carl Philipp Emanuel Bach and its architect Ernst Georg Sonnin. The top of the tower is accessible by lift, but it is far more rewarding to climb the 449 steps up to the viewing platform, which affords a spectacular panorama of the city, its harbor, and the Elbe River. Twice a day, at 10:00 A.M. and 9:00 P.M. hours, a watchman plays a trumpet solo across the rooftops, as he has done for the past 300 years. For Hamburg clings firmly to traditions, and nowhere more so than in the church which has come to symbolize this city.

The Michel, as it is locally known, overlooks the harbor (main picture)

View of the cathedral's famous organ and the gallery below (above)

St. Michaelis hosts some first-class music concerts, especially around Christmastime (below)

A symbol of the West

The Gedächtniskirche in **BERLIN** was destroyed in World War II – A modern extension has made it a city symbol

Berlin has two diocesan churches, one Catholic and one Protestant. Both are in the middle of the city, near the Schlossplatz (Palace Square), and both are quite famous. The Catholic cathedral of St. Hedwig, a classical domed, central-plan building, is the work of two renowned Berlin architects, Knobelsdorff and Boumann.

Another architect of importance for Berlin was Karl Friedrich Schinkel. He built the Protestant cathedral next to the Stadtschloss (Palace), but the last German Kaiser did not consider it grand enough and ordered it to be demolished. He then commissioned the late 19th-century architect Julius Raschendorff to erect a new building on the site. This was also a central-plan building and, though many people think it ugly, its dome is an indispensable part of the Berlin skyline, like the domes of the New Synagogue or the filigree glass dome on top of the Reichstag building.

The church attracting most attention is in a different part of the city, in the Charlottenburg district, at one end of the famous Kurfürstendamm. The Kaiser-Wilhelm-Gedächtniskirche (Kaiser Wilhelm Memorial church) is a ruin and a new building all in one. The decision to build this church is explained in its name. It was to be a memorial to Kaiser Wilhelm I of the House of Hohenzollern, who died in 1888 at the age of 91.

Romanesque model
The nouveaux riches of Charlottenburg, which at that time was still an independent town, were preparing to compete with the old, imperial capital in the east. The Kurfürstendamm and the neighboring streets were being lined with prestigious apartments for the well-to-do. The Charlottenburg end of the street was intended to be a showplace of prestigious architecture. The square where it was to start was later named Auguste-Viktoria-Platz, after the daughter-in-law of Wilhelm I and eldest daughter of the legendary British queen, Victoria.

The Kaiser-Wilhelm-Gedächtniskirche was finished in 1895, having taken four years to build. The architect was Franz Schwechten. Fully committed to the spirit of historicism, he decided in favour of the Late Romanesque style that can be seen in the great German cathedrals along the Upper Rhine. The burgeoning nationalism of the end of the nineteenth century saw the medieval era of the Salier and Staufer dynasties as a particularly brilliant period in German history.

Schwechten created a central-plan building with a ground plan in the form of a Latin cross. The main tower on the west front was 371ft (113m) high. The interior was richly and amply furnished, uniting the traditional style of Christian religious buildings with that of nationalist-monarchist architecture, along with unmistakable echoes of the imperial cathedral in Speyer.

Left in ruins
When Charlottenburg was incorporated into Greater Berlin after World War I, the Kurfürstendamm became the popular street for shopping and strolling that it still is today. The cinemas where the most important film premieres took place were located here, and the artists' quarter was founded and flourished around the Gedächtniskirche.

All this came to an end with World War II, which left the Kaiser-Wilhelm-Gedächtniskirche in ruins with its towers broken off. An intense public debate began as to whether it should be demolished and what should replace it. In the meantime, the city was politically divided, though the Wall had not yet gone up. In 1956, the West Berlin authorities announced a competition, which was won by the architect Egon Eiermann.

He suggested a new building, with the remains of the towers of the old Gedächtniskirche integrated into it. In 1959, the foundation stone was laid in the square that is now named after August Bebel, the Socialist leader. The

work was finished on 14 December 1963. By this time, the Wall erected by East Berlin had been in place for two years. The old/new church unexpectedly found itself elevated to the status of a symbol of West Berlin's desire for self-determination.

Besides the ruin of the old tower, now no more than 207ft (63m) high, Eiermann's church includes a low, octagonal building and a new, hexagonal tower, 174ft (53m) in height. Both are built of honeycomb-shaped, concrete slabs, with blue glass openings. The new tower houses wedding and baptism chapels and, in the old tower, there is a hall of remembrance for Schwechten's ruined building.

This boldly designed church initially aroused strong feelings, 'Jesus' power station' being the most polite term of abuse. Since then, however, Berlin has come to terms with the building, which has become one of the city's most photographed sights.

GETTING THERE:
Via Tegel international airport. Good rail and motorway connections from all directions

OPENING TIMES:
Usually 9:00 A.M. – 7:00 P.M. daily. Hall of remembrance in the ruined tower, Mon-Sat 10:00 A.M. – 4:00 P.M.

SPECIAL INTEREST:
Bathed in blue light, the interior of the church transmits a unique atmosphere of peace and harmony

A modern, colorful tower designed by Egon Eiermann has been built next to the ruin of the old church (main picture)

Interior of the new church (above)

The old Kaiser-Wilhelm-Gedächtniskirche was built at the end of the nineteenth century in the Neo-Romanesque style, representing the spirit of the Prussian monarchy (below)

A testimony to courage

St. Nicolai in **LEIPZIG** helped to start the demonstrations which led to the downfall of the GDR

North Sea

Leipzig
GERMANY

GETTING THERE:
Flights to Leipzig airport. By motorway from all directions. Good rail links

OPENING TIMES:
Usually from 10:00 A.M. – 6:00 P.M. daily, although occasional changes may occur at short notice

SPECIAL INTEREST:
The Classical-style paintings in the altar section

The tower with its panoramic views was used as a watchtower for fires, right up until the twentieth century (above, left)

The central nave clearly bears the hallmark of Classical design features. The interior of the church was redesigned between 1784-97 by Johann Friedrich Carl Dauthe and Adam Friedrich Oeser (above, right)

The church's exterior façade accurately mirrors the different phases of construction (below, right)

74

Leipzig is very much a commercial center. It began life in the Middle Ages at the crossroads of two important trade routes. It was first mentioned in records as a settlement of merchants, who dedicated the church to their own particular patron saint, in this case the former bishop of Myra whose name was Nicolai, or Nicholas. Leipzig continued to grow in importance, largely due to its commercial role as a trading center for the buying and selling of goods. Between 1156 and 1170, when Leipzig was granted the status of a town, it became host to the caliber of markets which ultimately spawned Germany's most famous trade fair.

The parish church of St. Nicholas remained the new town's principal church. The oldest part of it was a stone basilica, built on land which formerly belonged to a graveyard. Its west front was topped by traditional, Romanesque twin towers. The town and its population grew. The church of St. Nicholas soon began to seem too small, and steps were taken to enlarge the building. An eastern apse was added, followed by the North chapel, both Gothic in style and preserved to this day. In 1452, the cathedral acquired its first set of bells. Not only did the bells summon the faithful to church but also rang out to warn the townsfolk of any outbreaks of fire. The tower of the church of St. Nicholas continued to serve as a fire watchtower right up until 1916.

Conversion to a hallenkirche
In 1507, it was decided to make some radical changes. Only the west section and the Gothic east choir remained unaffected. In 1525, the bishop of Merseburg, who was responsible for Leipzig, inaugurated the finished building, now a spacious, Late Gothic-style hallenkirche (hall church).

It was the year that the Peasants' Revolt ended, which, in turn, would not have broken out had it not been for the Reformation. Martin Luther's famous debate with conservative theologian Johannes Eck took place in Leipzig. During the ensuing religious clashes, the new doctrine was embraced by the whole of the Electorate of Saxony and, from 1539 onward, all church services in Leipzig's church of St. Nicholas were conducted according to evangelical rites. Johann Sebastian Bach, that great exponent of church music,

played not only in St. Thomas' church but also in the church of St. Nicholas, his first introduction to Leipzig.

The next phase of construction also began round about that time. Once again, the building had fallen into disrepair. The old, Romanesque portal was on the point of collapse. It was therefore demolished and replaced by the portal you see today. The interior then underwent extensive renovation between 1784 and 1797. The church of St. Nicholas became a Protestant church in the Classical style, with well-defined lines and light colors. It became as much a haven of reflection and platform for outspokenness as a place of prayer and communion.

New artistic furnishings were acquired, both for the altar section

and for the entrance. These were the work of Friedrich Oeser, an important figure in the history of German Classicism. Born in Bratislava, he was educated in Vienna before moving to the Electorate of Saxony, where he was appointed painter to the court. His style made a smooth transition from Late Baroque to Classicism. Johann Wolfgang Goethe, who was himself a gifted artist, had spent several years studying in Leipzig as one of Oeser's pupils.

Leipzig's prayers for peace
The latest building work on St. Nicholas' church was carried out at the beginning of the twentieth century, when the present-day exterior façade was built. The Late Gothic style of the main body remained,

although its stylistic origins are only discernible on closer inspection.

Since that time, any work undertaken has been solely for the purpose of repairing age-related damage and that caused by environmental factors. The paintwork dating from the Classical period has remained intact. In acknowledgment of current ecological concerns, solar energy equipment was installed following restoration of the south roof in 2000.

The word 'ecology' inevitably carries political overtones. One of the fundamental principles propounded by the emerging opposition forces in the former GDR was the preservation and protection of the natural environment. It is mainly thanks to the evangelical church, which provided them with refuge and protection, that these forces had the opportunity to come together in the first place.

Prayers for peace were held here every Monday from 1982. People who were desperate to leave the GDR found themselves alongside those striving for radical changes at home. The prayers for peace developed into demonstrations, which became increasingly forceful until they culminated in that powerful demonstration of 9 October 1989 on Leipzig's ring road. It was obvious to everyone that this marked the beginning of the end for the Communist regime in East Germany. In the words of Christian Führer, past and present pastor of the church of St. Nicholas: "This church has been a godsend not just for one single group, one denomination, one sector of the population, but for the whole country."

The stone bell

The Frauenkirche in **DRESDEN** became a symbol of destruction caused by World War II

The Frauenkirche (church of Our Lady) in Dresden was once one of the most important Baroque Protestant churches in Germany and an emblem of the city. For more than 40 years after the bombing raids of February 1945, the ruins served as a war memorial symbolizing the destruction of Dresden. Since the decision was taken to restore it to its original form, it has been seen as a symbol of the collective desire of the inhabitants to preserve their city as it used to be, and of the German people's efforts to help them.

Before the Baroque Frauenkirche, there was a church of the same name dating from the Gothic period. It soon became too small, as several suburbs of Dresden became part of the parish. In addition, the building was crumbling. In 1722, George Bähr, the master carpenter to the Dresden City Council, a native of Fürstenwald in East Brandenburg who had become known through church building in the Kursächsen area, was entrusted with the task of building a new Baroque church. The old Frauenkirche was to remain open during the building work, to ensure the spiritual needs of the congregation were provided for.

The planning was not straightforward. Bähr's first design took the form of a Greek cross with octagonal galleries. He dispensed with a façade, because of the close proximity of the surrounding buildings. This design met with skepticism on the part of the authorities.

Foundation stone laid in 1726

The ensuing negotiations dragged on until 1725. Johann Christoph Knöffel, a pupil of the great Pöppelmann, was asked for his opinion on Bähr's plans. Knöffel put forward a formal counter-proposal for a circular central-plan building on a rectangular ground plan. The authorities liked the idea and passed it on to Bähr, who integrated it into his design. In 1726, the amended plan was approved and the foundation stone laid.

By the end of 1726, the foundation walls of the choir were already in place. In 1727, work began on demolishing the old church. By the end of 1732, the new building had reached the cornices.

Now it was a matter of putting on the dome. Bähr had the bold idea of making it entirely of sandstone but, at first, people had reservations about the mechanics of it. In the course of an agonizingly long decision process, all the reservations were overcome. While this was going on, the body of

the church was consecrated, and Johann Sebastian Bach played the organ built by Gottfried Silbermann.

This took place in 1738. Bähr had died shortly before. Johann Georg Schmid, a relative and pupil of his, took over the direction of the work, which was completed in 1743. With its unusual height and conspicuous elongated dome, the church immediately claimed a place in the image of the city.

The Protestants' church

The interior conformed to the way Protestant church buildings had developed since the beginning of the Reformation. The sung and spoken word form the core of Protestant services, with the altar, organ, and pulpit being arranged and visually emphasized with this in mind. Seats are provided for worshippers as a matter of course. Four circles of box-pews ran round the edge of the building. The altar was the work of Johann Christian Feige and Benjamin Thomae, and the Venetian painter Johann Baptist Grone decorated the dome with images of the four evangelists and the four cardinal virtues.

It was a Protestant church in a predominantly Protestant city, whose royal family nevertheless adhered to the Roman Catholic faith and had in the Hofkirche (the Roman Catholic cathedral) a fairly conspicuous church of their own. Bähr's dome, the 'stone bell', now stood close to it, signaling the aspirations of the common citizens who built it. The skyline as seen from the Neustadt bank of the Elbe, which has become a part of German cultural history, captivated first the great Canaletto and then the many representatives of the Dresden School who followed in his footsteps.

The Allied air raids on Dresden, which had remained intact until then, took place on the nights of 13 and 14 February 1945, towards the end of World War II. First explosives, then firebombs, were dropped in several waves, causing a so-called fire storm which took hold of and destroyed the entire Old Town. The Frauenkirche

too was burned down. The tower remained standing to begin with, and the dome did not fall until the next day. For 45 years, the ruins remained as a sombre backdrop, with the statue of Martin Luther preaching in the foreground. While other historic buildings in Dresden rose from the ashes, the Frauenkirche was deliberately left as a ruin. The atheist German Democratic Republic had no great interest in rebuilding a church.

All this changed in 1990. Since then, rebuilding work has been going on, with the help of contributions from the citizens and donations from all over the world. The stones rescued from the old building have been sorted and recorded and will be put back in their original places. The crypt is already finished and the first services have been held. The entire project should be completed by 2006.

GETTING THERE:
Dresden has an international airport. Good rail and motorway connections from all directions

OPENING TIMES:
The rebuilding of the cathedral will probably be finished in 2006. Until then, only those attending services may enter. Guided tours are possible

SPECIAL INTEREST:
The statue of Luther in the square in front of the cathedral. Around it, the builders' store-yard with the old stones ready to be put back in place

Historic photo of the old Frauenkirche from 1893 (main picture)

State of the building work in 2003. The exterior façade and the interior are largely complete. Work on the dome is in progress (above)

The ruin with the fallen statue of Martin Luther in 1945 (below)

The first skyscraper

COLOGNE cathedral was finished after taking more than six hundred years to build – a miracle of Gothic architecture

GETTING THERE:
Via the international airport at Düsseldorf. Good rail and motorway connections from all directions

OPENING TIMES:
Daily 9:00 A.M. - 7:00 P.M. No entry to tourists during services

SPECIAL INTEREST:
The art treasures in the treasury

Standing before the west façade of Cologne cathedral, there is always a feeling of stunned amazement. As if by magic, the gaze is drawn upwards to the towers. Inside, too, the visitor is overcome by the 'shock of Cologne'. In the most impressive cathedral in the world, there appears nothing to keep people anchored to the ground. The church can hold 20,000 worshippers, and that was the number that gathered there to celebrate its completion. A *Te Deum* for a vision. For one of humanity's craziest visions.

Why Cologne, exactly? Why just here by the Rhine? On the site where the cathedral with its lacy towers now stands, surrounded by surging traffic and plagued by the unsleeping station, there was once a heathen temple. Various churches followed, the last of which was a five-nave, Romanesque basilica. When the fresh breeze of Gothic blew over from neighboring France, the people of Cologne were no longer satisfied with this church. They demolished the building and, in 1248, Archbishop Konrad of Hochstaden laid the foundation stone of a cathedral that – setting modesty aside – was to be the biggest ecclesiastical building in the world. To a great extent, it was modeled on the cathedral at Amiens, including the perfect system of buttresses. There was, however, a real treasure within the walls.

In addition to many other relics, Cologne had the bones of the Three Magi, which the Emperor Barbarossa had brought from Milan to the Rhine as spoils of war. Such was their power to attract that, after being crowned in Aix-la-Chapelle, the Holy Roman Emperors came here to pay homage at the shrine of these eastern saints.

The crane remained

For a century, good progress was made on the building work. In 1322, the extension of the choir was completed and work began on the west front. Eighty years later, the south tower was completed up to the height of the carillon. With its slender, bundle pillars, the choir in particular had people gazing as if at a miracle. It was (134ft) 41m long, 148ft (45m) wide, and a fabulous 141ft (43m) high; the 56ft (17m)-high clerestory windows provided a real thrill in the dark Middle Ages. In 1333, Petrarch called this cathedral "the very highest."

Around 1500, the flight of the phoenix was over. With the discovery of America and new scientific knowledge, the startled people turned their attention from heaven to earth and forgot about the cathedral. Building work was officially abandoned in 1560, though the crane, which for more than a century had hoisted building material up to the dizzying heights, remained fastened to the top of the tower like a giant octopus – a constant reminder that work might possibly resume.

After the cathedral suffered devastation at the hands of Napoleon, salvation arrived at the beginning of the nineteenth century. Gothic was rediscovered, and leading figures such as the Cologne art collector Boisserée, the poet Johann Wolfgang von Goethe, and the leading architect Friedrich Schinkel came out in favor of perfecting the greatest ruins of the western world.

The most enthusiastic of all, however, was Wilhelm IV, the romantic king of Prussia, as he saw the completion of the building as symbolic for Germany. In 1842, he laid the foundation stone for the resumption of work, and the cathedral was officially opened in 1880. After more than six hundred years, the new wonder of the world on the Rhine was finished and the people of Cologne held a gigantic celebration – something they are extremely good at. With its thousand spires and highly intricate, integrated craftsmanship, the west front is extolled today as the most phenomenal of its genre.

The shrine of the Magi

Inside the cathedral, it is in fact the parts that were completed in the Middle Ages, such as the choir, that inspire the modern art-lover. In addition, there are the countless art treasures, with the shrine of the Magi holding the place of honor. It is one of the most beautiful examples of the medieval goldsmiths' art. Other outstanding pieces are the Gero Cross, the tomb of Konrad of Hochstaden, and the choir stalls which, with 104 seats, make up the biggest group of medieval choir stalls in Germany.

But what would the cathedral be without its surroundings? When the 'Domplatte', a kind of terrace on stilts, was created at the time of the major renovations in the nineteenth century, Baroque houses and even two churches were mercilessly swept away.

Nowadays, the square in front of the cathedral is a unique melting pot of cultures. Artists transform the paving stones; people juggle, chat, and flirt. Yet they remain astounded by the 'world's first skyscraper'.

Evening atmosphere outside a millennium building: Cologne cathedral, and in the foreground the Rhine with the historic iron railway bridge (far right)

Statue of St. Christopher in the central nave of the cathedral (above, left)

Cologne cathedral in 1824 before building work began again. Steel engraving of 1857 after a drawing by the architect Ernst Zwirner (below, left)

The brilliance of Baroque

VIERZEHNHEILIGEN is a late masterpiece by Balthasar Neumann. The interior is a feast of Rococo

The story begins with a holy legend. In the fall of 1445, a Frankish shepherd, Hermann Leicht, was driving his flock home to the Cistercian monastery of Langheim on the left bank of the River Main when he glimpsed a child crying in a field. No sooner had he seen it than the vision disappeared. A year later, he saw the child again. This time, the figure was wearing a red cross on its chest and was surrounded by 14 other children. They told the shepherd that they were the 14 saints, who helped people in need, and requested that a chapel be built in their name.

Three weeks later, a woman was miraculously healed, whereupon the Abbot yielded to the entreaties of the shepherd and erected a little chapel. Pilgrimages to the spot began soon after, attracting pilgrims from near and far: Thuringia, Saxony, and Franconia. They included prominent figures, such as Albrecht Dürer, the Nuremberg painter.

The chapel burned down several times. Each time, it was rebuilt on a larger and grander scale. Eventually, around 1735, Stephan Mösinger, an ambitious young abbot, decided to replace the chapel, which had become somewhat dilapidated and much too small, with a church which could accommodate the vast numbers of pilgrims. He commissioned the region's master architect, Gottfried Heinrich Krohne of Weimar, a Protestant, with the task but his designs met with opposition on the part of the then bishop of Bamberg. Mösinger made sure that henceforth Balthasar Neumann would also be involved in the planning.

Constant strife

Neumann was an outstanding architect of Upper German Baroque. Born in 1687 in Bohemia, he served his apprenticeship in a foundry, before becoming an artillery engineer. The mathematical and statistical knowledge he acquired during this time served him well in his later architectural work. In 1719, he took charge of the bishop's construction project in Würzburg and supervised the work being carried out on his residence there, one of the most magnificent Baroque palace complexes in Europe. Many more commissions followed and Vierzehnheiligen was one of his later projects.

No architectural project could have caused him more problems or trouble. The laying of the foundation stone took place in April 1743 and the craftsmen came from nearby Staffelstein. The first walls were erected, with the yellow sandstone used as a building material coming from a local source. While checking on the progress of the building work nine months later, Neumann discovered that his design was being consistently altered and undermined. He complained to the bishop, who immediately ordered that everything Lutheran should be removed and a proper Catholic church built in its place. Krohne was dismissed.

Balthasar Neumann now took over the project with renewed vigor. He tried to incorporate Krohne's existing plans by adapting them to suit his own needs. He remained dedicated to this building project until his death in 1753. The church was not completed until much later, in 1772, and it was another three years before work on the interior was finished around 1775.

Vierzehnheiligen is a successful combination of basilica and Baroque vaulting. The galleried interior is flooded with light and reminiscent of a ballroom. The focal point is the altar of Mercy forming an oval in the center of the main rotunda, flanked by four pillars. Two smaller ovals are laid out either side of the central one. This was Neumann's inspired solution to incorporating Krohne's original design.

Memorial to the 14 saints

From the outside, Vierzehnheiligen gives the appearance of an impressive Baroque church with a monumental twin-towered façade, visible from afar. The interior is pure Rococo, that ornately elegant style from the mid-eighteenth century which directly preceded Classicism. The interior decoration was the work of Mainz artist Giuseppe Appiani, the Elector's official painter at court. He created the frescoes and altar paintings, while the stuccowork is attributed to Johann Michael Feuchtmayr, who created the altar of Mercy. Statues of the 14 saints are grouped around the altar on different levels.

The church experienced several disasters after its completion. It was struck by lightning and suffered flood damage, while soot from the candles tarnished the stucco decorations. An extensive program of restoration was undertaken towards the end of the twentieth century, to restore the building to its original glory.

GETTING THERE:
By car via motorway from Bamberg to Vierzehnheiligen near Lichtenfels

OPENING TIMES:
Usually 10:00 A.M. - 6:00 P.M. daily, except Sunday morning

SPECIAL INTEREST:
Pilgrimages and processions take place in May and September. Coburg, 12.5 miles (20km) to the north, is well worth a visit

View from the organ gallery onto the altar of Mercy, the centerpiece of the rotunda, to the main altar beyond (main picture)

The main Baroque façade is dominated by its magnificent twin towers (center)

The pulpit in this pilgrimage church, dedicated to the 14 saints (right), is an outstanding example of ornate Rococo

Royal German Romanesque

The cathedral of **SPEYER** was built as a burial place for the Salian dynasty

German rulers in the Middle Ages did not have a national capital city. They were constantly on the move with a great train of advisers, guards, and court officials in tow, visiting the far-flung regions of their empire. They stayed in palaces, bishops' residences, or monasteries, from where they conducted their official business. It was only in death that their journeying ceased and they finally came to rest in one place; normally, in a particular church, in which they and all the rest of their dynasty were buried.

The second royal dynasty in the country were the Salians of Rhine-Franconia, who came to power after the Saxon Ottonians. The first Salian king, Conrad II, Duke of Worms and Speyergau, was elected in 1024. Members of the Salian family had traditionally been buried in Worms cathedral. Conrad decided, presumably in the light of his new-found eminence, to build a new burial place in the old cathedral city of Speyer. Since Speyer's church was greatly inferior to the cathedrals in the neighboring cities of Worms, Mainz, and Basel in terms of size and importance, he laid the foundation stone for a brand new cathedral.

Pantheon of imperial magnificence

When he died in 1039, he was buried in Speyer cathedral, despite the fact that it was still under construction. When his wife Gisela died some time later, she, too, was laid to rest in the middle of what was still a building site. All of Conrad's royal successors, provided they were members of the Salian dynasty, together with some of their wives, were buried here. Even royal rulers from other dynasties were occasionally laid to rest here, including Rudolf, the first Habsburg to be elected German king. The royal crypt contains the tombs of altogether 13 German rulers and five bishops, as well as a collective grave, placing Speyer on a par with Ste. Denis near Paris. German people regard Speyer cathedral as a national pantheon of medieval imperial magnificence.

Present-day Speyer is a well-to-do little town. Its fame derives largely from its glorious past: imperial diets were once convened here and, on a hill above the Rhine, guarding the royal tombs of the Salian dynasty, stands the cathedral, one of the three great cathedrals in the Upper Rhineland. Apart from the later addition of a Gothic sacristy and the Baroque roof on the tower crossing, the building is predominantly Romanesque in style, thanks mainly to the fact that the main shell of the cathedral had been more or less completed by 1106 under Henry IV, grandson of the original founder.

It is a building of massive proportions, measuring 440ft (134m) in length, 46ft (14m) in breadth, and rising to a height of 98ft (30m) above the central nave. There are two towers and a crossing tower at both the eastern and western ends. The original flat ceilings of the cathedral, which has its own baptism chapel as well as the St. Afra chapel, were later replaced with groined vaulting. The building is generally regarded as the first basilica on German soil.

Walls 20ft (6m) thick

The central nave is separated from the rest of the church by pillars, every second one of which is fronted by a half column, producing a rhythmical sequence of spatial units (known to architects as a 'compound system') which punctuates the space and avoids any potential monotony.

The design of the inner section is similarly echoed around the outside. All around the apse, choir, and long nave are dwarf galleries, purely by way of architectural detail. The recesses give an indication of the strength of the walls, which are up to 20ft (6m) thick in some places.

Speyer has comparatively few carvings of the kind commonly seen in other medieval cathedrals. One of the half pillars in the apse has a rather ingenuous relief depicting a human figure, an animal, a snake, and some trees in peaceful harmony with each other. At the base of another pillar is a carving of a grapevine, based on the metaphor of Christ in the Gospel of St. John.

Colored stone

The rest of the ornamentation is generally limited to mythical figures of flowers and animals. Even the portals, traditionally a favorite place in cathedral buildings for portraying scenes from the New Testament, remain unembellished. The beauty of the rounded arches lies in the variety of shades in stonework and the alternating layers of different colors of stone, an effect reproduced elsewhere the cathedral.

The west-facing façade was rebuilt in the nineteenth century in its present form (main picture)

A carving on a pillar in the East chapel depicting Samson slaying the lion (above, right)

The tomb of Kaiser Ludwig I dating from 1291 (center, right)

View of the vaulting in the crypt, dating from the eleventh century (below, right)

The lower part of the church is extremely spacious, comprising the entire choir section, the apse, and transepts. The tombs of the Kaisers still stand on their original site, although the mounds of earth, under which the tombs originally lay, were removed in 1902 in order to display the magnificent architecture.

This is not the only time that slight alterations have been made. Every now and then, restoration work, some of it unavoidable, has had to be carried out; for example, following a devastating fire during the twelfth century, and after 1683, when French troops ravaged the cathedral

during the Palatinate War of Succession.

An ambitious restoration program was undertaken in the mid-nineteenth century, which restored the west front to its present form. At the same time (it was a period of national preoccupation with the Romantic age), the entire interior was endowed with historic-style paintings. These paintings have since been removed. The cathedral of Speyer has been returned to how it was, or how it is thought to have been, 900 years ago.

'The foreign bonnets'

With its strange towers, the Frauenkirche in **MUNICH** has become a symbol of the city

GETTING THERE:
International airport about 19 miles (30km) from the city. Easily reached by train and car from all directions

OPENING TIMES:
The cathedral is usually open Mon-Sat 10:00 A.M. - 5:00 P.M. Closed on Sundays

SPECIAL INTEREST:
The Marienplatz and town hall, very close to the church. There are many traditional Bavarian beer-cellars in the neighborhood

Legend has it that Satan sneaked into the Frauenkirche (church of Our Lady) in Munich shortly after it was finished. He was overcome with delight and pleasure when he discovered that the master builder had forgotten to put in any windows, until he found out that he had merely been the victim of an optical illusion. For what he had taken to be a windowless exterior wall were the massive pillars separating the nave from the aisles and, of course, the exterior walls have proper windows. When the devil realized this, he flew into a rage. He stamped furiously with his cloven hoof and rushed out of the church in a whirlwind. The satanic imprint is still to be seen under the gallery and is known as the 'devil's footprint'.

Megalomania? Far-sightedness?

This tale originated in the Baroque era. At that time, there was still a gigantic altar obstructing the view of the central window of the choir. The 22 octagonal pillars, which stand in two rows and were once the cause of Beelzebub's great rage, are actually described as a wall. The aisles behind them rise to almost the same height as the nave and you can see the similarity to the Late Gothic hallenkirche (hall church). The star vault where the bundle pillars join the ceiling is also a Late Gothic feature.

The church 'Zu unserer Lieben Frau' ('of Our Beloved Lady') is spacious, holding around 20,000 people. When it was planned, Munich had just 13,000 inhabitants, so the building almost seemed like a sign of megalomania – or far-sightedness. Perhaps they had envisaged the future growth of the city and made their plans accordingly.

The previous building was smaller. It was a Late Romanesque church, dating from around 1230. The foundation stone of the present brick-built church was laid in 1468 by Duke Sigismund of Bavaria, of the house of Wittelsbach. His master builder was Jörg von Halsbach. Part of the building costs were paid from the ducal coffers.

Churches dedicated to Our Lady are generally parish churches and the same was true in Munich. Despite its extraordinary size, the Liebfrauenkirche simply functions as one of two ordinary, local, parish churches. The other was named after St. Peter and was much older than the city, being built as long ago as the tenth century. St. Peter's church has undergone a number of alterations. The 315ft (96m)-high tower with its Baroque spire is seen as another symbol of Munich, alongside the towers of the Frauenkirche.

The latter are a little higher – 325ft (99m), to be precise. They were already standing when the church was consecrated in 1494. A view of the city in Schedel's famous Nuremberg Chronicle shows them with flat roofs. The cupolas were not added until a quarter of a century later. Their shape is unusual, in Munich being known as 'die welschen Hauben' ('the foreign bonnets'). The models they were based on are certainly foreign, most probably Venetian.

Burial place of the Wittelsbachs

The Frauenkirche was originally planned as the burial place for the Wittelsbach family, but things have not turned out quite in that way. A few members of the family found their last resting place here, including the only emperor to come from that dynasty, Ludwig IV, known as 'the Bavarian', who died in 1347. The last king of Bavaria, Ludwig III, is also buried here. He took over the throne from his father Luitpold in 1912, and reigned until he was forced into exile after the revolution of 1918. He died in 1921 in Sávár in Hungary.

As well as the Wittelsbachs, there are also bishops buried in the Frauenkirche. In 1818, the seat of the diocese was moved from Freising to the Bavarian capital, and the Frauenkirche became its cathedral. Like the entire inner city of Munich, the Frauenkirche suffered serious bomb damage during World War II, which was cleared away after the war was over. The initial result was an almost bare interior. In the course of restoration, which was completed in 1993, many surviving fragments from the Gothic and Baroque periods were first archived, then later put on show – for instance, the 48 carved busts of prophets and apostles and the choir stalls by Erasmus Grasser dating from 1502.

On leaving the church, it is only a few steps to the Marienplatz in front of the town hall. Beer-drinkers, beggars, and idlers throng the square. Munich is heaven, according to the American novelist Thomas Wolfe. A proper Christian heaven needs a place of worship. In Munich, it is the Frauenkirche.

With their copper-domed caps, the twin towers of the Frauenkirche still dominate the Munich skyline (main picture)

When you enter the church, you are overwhelmed by the simplicity of the nave. Almost all the interior decoration was lost through bomb damage in World War II (below)

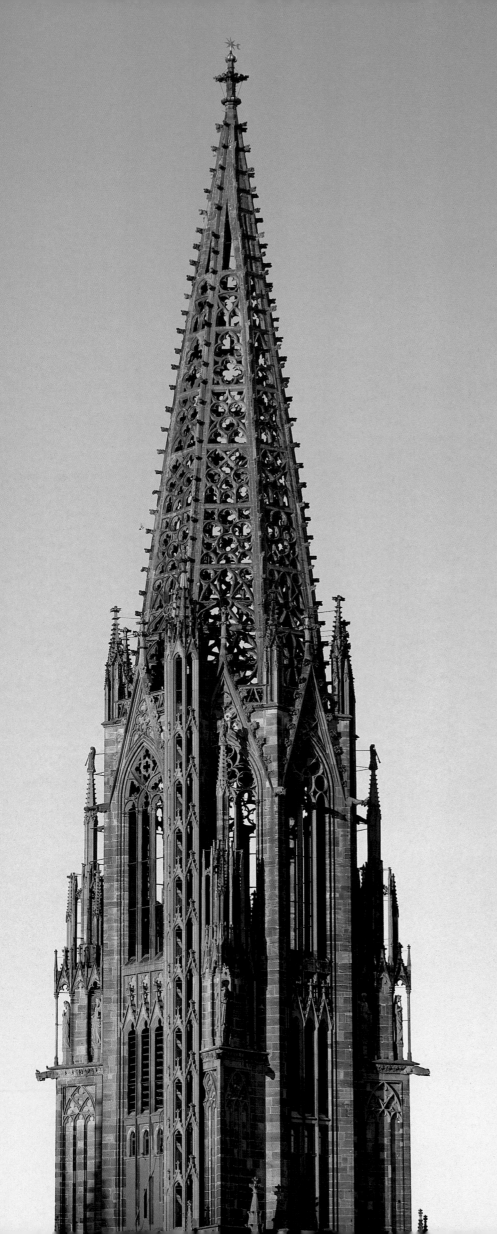

Supreme Gothic artistry

The minster in **FREIBURG IM BREISGAU** has a magnificent spire

Freiburg im Breisgau has had an unsettled past. Situated at the meeting-point of France, Germany, and Switzerland, the town has, in turn, belonged to each of these three countries. This has inevitably had an influence on its cultural development, although Switzerland, in this case, means Habsburg Austria.

Geographically speaking, the town lies between the southern part of the Black Forest and the Kaiserstuhl region. Freiburg has an economic foot in both these regions, which explains its affluence and architectural elegance.

Freiburg owes its existence to the Zähringer family. This noble dynasty died out long ago, but not before instigating, around 1200, the construction of the cathedral which would later serve as their burial place. A few parts of what was the original Romanesque building have been preserved: for example, the crossing, the transepts, and the lower sections of the so-called 'cock towers'. Echoes of neighboring Basel minster are clearly evident in the cathedral's architectural style.

Construction work began at a time when the period of Romanesque architecture was coming to an end. The increasingly popular Gothic style was quickly adopted in Freiburg, if only because of the town's geographical proximity to France, the country where it was born. A new architect, whose name is unknown, incorporated this emergent style into the ongoing construction of the long nave. His distinctive, personal signature can be seen in the traceried windows and the capitals, revealing the influence of yet another architectural model, namely that of the cathedral in neighboring Strassburg, the architect's home town.

Three centuries of construction

The crowning glory of his work, however, was the tower. Instead of the traditional, twin-towered façade, he opted for a single tower, a combination commonly found on rather less grand Romanesque churches in the region. The result was indisputably the finest

Gothic tower and spire in Germany, which culminate in an artistic pinnacle consisting of eight ribs separating elongated triangles of lace-like, stonework tracery. It is delicate rather than solid in appearance but, despite its filigree pinnacle, it manages to evoke an impression of unshakable strength. Tapering to a fine point, it soars upwards towards heaven and sublimity, the epitome of Gothic architecture.

The succeeding architect was Johannes von Gmünd, who trained under the great Parler family of architects, famed for their work both in Cologne and Prague. Johannes began work on the choir in 1354. Seventeen years later, he was followed by another architect, Hans Niesenberger, from Graz. The choir was finished in 1513, a magnificent masterpiece in what by now was the prevailing late Gothic style. Having taken three centuries to build, the consecration of the choir marked the completion of the Freiburg minster.

It is a church of exceptional proportions: 410ft (125m) long, 98ft (30m) wide, and reaching a lofty height of 89ft (27m) in the nave. These dimensions are similar to those of its sister churches in Basel and Strassburg. These two are cathedrals, however, and bishops' churches, whereas Freiburg's minster was no more than a parish church until it became an archbishopric in 1821.

Main altar by Hans Baldung 'Grien'

The altar is fashioned from the same reddish-coloured stone as Strassburg cathedral. The church has amassed a rich collection of art works, both inside and out, beginning with the elaborate carvings on the west portal, where the tympanum depicts the story of Jesus' life from his boyhood up until the Passion and Last Judgment. Either side of the porch are the famous statues of the prudent and foolish maidens.

These relate to a parable in the Gospel according to Matthew: the five foolish maidens are depicted holding their empty oil lamps upside down, while the prudent ones are holding theirs upright. Among the foolish virgins is a figure representing a synagogue with the corresponding insignia, a reference to the strong anti-Semitism which flourished during the High Middle Ages in Europe.

The cathedral boasts splendid stained-glass windows, particularly in the chapels radiating off the choir and above the main altar. These are the work of Hans Baldung. Born in the Upper Rhine region, he studied under Albrecht Dürer and was given the freedom of the city of Strassburg. The altar in Freiburg, depicting the crowning of the Virgin Mary, to whom the cathedral is dedicated, is considered one of his greatest works. His preference for green tones in his art earned him the nickname 'Grien' ('green').

GETTING THERE:
Flights to Basel international airport, about 38 miles (60km). Easily accessible via the Rheintal motorway. Good rail links

OPENING TIMES:
From 9:00 A.M. - 6:00 P.M. daily until further notice. No admission to tourists during services

SPECIAL INTEREST:
The weekly market in the large square around the cathedral

The cathedral spire represents a pinnacle of Gothic architectural achievement (main picture)

A statue of St. Andreas decorates one of the pillars in the long nave (above)

The altarpiece painted by Hans Baldung 'Grien' is one of the cathedral's finest treasures (center)

The minster as seen from the choir end. View of the long nave and tower. The square around the cathedral is a popular meeting place for local townsfolk (below)

Swiss cathedral-building

BASEL minster is decorated with fabulous, Late Romanesque sculptures

Basel
SWITZERLAND

Ligurian Sea

Mediterranean Sea

GETTING THERE:
Basel has an international airport. Good rail and motorway connections from all directions

OPENING TIMES:
Usually Mon-Fri 9:00 A.M. - 5:00 P.M., Sat 11:00 A.M. - 4:00 P.M. No admission to tourists during services and prayers

SPECIAL INTEREST:
The St. Gallus doorway

In Basel cathedral, there is a memorial to Erasmus of Rotterdam who is buried here. The famous scholar of the Reformation era spent many years in Basel, and his Greek edition of the New Testament was printed here by Johann Froben for in those days Basel specialized in book-printing. Partly as a result of its considerable commercial prosperity, the city was a center of humanism in Europe and receptive to the new cultural ideas of the times.

It is an area of ancient Celtic, Roman, and Alemannic settlements. The hill overlooking the Rhine on which the minster now stands presented a favorable site for the Roman fortification of Basilia. This was later replaced by a Christian church, whose naturally elevated site testified to the supremacy of God. Basel probably became a bishopric in the eighth century. The earliest written mention of a building dates from around 820.

The present basilica was completed in the late Romanesque period and was damaged by an earthquake in 1356. The repair work took place just as the Gothic style was coming into fashion. Built of reddish stone from the nearby quarries of Wiesental and Degerfelden, the cathedral took five hundred years to construct and provides important evidence from these periods of architectural design.

This can be seen, for instance, in the façade surrounding the main entrance. The pale layers at the bottom of St. George's tower form the oldest part of the building. The finial on the other, St. Martin's tower, was added in the year 1500. The names are those of the two saints whose statues stand at the bases of the towers, while the church as a whole is dedicated to the Virgin Mary. There is a statue of her standing between the two towers, along with Henry II, the last Emperor of the Saxon dynasty, and his wife Kunigunde. Henry was a deeply religious man, and was later canonized as a saint. He founded the minster together with his wife.

Other figures near the entrance are a foolish virgin and her devilish seducer. While she smilingly undoes her dress for him, all kinds of toads and snakes creep up behind him, signifying the depth of his depravity.

The famous St. Gallus doorway

These figures date from the end of the Romanesque period, around 1280. The sculptures on another doorway – the St. Gallus doorway located at the northern end of the transept – are about a hundred years older. It is named in memory of the Irish missionary who came to convert the people in the area around the northern part of Lake Constance at the end of the sixth century.

The doorway that bears his name shows Christ the Judge of the World with the apostles Peter and Paul, the wise and foolish virgins, the four Evangelists, and John the Baptist. Two angels blow the last trumpet for Judgment Day; the dead rise from their graves and prepare for trial. The St. Gallus doorway is the most important work of Romanesque sculpture in Switzerland and one of the earliest carved doorways in the entire German-speaking area.

The window above the St. Gallus doorway shows a huge wheel of fortune, a popular symbol of fate in the Middle Ages that probably goes back to the ancient Roman Fortuna (goddess of good fortune), who was often depicted holding the rudder of her ship. In this window, the mutability of the human condition is portrayed through many small figures clinging to the curved spokes of the wheel. The spokes were originally made of oak and were only replaced by sandstone in the nineteenth century.

Like the entrances, the façade of the choir is richly decorated with statues. You can see all kinds of animals,

including lions and a pair of elephants that clearly reveal that the sculptor had never encountered a real elephant. There is also much carving in the interior, for instance the relief showing St. Vincentius and the apostles dating from around 1100. The vaulted basilica with three naves and a transept has its burial chapels to the left and right connected in such a way as to give the impression of a five-nave church.

Late Romanesque decoration

The nave still bears all the hallmarks of its Late Romanesque origins, right down to the original decoration. The font, the pulpit, the paintings on the ceiling, the choir, and the choir stalls all date from the Gothic era. The towers suffered the most lasting damage from the earthquake of 1356. The minster originally had five towers, but only the two towers of the façade were rebuilt, 213ft (65m) and 203ft (62m) high respectively.

There is a cloister adjoining the cathedral, which was built in the Late Gothic period on Romanesque foundations. The bishops and the cathedral chapter used once to walk there; later on, members of well-known, middle-class Basel families were buried here. In the crypt of the minster is the oldest surviving tomb, that of a certain Bishop Rudolph, who died during the Hungarian invasion of 917.

Since 1529, the Minster has been a reformed church. The change of denomination left a certain amount of destruction in its wake, but was not

so radical as to prevent burial there of the great Erasmus, who remained a Catholic priest to the end.

**View of the nave
(above, left)**

**View of the cathedral
transept from the Rhine
(above, center)**

**Sandstone relief
showing the apostles
disputing, dating from
around 1100
(above, right)**

**The Late Gothic cloister
adjacent to the minster
(below, right)**

Southern German Baroque

The abbey church in **ST. GALLEN** once formed the focal point of a monastery, dating back to the eighth century

Gallus, or Gall, was an Irish monk, born in 550, who grew up in the northern Irish monastery of Bangor, near Belfast. In those days, Ireland was a center of learning and piety, and sent missionaries all over Europe. Gallus began his journey with a fellow priest, called Columbian. His travels as a missionary took him to Merovingian France, Burgundy, and Lake Constance. Here, he established a chapel and a cell in the Steinach valley, where disciples joined him. He was over 90 years old when he died.

A Benedictine monastery, dedicated to Gallus, was built on the site of his dwelling by the monk Otmar. It quickly grew in size and soon became rich and powerful. The town, which grew up around the monastery walls, as well as the canton in which it is situated were also named after St. Gall. The history of the abbey of St. Gallen stretches back over many centuries. Important manuscripts were produced here during the Late Middle Ages and Gregorian chants notated in neume, the forerunner of musical notation.

The monastery up until 1805

The abbey was granted its independence and ruled by bishops; for eight years during the Reformation it became an evangelical church, before reverting to Catholicism. The abbey's rule came to an end in 1797 in the wake of the French Revolution. Napoleonic troops camped for a time in the cathedral. The monastery was dissolved in 1805 and its minster was elevated to become cathedral of the newly-formed twin dioceses of Chur and St. Gallen.

Standing outside the church, the first impression is of a magnificent, Baroque cathedral. There is nothing to suggest that its origins date back to the eighth century. It is worth visiting the monastery's former wine cellars, which now serve as a lapidarium. This contains relics dating from that early period of its history. Within the cathedral, all that remains intact of the old Romanesque building is the crypt.

The ground-plan of St. Gallen cathedral adheres more or less to the original layout of the Gothic monastery church. It began as a Carolingian minster, completed in 837/839, after which it underwent frequent periods of enlargement and rebuilding, the last of which was in the mid-fifteenth century. It is known to have suffered several devastating fires during its history. Construction of the Baroque church began in 1623, involving architects from the Vorarlberg region. Work on the abbey as it stands today, particularly the interior, began in 1755.

Stucco ornamentation

The cathedral of St. Gall and Otmar, as it is now called after its two founders, is a pilaster church with a rotunda and double choir. It is a classic example of southern German Baroque, at least with regard to its interior, which to some extent outshines the exterior. Peter Thumb, Johann Caspar Bagnato, and Johann Michael Beer were among the architects who took part in the planning and building work, as was Gabriel Loser, one of the monks.

The end result was a church which, like the Vierzehnheiligen church in Franconia, successfully made the transition from Late Baroque to Rococo. One of the artists involved in Vierzehnheiligen was called Feuchtmayer. Another member of his family, Joseph Anton Feuchtmayer, created the choir stalls in St.

Gall and Otmar. Stucco ornamentation, typical of this period of architecture, features very prominently in the interior. The four altars in the rotunda, designed by Fidel Sporer, similarly feature highly elaborate stuccowork.

It is the rotunda, combined with its basilica, which makes the cathedral of St. Gallen exceptional. It is not so large that it dominates the building, nor is it situated above a crossing, since the church does not have a transept. It divides the nave into two symmetrical halves, with a choir on each side. Notwithstanding the high altar with its huge Baroque painting of the Ascension of the Virgin Mary, it is the rotunda that remains the focus of attention. The paintings here are equally remarkable, one of which is the *Advent of God*.

The ceiling frescoes are distinctly gloomy in color, forming a striking contrast to the brilliant white of the pillars and walls. There is a two-tiered organ, while the choir stalls are studded with an abundance of carvings; gilt figures before a light-colored background, all within a rocaille.

Famous abbey library

The former abbey buildings adjoin the cathedral and incorporate the abbey library, which once formed part of the monastery. This contains one of the oldest and most famous collections in the German-speaking world. The reading room is pure Rococo, like the church interior. Its treasures include a plan of the monastery dating from around 820, which is occasionally put on display. Its authenticity is well documented and it is nowadays acknowledged as the perfect blueprint for a building of this kind.

GETTING THERE:
By rail or motorway from Zürich

OPENING TIMES:
The church is usually open daily from 9:00 A.M. to 6:00 P.M. except Sunday, when it is closed to tourists during services and confession

SPECIAL INTEREST:
Main room of the abbey library with its magnificent interior

The abbey church of St. Gall's monastery, built between 1755 and 1766, is crowned with twin, Baroque towers (main picture)

Inside the church, the view down the nave and rotunda is framed by startlingly white pillars (below, right)

The manuscript room in the abbey library with its Rococo interior, designed by Peter Thumb, is world-famous (below, center)

St. Florian be praised

Anton Bruckner was once the organist at this abbey church in the Danube Valley near **LINZ**

GETTING THERE:
By rail from Vienna or Salzburg; by car via the Munich-Vienna motorway. Linz has its own airport

OPENING TIMES:
Usually open daily from 10:00 A.M. – 6:00 P.M., except during Mass and special services

SPECIAL INTEREST:
Concerts of church music featuring the Baroque Bruckner organ

Within the church itself, two items of special interest are the Bruckner organ (below, right) and the Passion altar by Albrecht Altdorfer (below, left). The altar panel, dating from 1510-12, depicts the *Widow Lucine recovering St. Sebastian's body from the sewer*

Panoramic view of St. Florian church and monastery (main picture)

There are many significant abbeys in Austria: Melk, Seitenstetten, Heiligenkreuz, Zwettl, Göttweig. Generally speaking, they all own extensive estates, while some practise viniculture and sell their own produce, as in Vienna. Tradition and art treasures, without exception, figure substantially in abbey life. The most important abbey of all, however, is that of St. Florian, near Linz in Upper Austria, a focal point of choral music.

The town is small, with a population of barely 4000 inhabitants. The saint after which it is named is the one traditionally invoked for protection against fire and flood, hence he is the patron saint of beer brewers, smiths, soap-makers, and chimney-sweeps. He was a Roman official, who lived in what is now Upper Austria and was martyred in 304, a victim of Christian persecution. The present monastery is built over his grave and evolved from a place of pilgrimage, the oldest segments of wall dating from the fourth century.

The first mention of a monastery on this site is in the eighth century. In 1071, Bishop Altmann of Passau initiated the restoration of the church and adjoining buildings. It was rebuilt in the Gothic style following a fire. The abbey is now in the hands of Augustinian monks belonging to a 12th-century Order based on the Rule of St. Augustine of Hippo.

The abbey and its church were rebuilt in the Baroque style in the seventeenth century. Provost Leopold Zehetner organized the renovation of the interior of the basilica, while

Provost David Fuhrmann ordered the entire monastery to be rebuilt. The signal for this was Austria's victory over the Turks near Vienna in 1683, as a token of gratitude for which the Kaiser made a pilgrimage to the tomb of St. Florian. The architect was Carlo Antonio Carlone of Milan, one of the many itinerant architects of the time. The foundation stone for the new abbey church was laid in 1686.

Wall and ceiling frescoes

The result of the renovation work is overwhelming. The impression of vastness in the interior is created by the side chapels, galleries, presbytery, and apse. The cupola is 118ft (36m) high; the ceilings are all vaulted. The stucco decoration on the walls is by Giovanni Battista Carlone, brother of the architect.

The frescoes by Innsbruck painters Johann Anton Gumpp and Melchior Steidl depict the Ascension of the Virgin Mary and the Martyrdom of St. Florian in vivid colors, covering a surface area of 5886 square yards (4921 square meters). It repre-

sents the first full ceiling fresco on this scale north of the Alps.

Carlone, the architect, began rebuilding work on the rest of the abbey buildings, in which the prelates' and imperial apartments are situated. Local architects, such as Prandtauer and Steinhuber, continued Carlone's work. In 1751, 65 years after it was begun, the ambitious project reached its completion. St. Florian is one of the most impressive Baroque buildings to be found anywhere in Austria and, despite the different architects who had a hand in its creation, its overall impression is one of uniformity and harmony.

The abbey has a large collection of paintings, displayed in their own gallery. Some of the pieces were originally intended for the basilica, in particular the St. Sebastian altar by Regensburg artist Albrecht Altdorfer, a master of the so-called Danube School. His significance stems partly from the fact that he was one of the first painters to endow landscape painting with renewed importance. His winged altar for the abbey is con-

sidered one of his main achievements; twelve panels and two predella side-pieces are still to be found in St. Florian. Some items have been lost, while others are in the Vienna Museum of Art.

Privilege for prelates

The choir stalls are carved with images of the Latin church fathers, the Virgin Mary, and the Archangel, all the work of Adam Franz and Jakob Auer. The pulpit is of black marble and depicts St. Augustine, founder of the Order, holding out his burning heart to the Holy Trinity.

The basilica church hosts a total of eight side chapels, each dedicated to a different saint and with its own marble altar. Beneath the basilica is the crypt, where until 1780 all the monks were buried. The prelates retain this privilege to the present day, while others go to their last resting-place in the priests' cemetery, adjacent to the basilica's main portal.

The crypt is directly beneath the high altar, the oldest part of the monastery buildings which are in early Gothic style. Here is the sarcophagus of Wilbrig, a pious hermit, who lived in the shadow of the monastery for many years and died in 1289. She is venerated as patron of the abbey.

The abbey is also renowned for its library and its musical activities. Of particular note is the Boys' Choir, whose most famous member was the composer, Anton Bruckner. His career as a professional musician began here in St. Florian, before he moved to Linz to continue his work. He maintained close links with St. Florian and, when he died in 1896, was buried at his own request in the church, underneath the big organ which he used to play and which now honors him with its name.

The cathedral of Jedermann

St. Rupert's cathedral in **Salzburg** is a famous example of Baroque art north of the Alps

GETTING THERE:
Very good rail and motorway connections from all directions

OPENING TIMES:
Normally open all day

SPECIAL INTEREST:
A performance of *Jedermann* in the square in front of the cathedral

View of the vault of the great dome and organ (main picture)

The entire cathedral complex with the inner court, the great dome, and the two towers of the main façade (below, right)

During the Salzburg festival: a performance of *Jedermann* in the inner courtyard in front of the main façade of the cathedral (below, left)

Probably the most famous part of Salzburg cathedral is outside the actual walls of the church – it is the steps. Every year, in the summer, the spine-chilling sound of Death calling Everyman rings out over these steps and across the adjoining Domplatz (Cathedral Square). Everyman, or Jedermann in German, is the title character of the Old English morality play adapted by the Austrian poet Hugo von Hofmannsthal, which has been performed at the opening of the Salzburg Festival for more than eight decades. *Jedermann* is a play in the spirit of early modern Christian transcendentalism, and the cathedral of St. Rupert and St. Virgil provides an appropriate backdrop.

It is one of a number of magnificent churches in Salzburg. The beautiful city on the Salzach has an exceptional wealth of Baroque architecture that has made it famous throughout the world. Its economic importance is due in part to the salt from which it takes its name.

In the beginning there were monasteries

The Celtic and Roman settlements were followed by a wave of Bavarian immigration. Then, at the end of the seventh century, the future St. Rupert,

a scion of the Upper Rhineland nobility, founded two monasteries.

Its cultural heyday was the Baroque period, when the prince bishops holding office here became patrons of the arts. During this time, Leopold Mozart and his son Wolfgang Amadeus were in the service of the court, and the royal city of Salzburg and its cathedral took on their present form.

The beginnings of the cathedral lie far in the past. As long ago as 774, there was a church on the site, dedicated to Virgil, a saint of Irish origin, who succeeded St. Boniface and came as a missionary to the surrounding Alpine region.

The cathedral was continually under reconstruction, as a result of seven fires. The eighth, in 1598, was particularly devastating in its effect. Archbishop Wolf Dietrich von Raitenau, one of the great Salzburg princes of the church and an obsessive builder, had the scene of the fire completely cleared. However, during excavations that took place between 1956 and 1958, it was still possible to uncover parts of the late Roman crypt – a pillared hall with three naves, each with three bays, adjoining the semicircular apse in the east.

Some of the sculptural decoration has also been preserved, for instance a capital beautifully decorated with acanthus leaves – a way of finishing off a column that was already a favorite in Greco-Roman antiquity. The only other survival from that earlier time is the High Gothic font.

Wolf Dietrich von Raitenau commissioned Vincenzo Scamozzi, one of the numerous itinerant Italian architects of that time, to plan an extensive new building.

Only 14 years to build

Wolf Dietrich's successor, Markus Sittikus, Count of Hohenems, did not lay the foundation stone until 1614. It was left to another Italian, Santino Solari, to carry out the work. He subjected Scamozzi's plans to a thorough revision and, in so doing, continually looked back to examples from his native land, notably the churches of St. Peter and Il Gesù in Rome and the cathedral of Como in Upper Italy. The total building time in Salzburg amounted to just 14 years.

St. Rupert's is a domed church, with a three-story façade divided by balustrades and statues and with twin towers. Its overall length is 256ft (78m), the width 233ft (71m), and the height of the central nave 102ft (31m). The cupola is 233ft (71m) high, with the two towers soaring to

256ft (78m). The cathedral holds around 10,000 people.

It is said to be the first example of the adaptation of Italian Baroque for use in ecclesiastical buildings north of the Alps, thus setting a precedent for the future of architecture and church building throughout the whole of Upper Germany.

Solari consciously set the individual parts of his building alongside one another to create a striking contrast, for instance in the construction of the façade which, with its facing of white Untersberg marble, stands out clearly against the exterior walls and the choir area.

There is a single nave with barrel-vaulting and high side-galleries. Between the massive double pilasters on either side there are individual interconnected chapels.

Shining light from on high

The eastern part of the cathedral is a triconchos – three, linked, semicircular apses in the form of a clover leaf – with the octagonal dome rising above them. The shining light entering from above clearly separates this area from the semidarkness of the nave. The entire interior of the cathedral was extravagantly decorated with fine plasterwork, using Santino Solari's designs. There are a total of 11 altars in the cathedral.

During the last war, St. Rupert's was badly damaged by an American air raid and the dome collapsed. Rebuilding work lasted until 1959.

There are three portals leading into the cathedral, with the figures of four saints standing in front of them. These are the two apostles Peter and Paul and the two patrons of the city and the church, Virgil and Rupert.

The sculptures date from the second half of the seventeenth century and are of gigantic proportions. They gaze out calmly over the costumed actors who declaim the verses of Hofmannsthal's *Jedermann* at their feet, seeming to preside over the whole cathedral square with its magnificent backdrop. Thus they continue, though the voices fall silent and the summer festival ends.

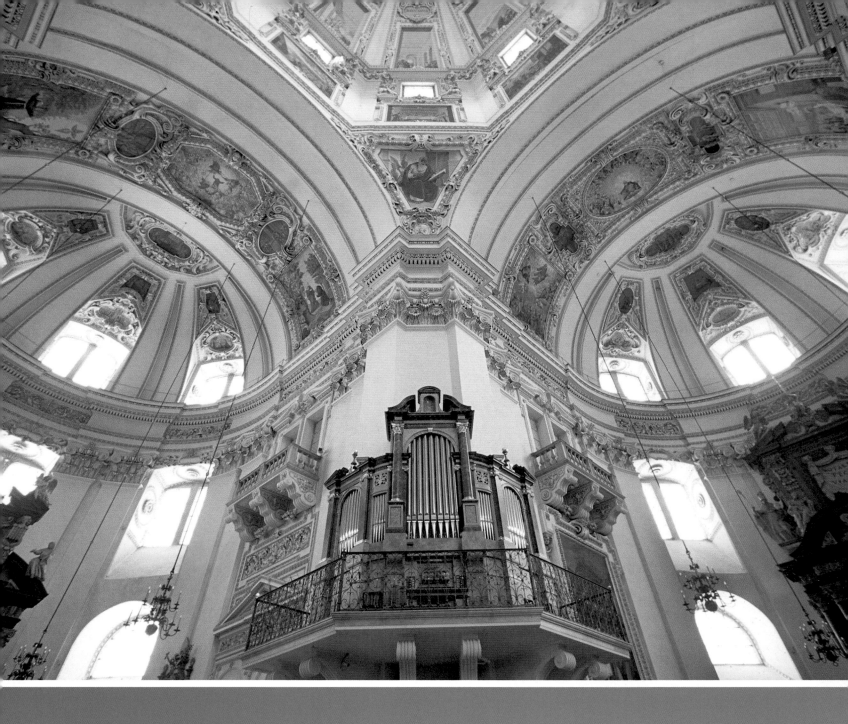

The 'Steffl', symbol of Vienna

St. Stephan's cathedral in **VIENNA** has the most solemn interior in the world, according to its admirers

Vienna
AUSTRIA

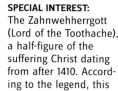

Adriatic Sea

Vienna is a Baroque city. All the surviving palaces and almost all the churches are dressed in the architectural trappings of the Counter-Reformation. The Gothic buildings so commonly encountered in other cities in central and western Europe are largely missing here, though with two notable exceptions: Maria am Gestade (St. Mary's on the Bank), the church of the medieval Danube boatmen, and St. Stephan's cathedral.

As Vienna's biggest church, it is naturally conspicuous. It has accompanied the historical development of the city from the High Middle Ages to the present day, faithfully mirroring these events. Its tower, nicknamed the 'Steffl' by the locals, has become the symbol of the city.

St. Stephan's stands on the site of a pagan shrine, which was replaced by a chapel after the conversion to Christianity. Bishop Reginmar of Passau initiated the building of the cathedral in 1137. Only a parish church was planned but the size reveals a secret, more far-reaching ambition. The cathedral was consecrated in 1147, being named after an early pope.

Creation of the bishopric

The basilica, which has three naves and a transept, matched the size of other Romanesque cathedrals. After a big fire, the new Gothic building was begun in 1230-1240. The exterior walls of the hall were erected first, enclosing the entire Romanesque transept. This resulted in the new church, including the west front, ending up much wider than its predecessor. Two chapels were added to the building known as the Westwerk, which had become too narrow.

By around 1430, the walls of the nave were standing; the roof was put on after 1440. The building of the south tower had started around 1360. It was completed in 1433 by the Bohemian master builder Hans von Prachatitz. Work began on the north tower in the mid-fifteenth century, but it was to remain unfinished. Chapels were built and altars were set up. The building was completed by the end of the fifteenth century and, at the same time, the expectations raised by the extraordinary size of the building were fulfilled. Vienna became a bishopric in 1469.

Judgment day outside the cathedral doors

St. Stephan's is one of the most impressive of all Gothic cathedrals. The Riesentor (Giant Gate) at the north-west end of the nave – it takes its name from the old word 'Riestür'

meaning portcullis – is a Late Romanesque, 'funnel' portal. Like the rest of the Westwerk, it was incorporated from the previous Romanesque building. In the niches in the outer wall of the portal, there are statues of St. Stephan, Samson from the Old Testament, and one of a sitting judge, which suggests that a court was held in front of this gate.

Inside, the nave displays the fine fan vaulting of the Late Gothic period with the richly carved pillars ornamented with baldachin statues. The hall choir has three naves. It is always in semidarkness. Adolf Loos, a Viennese, avant-garde architect of the Reform period around 1900, called it the "most solemn church interior in the world."

Famous tombs

There are various masterpieces of Gothic stone carving, such as the pulpit with its images of the four Fathers of the Church and, under its stone steps, the self-portrait of the man who created them, Anton Pilgrim from Brno. He also carved the Orgelfuss (organ base) of 1513 and this, too, bears his self-portrait. Close to

the pulpit is the statue dating from 1325 known as the Dienstbotenmadonna (Servant's Madonna), so named because it is said to have succeeded in helping a maidservant unjustly accused of theft.

The statue of St. Christopher in the choir is the work of the Dutchman Niclas Gerhaert von Leyden. St. Christopher was the favorite saint of Emperor Friedrich III, who donated a sumptuous altar to the cathedral. His tomb is also to be found in the cathedral. There are a large number of other tombs, including that of Prince Eugene of Savoy. In the sacristy is the entrance to the tower staircase, which has 418 steps reaching a height of 236ft (72m). From the top, provided the weather is fine, you can see as far as the foothills of the Carpathians to the east and Moravia to the north.

Altogether, the tower measures 449ft (137m) in height; its opposite number on the north side can only manage 197ft (60m). Under the north tower is the entrance to the catacombs, an extensive crypt containing the tombs of 15 Habsburg members. Since 1953, the archbishops of Vienna have also been buried here.

The Gothic cathedral stands in the middle of Vienna and is surrounded on all sides by busy squares (main picture)

The patterns on the tiled roof are part of the traditional decoration of the church. The national coat-of-arms on the roof and the inscription 1950 are a reminder of the rebuilding of the cathedral after heavy damage sustained during WWII (above)

View of the nave with the high altar (below)

The Karlskirche in Vienna

Built by Emperor Charles VI to celebrate victory over the Turks and to give thanks for an end to the plague

Vienna
AUSTRIA

Adriatic Sea

GETTING THERE:
Flights to Vienna-Schwechat international airport. By tram to Karlsplatz

OPENING TIMES:
Usually open all day every day, except Sunday morning when services are in progress

WHEN TO GO:
May/June or August/September

SPECIAL INTEREST:
The architecture of the Karlsplatz as a whole, which blends perfectly with the style of the church

The frescoes on the dome ceiling, created by Johann Michael Rottmayr between 1725 and 1730, depict St. Borromeo's intercession for protection from the plague (below, left)

On two occasions in history, the Turkish forces of the Ottoman Empire laid siege to Vienna during their Balkan campaigns; the last was in 1683. The building of the church situated in Vienna's Karlsplatz (St. Charles' Square) was partly a way of giving thanks to God that the attackers had been repelled.

The other event that prompted its construction was a major epidemic of the plague, which swept through the Austrian capital in 1713 claiming 8000 lives. The Habsburg emperor, Charles VI, vowed that he would build a church if the plague would only come to an end. The foundation stone was duly laid outside the actual town, on the empty, partially vine-clad slopes of a hill on the far side of the Wien river valley.

It was designed by Johann Bernhard Fischer von Erlach, one of Austria's greatest Baroque architects, whose work extends to many other buildings in Vienna. He and his equally talented son, Joseph Emanuel, supervised construction of the Karlskirche, which was completed in 1739 and built at a cost of 304,000 guilders. The money was raised by the crown lands, as well as from fines collected from the City of Hamburg.

Minaret-style pillars

The church has been referred to as Vienna's own Hagia Sophia and it is easy to see why it might be considered a deliberate amalgamation of Christian and Muslim influences. This impression undoubtedly arises from the two slender pillars flanking the portal. These, no doubt intentionally, resemble minarets, despite the fact that they are primarily modeled on the Trajan's Column in Rome. The rotunda and its cupola, together with these columns, are reminiscent of a mosque although domed churches of this kind are an equally common feature of ancient Christian architecture. While obligatory in Orthodox churches, what better example of a domed Christian church could there be than Catholicism's most important holy building, namely St. Peter's basilica in Rome? Even the Hagia Sophia itself in Istanbul originally began life as a Christian church.

Borromeus, a patron saint

"I desire to fulfil my vow before those who fear God," reads the Emperor's dedication inscription. The church is dedicated to St. Charles Borromeo, cardinal and archbishop of Milan, who died in 1584. He was related to the Medici family and a fervent opponent of the Reformation. He was greatly acclaimed for his work during the plague outbreak between 1570 and 1576, for which he was later canonized. Since then, he has been regarded as the patron saint who provides protection against the plague. The church of St. Charles in Vienna, named in his honor, is the most important memorial to Borromeo anywhere outside Italy.

In front of the central dome is a pillared porch, built in the style of a Greek temple. The two columns represent the Herculean pillars of the Empire, as well as of the "Determination and Courage" motto of the Emperor who built it. Each of the pillars symbolizes one of these qualities. They are capped with an eagle and crown, the insignia of earthly sovereignty. The spiral reliefs on the pillars not only depict scenes from the life of St. Charles Borromeo but also extol the virtues of various rulers, from Emperor Charles the Great to Emperor Charles VI.

The mighty dome

The interior of the church is built to an oval plan, rigidly adhering to a logical design while creating an overall impression of coolness. Its dominant feature is the ceiling fresco, created between 1725 and 1730 by Johann Michael Rottmayr. It depicts St. Charles Borromeo interceding with the Holy Trinity for protection against the plague. He is surrounded by all kinds of allegorical figures. The frescoes in the curved choir, side chapels, and organ gallery are likewise the work of Rottmayr. The saint is

also depicted above the high altar, ascending to the light of God. Although the design for this is attributable to Fischer von Erlach Senior, the finished work was produced by the stucco artist, Camesina.

The Karlskirche used to be surrounded by other buildings. Below it was once a cemetery belonging to the Bürgerspital hospital; next to it was the Baroque Rochus chapel, demolished in 1790. Karlsplatz, in which the church now finds itself situated, was not built until the end of the nineteenth century. It was created mainly as a result of the construction of the city's tram system.

The Karlsplatz station pavilion, designed by Otto Wagner, is a fine example of Art Nouveau (Jugendstil) architecture and blends well with the Karlskirche, as does the Secession building on the other side of the Plaza, created by Josef Maria Olbrich. Its unmistakably Islamic-style dome also seems to mirror the Karlskirche.

In the center of the Karlsplatz is a water feature with a large sculpture by Henry Moore, entitled *Hill Arch*. Its Baroque style might almost be interpreted as a tribute to the spirit of this square, and to Vienna as a whole.

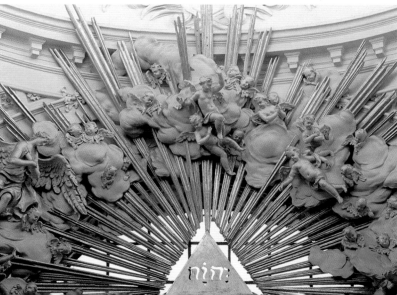

Viennese Baroque at its best. Nevertheless, the dome of the Karlskirche and the pillars flanking the main entrance – which could easily be mistaken for minarets – reflect elements of Islamic mosque architecture (main picture)

The sumptuous gilt ornamentation above the high altar is a magnificent sight (below, right)

High above the Moldau

St. Vitus' cathedral in **PRAGUE** is Peter Parler's finest achievement and the city's most famous landmark

North Sea

•Prague

CZECH REPUBLIC

GETTING THERE:
International airport on the outskirts of Prague. Rail links from all neighboring countries

OPENING TIMES:
Usually 9:00 A.M. – 7:00 P.M.; Nov-Mar until 4:00 P.M. No admission to tourists during services

SPECIAL INTEREST:
Golden Lane in Hradcany near the cathedral with its former tradesmen's houses

The cathedral's east façade is a fine example of filigree stonework (above)

The Wenceslas chapel contains a statue of St. Wenceslas, surrounded by frescoes depicting scenes from his life (below, center)

In spite of its immense height, the central nave is not at all overwhelming: the light flooding in through the windows lends the pillars an ethereal quality (below, right)

A bust of the the cathedral's architect, Peter Parler, can be seen in the gallery (below, left)

It is a little known fact that, during the High Middle Ages, Prague was second only to Paris as the most important city in Europe. What began as an insignificant little settlement gradually grew into an extremely important center of power, thanks to a steady influx of Slavs, Germans, and Jews. The area known as Hradcany, that unique collection of buildings above the Moldau which includes the cathedral of St. Vitus, bears testimony to its former greatness.

It took six hundred years for Prague cathedral to become what it is today. There were earlier buildings on this site. A Romanesque basilica, consecrated in 1096, was replaced by a new building in the mid-fourteenth century, after Prague became an archbishopric. It was commissioned by Charles IV of Luxemburg, who chose Prague as his seat of residence and also founded Prague University. The first architect to be involved in the project was Mathias of Arras, who had previously worked in Avignon. It is to him and his successor, Peter Parler, that the cathedral owes its design.

Parler came from one of the foremost artists' families in late medieval Europe. His father was one of the architects of Cologne cathedral and, after his death, his sons Wenzel and Johann continued his work in Prague.

Rhineland origins

Broadly speaking, the design of St. Vitus' cathedral is based on that of the early Gothic cathedrals of southern France; under Peter Parler's influence, this rather rigid architectural style, also known as 'doctrinaire Gothic' was relaxed and modified to a certain extent, with the result that some of the cathedral's features almost verge on the Baroque. The 'vesica piscis' design featured in the tracery, for example, illustrates the influence of English Gothic. Peter Parler moved away from the traditional style of ribbed vaulting, introducing instead a criss-crossing design of ribs produced by intersecting triangles.

The exterior clearly illustrates Parler's Rhineland roots: the choir supports are reminiscent of those in Cologne cathedral. One of the cathedral's gems is the Wenceslas chapel, consecrated in 1367. It was named after Václav, a medieval Czech ruler, who brought Christianity to Bohemia and was murdered by his brother. He was buried in the chapel of St. Vitus, which he had founded, and the Wenceslas chapel now contains his tomb.

Peter Parler's design for the vaulting consists of an intricate network of criss-crossing ribs and delicately fashioned portals. He was the first European architect to experiment with pendentive vaulting, an example of which can be seen in the old sacristy. The south-facing tower is also Parler's innovation. It had been customary for Gothic cathedrals to have a west-facing, twin-towered façade. Parler dispensed with this tradition and St. Vitus's main façade faces south, overlooking the town.

Portraits in stone

One of the cathedral's main art treasures is its gallery of 21 busts in the triforium, representing contemporaries of Emperor Charles IV. These depict members of the House of Luxemburg, archbishops, and cathedral sponsors, as well as the two architects Peter Parler and Mathias von Arras. These figures are not of the traditional genre of stylized or idealized portrayals that were customary for the High Middle Ages. They are, on the contrary, true likenesses. The bust of Peter Parler shows a man with a trimmed beard, high forehead, and combed-back hair. His expression is at once resolute and melancholy.

He died in 1399, after which time the pace of work on the cathedral slowed considerably. When third and fourth levels were eventually completed, they reflected a distinctly Late Gothic style of architecture. Work continued under two new architects, Bonifaz Wohlmut and Hans von Tirol, who introduced Renaissance elements into the design, including the south tower. After this, construction ceased for a time.

Apart from a few, fairly half-hearted attempts in the eighteenth century, building work did not resume in earnest until 1842. The similarities with the cathedral of Cologne, the great Peter Parler's home town, are unmistakable and St. Vitus, like its sister project on the banks of the Rhine, should be seen within the context of the national Romantic movement sweeping Europe at that time.

Official opening in 1929

Following years of German-Austrian domination, it was important for Prague to revive its flagging sense of Czech national identity. It is not without irony that the architects who were then in charge of the construction of St. Vitus bore German names: Andreas Kranner and Joseph Mocker. They gave the long nave its present form. The finished cathedral was finally consecrated in September 1929.

Apart from the Wenceslas chapel, some of the cathedral's most impor-

tant treasures include the Vladislav Oratory, completed in 1493 and attributed to Benedikt Ried, as well as the organ gallery by Renaissance artist Sebastiano Serlio. The cathedral also boasts murals, statues, and altarpieces by artists from all over Europe, as well as the Imperial Habsburg Mausoleum and the tomb of a Baroque field marshal. Joseph Emmanuel Fischer von Erlach designed the tomb of St. John of Nepomuk, a martyr from Prague and popular saint. He was a cleric, who was drowned in the Moldau on the orders of the king. He was buried in St. Vitus' cathedral and beatified in 1729.

Nowadays, the cathedral of St. Vitus is a national monument, constantly thronged with tourists. Once through its portals, however, they can lose themselves between the pillars and balustrades of this majestic edifice which has managed to triumph over everything.

Under Stephen's crown

St. Martin's cathedral in **BRATISLAVA** was where the kings of Hungary were crowned

GETTING THERE:
The city has an international airport. By car from Vienna, about 40 miles (65km) via the A 1 and E 58

OPENING TIMES:
Best visited as part of a guided tour of the city. Times obtainable from the city tourist office

SPECIAL INTEREST:
St. John's chapel with the sarcophagus of St. John the Patriarch

The pale sandstone cathedral of St. Martin (main picture)

On 25 September 1825, Carolina Augusta was crowned Queen of Hungary in Pressburg cathedral (below, left). Emperor Francis I is seated under the canopy (colored etching by J. A. Schlosser)

Bratislava: view of the city from the east, with the castle and St. Martin's cathedral. Copper engraving of 1740 with later coloring (below, center)

Martin of Tours, who was later canonized as a saint, was the son of a military tribune and had a glittering career as a soldier in Roman-occupied Gaul. When he went out one icy, winter evening, he met a ragged, old man who begged him for alms. Martin had neither money nor food for him, so he took his sword and cut his cloak in two, giving half to the freezing man. The following night, he dreamed that the beggar had been Jesus. Martin was baptized, left the army, and retired to a hermitage, which later became one of the first monasteries in Europe. In 371, the people elected him bishop of Tours. He died aged 80, while on a visit to another foundation.

He was one of the first saints not to have died a martyr's death. He soon achieved exceptional popularity among church folk as a result of what came to be known as the 'miracle of the cloak'. The incident became the subject of many pictures and was seen as an example of compassion in action. St. Martin is the patron saint of, among other places, the Burgenland province of Austria with its many Hungarian citizens, as he was born in Pannonia in Hungary. This was also where he undertook his first missionary work.

The metaphor of the divided cloak

The dividing of his cloak can also be interpreted as a political metaphor for the separation of things that really belong together. The Hungarians can find examples of this in their national history. So can Slovakia, where Hungarians still represent a large ethnic minority. The capital of Slovakia is now known as Bratislava. It used to be called Pressburg and its Hungarian name is Poszony. For more than two hundred years, Bratislava was also the capital of the kingdom of Hungary and the cathedral of St. Martin in Pressburg or Poszony was where the kings were crowned.

Baroque embellishments

Between 1541 and 1784, therefore, this was where the Magyar crown of St. Stephen was placed on the heads of rulers from the house of Habsburg. The crown of St. Stephen is recognizable by its slightly crooked cross. A gilded copy of the crown, one meter high and weighing 662lb (300kg), has adorned the 19th-century steeple of St. Martin's cathedral since the 1940s. Restoration of the tower became necessary after it was struck by lightning. Much earlier, it had been the tower of a defensive wall, forming part of the city's medieval fortifications.

The cathedral can reflect on a history not unusual for old cathedral churches. At first, there was just a small, Roman basilica dating from 1221. Alterations to the building began in the fourteenth century, when it was widened to create a three-nave church. In the fifteenth century, the old presbytery was replaced by a Late Gothic building with a stellar vault. The architect was probably the same Hanns Puchsbaum who left his mark on Ulm cathedral and St. Stephen's cathedral in Vienna. The north door with a relief of the Holy Trinity survives from that period.

At the beginning of the eighteenth century, the office of archbishop was held by Emmerich Eszterházy, a member of the famous noble family. He had the cathedral of St. Martin entirely redecorated in the Baroque manner. His most important assistant in this task was the Late Baroque sculptor from Vienna, Georg Raphael Donner, who was also responsible for work on Schloss Mirabell in Salzburg and the fountain in the Neue Markt in Vienna, which is named after him. His speciality was lead casting, and a major commission in this regard was a figure of St. Martin for the cathedral in Bratislava.

It was originally intended for the high altar but has not been allowed to stand there for many years, as the nineteenth century saw the removal of Baroque additions to reveal elements of the old Gothic building. Donner's huge statue found its way into the south-east nave. It shows St. Martin in the act of cutting the cloak, seated on a rearing horse. He is portrayed as a contemporary nobleman with identical features to those of Eszterházy, who commissioned it.

Maria Theresia, the last to come

Donner was also responsible for the decoration of the chapel of St. John. It is dedicated to St. John the Almsgiver, the patriarch of Alexandria, whose bones are housed there in a sarcophagus under a baldachin, flanked by six angels. In addition, the archbishop and commissioner of the work, Imre Eszterházy, also arranged for his own burial there.

St. Martin's cathedral in Bratislava is almost more important as an historic site than for its architecture. The pale sandstone building nestles in the shadow of the castle, an imposing structure built on a rock overlooking the bank of the Danube. The last ruler to reside here was the Empress Maria Theresia. As she was crowned in Pressburg, her name also appears as the penultimate on a memorial tablet on the north side of the presbytery. No more kings of Hungary would be crowned here; ultimately, there would be no more kings of Hungary.

Where kings were crowned

The Mátyas templom in **BUDAPEST** was first mentioned in 1247

HUNGARY
Budapest

Adriatic Sea

Mediterranean Sea

GETTING THERE:
Via Budapest international airport. Good rail connections from Vienna, Berlin, and eastern Europe. Motorway from Vienna

OPENING TIMES:
Until further notice, daily 8:00 A.M. - 8:00 P.M. No sightseeing during Masses

SPECIAL INTEREST:
The Black Madonna in the Loretto chapel

The roofs of the Matthias church are covered with colorful majolica tiles laid out in geometrical patterns (below, left)

The Matthias church on the castle hill, with its colorful roof (main picture)

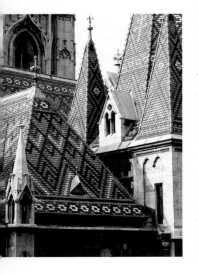

The capital of Hungary is Budapest. It has two million inhabitants and stands on both sides of the Danube, which flows due south at this point. Higher up river, a little to the north near the city of Vécs, is the start of the famous bend known as the Danube Knee. The left bank of the Danube is hilly, as the Buda mountain range ends here, whereas the right bank remains fairly flat, where the Small Hungarian Plain or Kisalföld begins.

Buda and Pest only became a single city in 1872. Until then, there were two separate administrations and two different urban cultures. Pest was mainly inhabited by the middle classes – manufacturers, tradesmen, ordinary people – whereas Buda was the home of the court, the nobility, and the court officials.

Buda is the older of the two cities. The Celts had already settled here before the Romans arrived in about 10 BC. The latter named their settlement Aquincum, deriving from the word aqua, Latin for water, because hot springs flow from the foot of the Castle hill.

Very little has survived from that epoch – no ancient theater, no triumphal arch, no old mosaics. Later invaders – Vandals, Avares, Slavs, and, in the last wave of migration, the Magyars – destroyed almost everything. The Magyars settled here but had to fight off the Mongols and the Turks. Apart from relics of the years of Turkish occupation, the only important architectural monuments in Budapest date from the age of feudal absolutism and the Baroque.

In Trinity Square

Among these architectural monuments are the Mátyas templom (church of Matthias) on the castle hill and the castle itself. The amusing Fisherman's Bastion, – a favorite subject for tourist photos with its pinnacles and battlement walks running part of the way round the hilltop – might look like a fortification, but is actually the product of 19th-century, Nationalist Romanticism.

This bastion is called Hálaszbástya in Hungarian, and was built by Frigyek Schulek, Budapest's most important historicist architect. The other bulwarks may be less striking, but they are older. The Transylvanian Bastion is the work of an Italian fortress-builder of the Baroque era.

Behind the Fisherman's Bastion is Trinity Square or Szentháromság tér. It is bounded on one side by the old town hall of Buda, which has a most beautiful Baroque façade. The Holy Trinity column was erected to commemorate an outbreak of plague, and is the equivalent of the Baroque plague columns found in Austria. The square is dominated by the Gothic Matthias church.

It was actually supposed to be called the church of Our Lady or, more correctly, the church of the Mother of God in the Buda Mountains. At any rate, that was once its name. Its Gothic architectural features were added later and are the work of the aforementioned Frigyek Schulek. The church has a long history, however. One of the first documented references dates from 1247.

mosque. When Buda was Christian once more, the mosque again became a church. It was entrusted first to the care of the Franciscans, and then to the Jesuits.

Last coronation in 1916

The kings of Hungary were crowned in this church, despite the fact that those who were members of the house of Habsburg mostly lived in Vienna and were also emperors of Austria. That was the case with Franz Joseph and his wife, the slender Elizabeth of Bavaria, nicknamed Sissi. They were crowned in 1867, with Franz Liszt composing a Mass especially for the occasion.

After that, Frigyek Schulek undertook a comprehensive rebuild. The last king to be crowned here was Charles IV of Hungary in 1916, who was also the last Habsburg to rule Austria. Two years later, the Central Powers lost the First World War and Hungary gained its independence, with Austria subsequently becoming a republic.

The church has two towers. The smaller one is named after King Bela IV, who ruled the country after the Mongol attack. It is covered with majolica tiles from the famous Zsolnay factory in Pécs. The bigger tower is 262ft (80m) high. It is named after Matthias Corvinus and, from the second floor upwards, is octagonal in form. Entrance is through St. Mary's Gate, a medieval monument which has been preserved to this day.

The Loretto chapel houses the Black Madonna, darkened by candlesmoke, and in the Trinity chapel are the bones of King Bela III. Inside the church, there are frescoes of scenes from Hungarian history. These, too, are probably the work of Frigyek Schulek.

**Interior of the church
(below, right)**

The original building underwent numerous additions and alterations as its importance increased. In 1308, Charles Robert of Anjou was crowned king of Hungary here. In 1385, Sigismund of Luxembourg went through the same ceremony in the same place. In his reign it became customary to hang in the church the banners captured by victorious military expeditions. Hungary's most important Renaissance monarch, Matthias Corvinus, then gave it its new name. He was twice married in this church and his coat of arms, a raven with a ring in its beak, has hung on the south tower ever since.

In 1526, the Turks arrived and set fire to the church. Enough of the walls remained for the victorious Sultan Suleiman to hold a thanksgiving service there, and it then became a

Classical splendor

The cathedral in **ESZTERGOM** is at the heart of Hungarian Catholicism and the seat of the archbishop

The little town of Esztergom, or Gran, stands on the banks of the Danube to the north of Budapest and on the frontier with Slovakia. With its hot springs, it is not only a spa but also a popular destination for visitors. It also claims to be one of the oldest towns in Pannonia.

Pannonia was the Roman name for this central Danube province. Following the fall of their empire and the migrations which followed, various tribes made their way here, Germanic as well as non-Germanic, including the Huns and the Avars. Both were

nomadic horsemen of Asiatic-East European origin, and were later followed by the Magyars. They conquered Pannonia towards the end of the ninth century and settled there. Their leader was a grand prince by the name of Árpád.

One of his successors, Geza, founded the settlement of Esztergom in 970 and made it his main residence. Having also embraced Christianity, he built Hungary's first Christian church here. His son and successor was born in Esztergom. He was called István or Stephan and,

during Christmas 1001, was crowned Hungary's first king in the castle of Esztergom. The crown is said to have been provided by Pope Sylvester and one of its distinctive features is a slightly crooked Greek cross.

Stephan imposed Christianity on the country, in some cases by force. He introduced administrative structures and a central ecclesiastical body modelled on western European examples. The Archbishop's main seat was Esztergom. Following his death in 1038, Stephan was canonized and became Hungary's patron saint.

Esztergom remained the capital of Hungary. It reached its peak in the years up to 1196 when the Hungarian monarchs turned their attention downriver to Buda, where they established their new seat of power. Only the archbishop's seat remained in Esztergom. In the mid-thirteenth century, central Europe, including Hungary, was attacked by Mongol hordes, who laid siege to Esztergom. It managed to hold out but Hungary subsequently suffered many internal upheavals. The Árpád dynasty died out. The Empire regained strength and from 1443 was ruled by King Matthias I Corvinus.

He was one of the great men in European history, a Renaissance prince of considerable power who possessed an extraordinary appreciation of culture. He developed Esztergom into an important center of education. When he died, his empire soon disintegrated and, soon afterwards, the Turks marched into Pannonia and seized power. Sultan Suleyman crushed Hungary in a devastating defeat at the battle of Mohács, after which he conquered the entire country, including Esztergom. It remained under Turkish rule until 1683, when Poland's king, Jan Sobeiski, liberated Esztergom.

A visit by Hans Christian Andersen

The town and castle remained in Hungarian hands when the Turks launched a fresh onslaught on Hungary a century later and, even though the new capital was Buda, Esztergom retained its importance as a special focus of Hungarian history and national identity. It continued to be the seat of the archbishop, the primate of Hungary.

In 1843, the Danish fairy tale writer, Hans Christian Andersen, who was also a keen tourist and travel writer, took a riverboat trip up the Danube. "We are approaching Gran (Esztergom)", he recorded. "Up on top of the cliffs, in the middle of the ruined fortress, there is a church being built: the town itself is on level ground amid green trees; a cloud of butterflies flew out of these across the Danube…."

Andersen experienced the construction of Esztergom cathedral at its halfway stage. Work began in 1822, and it was completed in 1864. The opening ceremony featured a Mass by Franz Liszt, specially composed for the occasion. He conducted its première performance himself.

A 328ft (100m)-high cupola

The Classical-style basilica is the largest church in Hungary and the third largest church on the continent. It is 387ft (118m) in length and 131ft (40m) wide. It stands on Castle Hill, visible from miles around. It is modeled on St. Peter's basilica in Rome and, like St. Peter's, combines a basilica and central building, crowned by a 328ft (100m)-high, central dome. The porch is supported by 22 Corinthian pillars.

The left side aisle contains the Bakócz chapel with its lovely, red marble walls. It is much older than the rest of the building, having been commissioned at the beginning of the sixteenth century. It is the only surviving example of Renaissance architecture in the country. During building work, it was carefully dismantled into 1600 pieces, then reconstructed stone by stone in its current location. The basilica boasts a treasury with an extensive collection of ecclesiastical treasures, including the Matthias Corvinus Cross. The Latin word 'corvinus' means 'raven', a bird which is regarded as intelligent and adaptable. There was never any doubt about the intelligence of Matthias Corvinus.

The cathedral's main portal with its mighty dome in the background (main picture)

In the heart of the Old Town of Esztergom, the cathedral dome dominates the skyline (below, right)

Emperor Sigismund's drinking horn, fashioned from bison horn and decorated with silver, dating from around 1400. Sigismund gifted it to the cathedral during his lifetime (below, left)

Jesuit Baroque in Slovenia

The sumptuous interior of the cathedral of St. Nicholas in **LJUBLJANA** seems to echo the country's exuberant character

GETTING THERE:
Flights to the city's international airport. By rail or motorway from Italy and Austria

OPENING TIMES:
Usually open every day, but closed between 12:00 P.M. and 3:00 P.M. No admission to tourists during services

SPECIAL INTEREST:
The frescoes by Guilio Quaglio

View of the altar and Baroque interior of the cathedral of St. Nicholas (above)

Aerial photo showing the pleasing design of the cathedral with its twin towers and large dome (below, left)

A Baroque figure on one of the columns (below, right)

His ambition was to become a priest, but his genius stopped him fulfilling this dream: Andrea Pozzo (1642-1709), the architect who designed Ljubljana's ornate cathedral church, was a Jesuit, but was never ordained as a priest. His talent was so remarkable that the Order could not afford not to capitalize on it. He was sent to Savoy, Milan, Como, and Rome, and finally to imperial Vienna in the hope that the buildings he designed there would put the Roman Catholic faith on the map.

This man of many talents was born in 1642 in Trento. He was a gifted painter, stage designer, and art theoretician. His influence played a major role in the development of what became known as Jesuit Baroque, which he then introduced in Slovenia in his design for the cathedral of St. Nicholas in Ljubljana. The cathedral rises majestically in the heart of the city, its design reminiscent of the Chiesa del Gesù in Rome, and is generally regarded as Pozzo's finest achievement.

First mentioned in 1144

Italy and Slovenia have much in common, even if only on account of their geographical proximity to one another, for trends in art and architecture have never had any difficulty in crossing frontiers. Early in the first century BC, the Romans established a military camp on this site, calling it Julia Emona. During the sixth century, the settlement was destroyed by the Huns. Slavs eventually settled here on the banks of the Ljubljanica River in the seventh century.

The first documented mention of the town was in 1144, under the German name of Laibach. It was awarded the status of a town in 1260. In 1276, as the capital of the duchy of Carniola, Ljubljana was absorbed into the Habsburg Empire where it remained for over 600 years – apart from a very brief period under Napoleonic rule when Ljubljana was the government seat of the French Illyrian Provinces.

In the shadow of the church

In 1918, Ljubljana became part of Yugoslavia and, in 1945, capital of the semi-republic of Slovenia. In 1991, it finally became the principal city of a fully independent Slovenia. Its long history has always been played out against the background of the cathedral, one of the city's main landmarks along with its towering castle, fountains, bridges, and cafés.

In the thirteenth century, a Romanesque church occupied the spot where the cathedral now stands, dedicated to St. Nicholas, patron saint of fishermen and boatmen. In 1361, a Gothic church was erected on the same site, which was burned to the ground by the Turks in the fifteenth century. At the start of the eighteenth century, the Dolnicar brothers, who were members of the Academia Operosorum, a scientific society campaigning for reforms, set about organizing the building of a Baroque church, commissioning Andrea Pozzo with its design. It was consecrated in 1707, although the dome was not added until 1841. The keystone from the old church was used for the new building and a statue depicting the suffering of Mary, Mother of God, was also integrated into the new church.

Decorated in marble

The cheerful landscape of Slovenia with its forests, meadows, and river valleys appears to be echoed in the interior of the church, which is a feast of pink marble, stucco, and carvings. The magnificent frescoes depicting the life of St. Nicholas were created from 1703-1706 and 1721-23 by Guilio Quaglio, who had already made his name in Italy as a painter. Matevz Langus painted the altarpiece, which likewise portrays episodes from the life of the cathedral's patron saint. He also decorated the ceiling of the dome with scenes from the life of the Virgin Mary. The Corpus Christi altar in the transept is the work of Francesco Robba, an important Slovenian sculptor who also created the fountain outside the town hall representing the rivers of Carniola.

Choir stalls in 'Art Nouveau'

The pieces by Ljubljana's 'chief architect' Josef Plecnik within the cathedral will be of particular interest to art enthusiasts. Plecnik was a student of Otto Wagner and in the 1920s and 1930s made a major impact on the city, introducing a new style and dispensing with the familiar elaborate ornamentation, making Ljubljana not only a city of Baroque, but also of Art Nouveau. The choir stalls he designed for the cathedral are an example of his versatile talents. Two

stunning bronze doors were added in 1996 to commemorate Pope John Paul II's visit.

The priests' seminary, with its gigantic portals and massive figures of Atlas outside, was by way of an addition to the cathedral and contains a priceless library. Its Baroque interior features a ceiling lined in illusionist paintings, representing an allegory of theology as well as hope and love.

Tu felix Ljubljana! Oh fortunate city, to possess such a cathedral and temple of learning!

Bastion against the Turks

The cathedral in the Croatian capital of **ZAGREB** was converted into a fortress in the sixteenth century

GETTING THERE:
Flights to Zagreb international airport. By rail from central or eastern Europe. New motorways under construction from north and west Europe

OPENING TIMES:
Usually open every day

SPECIAL INTEREST:
The cathedral treasury

An aerial photo shows the cathedral surrounded by its fortress walls and fortified towers (main picture)

The cathedral's twin Neo-Gothic towers, illuminated at night (below, left)

View of the main nave with high altar (below, center)

Where else, outside Vienna, might you expect to find such a collection of busy coffee houses, full of women in elegant hats, where the men sit buried behind their newspapers for hours on end? In some parts of Zagreb, you could be forgiven for imagining yourself in Vienna. This is hardly surprising, considering that for hundreds of years the city's culture and lifestyle were influenced by the Austrian capital. By contrast, however, the scene in the Dolac, the large marketplace in the shadow of the cathedral, could not be more different: here, you will find mountainous piles of vegetables, chickens being plucked, and goat's cheese being sold. This is Zagreb, a city caught between the past and the present. Wherever you look in the Old Town, you will find buildings of yellow Schönbrunn-style stone side by side with constructions from Croatia's medieval past.

The highest spires in the Balkans

Zagreb is one of the oldest cities in Europe, exuding a strong sense of history at every turn. This is certainly true of the cathedral of the Assumption of Virgin Mary. Its imposing spires, rising to 341ft (104m) and 344ft (105m) respectively, are the highest in the Balkans and add to the cathedral's majestic appearance. It measures 253ft (77m) in length and 151ft (46m) in width and can accommodate 5000 people – a church truly fit for a bishop. A plaque inside the cathedral serves as a reminder that links with the Holy See in Rome were already in place 1300 years ago.

In the days of the Roman Empire, the area now occupied by the present-day Zagreb archbishopric was known as the province of Pannonia Savia. The bishopric of Zagreb was established in 1093 by King Ladislaus, who also commissioned the building of a church. The resulting Romanesque-style cathedral was consecrated in 1217, but was so badly damaged in a Tatar attack 25 years later that Bishop Timothy decided to build a new church in the Gothic style. The east section of the basilica was built between 1264 and 1284, while the main section slowly took shape over the next two centuries. Construction ceased completely at the beginning of the sixteenth century in the face of the threat of a Turkish invasion. Instead, a defensive ring of fortifications, incorporating Renaissance towers, was built around the cathedral.

In 1527, Croatia joined the Austrian Habsburg Empire, hoping to benefit from the protection of this mighty dominion in its defense against the Turks. During its wars against Turkey, however, the city still suffered heavily, with fires inflicting severe damage on the cathedral. It was not until the end of the seventeenth century that a period of peace and new-found affluence returned. In 1718, Zagreb became the capital of Croatia, a kingdom allied to Hungary, and soon became the new cultural center of the country.

Earthquake damage

During the ensuing years, the cathedral was furnished with precious Baroque marble, new organs were ordered, and more than 30 altars installed. In 1880, the church was so badly damaged by an earthquake that it had to undergo substantial renovation work. The cathedral owes its present appearance to the Viennese architects Von Schmidt and Bolle. They built the twin-towered façade in the Neo-Gothic style, and this has since become one of the city's most famous landmarks.

The pews date from the Renaissance period and were created by a Florentine master craftsman around 1520. The pulpit is a magnificent masterpiece of Baroque ornamentation; it is lavishly decorated with figures of angels, thus softening the otherwise austere atmosphere of Gothic architecture. The numerous Baroque altars, dedicated to famous saints or the Passion of Christ, are also sumptuously decorated. A number of paintings date from the fourteenth century, one of the later paintings being attributed to Albrecht Dürer.

A new place of pilgrimage

Zagreb cathedral boasts one of the finest treasuries to be found anywhere in Europe. Sacred as well as secular works of art spanning nine centuries are on display here, including monstrances, chalices, hand-written medieval documents, and tapestries, as well as a 10th-century, ivory diptych.

Of particular note is the sarcophagus of Cardinal Alojzije Stepinac, who came from a family of Croatian peasants and was imprisoned for many years on account of his open commitment to Christianity. Due to his defense of church interests in the face of the Communist regime, he was put on trial by Marshal Tito in 1946 for alleged collaboration during World War Two and placed under house arrest, where he died in 1960.

He was passionately revered by the people, long before Pope John Paul II proclaimed him a saint in 1998. Since then, however, there has been no end to the pilgrims flocking to pay homage at his silver tomb.

The monastery of Rila

These Orthodox church buildings are the national shrine of Bulgaria and are central to the country's history

BULGARIA
• Rila   *Black Sea*

Mediterranean Sea

GETTING THERE:
By bus or by car from Sofia, about 69 miles (110km) south along the E 79. Then, about 16 miles (25km) eastwards along the Rilska valley to the monastery

OPENING TIMES:
Usually 10:00 A.M. – 6:00 P.M. daily

SPECIAL INTEREST:
The collection with the monastery documents and Rila Cross

The monastery church of Rila was rebuilt in the nineteenth century after a serious fire. View of the main entrance and dome (main picture)

The monastery complex (below, left). The church stands in the center of the inner courtyard

Frescoes in the arcade (below, center) and a 19th-century ceiling fresco of God the Father (below, right)

An independent Bulgarian state has been set up three times in the course of history. The first time was in the Middle Ages, when a great Slavic empire, practising Orthodox Christianity, developed in the southern Balkans. In Old Church Slavic it possessed a written language with its own special script, Cyrillic, developed from the Greek alphabet. At the height of its influence, Tsar Simeon the Great of Bulgaria was also Emperor of Byzantium.

Under his successors, the empire crumbled and almost two centuries passed before a new one was created. This one had an even shorter lifespan than the first. It was subjugated first by the Serbs and then by the Turks. Bulgaria remained a province of the Ottoman Empire for more than five hundred years, and only the Russo-Turkish War of 1877 brought the Bulgarians the autonomy they had sought to achieve so many times in the past.

Such enduring resistance against a foreign culture is remarkable. Turkish rule, though known to the Bulgarians as the 'Turkish yoke', was not so totalitarian and harsh as not to tolerate ethnic and religious differences, and it was the Orthodox Christians who coordinated and promoted this vigorous resistance.

It began as a hermitage
The monastery of Rila had an outstanding part to play in all this. The word 'outstanding' can be taken literally. The Rila Mountains, where the monastery is sited, are the highest of several mountain ranges in Bulgaria. The monastery itself lies at a height of 3763ft (1147m), in a valley that is not easily accessible. It developed from the hermitage of a 10th-century monk by the name of Ivan Rilski. He was revered for his piety but became even more famous after his death,

when his bones acquired the reputation of being able to work miracles. As precious relics, they travelled as far afield as Hungary, before returning to Bulgaria and the monastery of Rila.

Symbol of resistance
The monastery buildings also date back to the tenth century. Ivan Rilski, together with his followers, built the accommodation for the monastic community, which lived through turbulent times until the rulers of the second Bulgarian empire confirmed its special status through donations and privileges.

Even the Turkish sultans guaranteed it special status, although it was later pillaged and fell into decline. The return of the bones of Ivan Rilski in 1469 brought about a change. The extravagant processions accompanying the transport were a conspicuous sign of the people's desire for self-determination and, since that time, if not before, the monastery of Rila has been considered both a national treasure and a symbol of Bulgarian resistance. This intense participation in the national liberation movement was respected even by the atheistic communists and, as a result, they left the monastery largely untouched.

Its situation has changed over the course of the centuries. In Ivan Rilski's day, the buildings were about 2 miles (3km) further to the northeast. The present site was not chosen until 1335. Fires resulted in damage that had to be cleared away. Today, the monastery is a national cultural monument and a flourishing business enterprise. Huge numbers of Bulgarian and foreign tourists guarantee employment and profit, with the monks being experienced managers.

Bell tower of 1335
The ground plan of the monastery complex is an irregular square. The domestic buildings, such as the kitchen, bakehouse, dairy, refectory, and hospital are housed in long buildings with wooden galleries and colorful arcades, with the monks' cells leading off them. The monastery has two gates. In the middle of the courtyard is the 75ft (23m)-high stone bell tower of 1335, with the church standing next to it.

The church is dedicated to the Nativity of Christ, and is reckoned to be the biggest in any of the surviving Bulgarian monasteries. It is a basilica with three domed towers, built as late as 1834-1837 after a particularly bad fire. Inside, there are wall paintings of

Biblical scenes and characters, with images of angels, demons, and martyrs surrounded by flowers, birds, and twining tendrils. They were painted between 1840 and1848.

The sanctuary is very impressive with its three-door iconostasis, which is entirely covered in gold leaf and arrayed with countless mosaics and ivory carvings. In the north wing of the monastery is a museum, whose collection includes the monastery documents, drawn up by a tsar named Ivan, and the Rila Cross, the work of an 18th-century monk by the name of Rafael. It is decorated with the tiniest miniatures of 140 Biblical scenes and a total of 600 figures. It took Brother Rafael 12 years to create the cross, and it is said that he ruined his eyesight in the process.

Jewel of the Ukraine

The magnificent cathedral of St. Sophia in **KIEV** with its cluster of domes

GETTING THERE:
Flights to Kiev's international airport. Rail links from Moscow, or from Vienna and Berlin in western Europe

OPENING TIMES:
Daily, except Thurs, 10:00 A.M. - 5:00 P.M. Subject to change at short notice

SPECIAL INTEREST:
The Monastery of the Caves in the Pechersk district

The Ukraine has only existed as an independent state since the collapse of the Soviet Union in 1991. The capital of the Ukraine is Kiev, which has, of course, been a capital city once before: of a kingdom bearing the same name.

By the ninth century, the Slavic tribes which had settled between the Bug and the Don rivers had grown tired of their constant feuding and decided to invite foreign powers to intercede in order to stabilize the situation. Their choice fell on the Varangians or Vikings, led by Dir and Askold. Their rule commenced in 862 with Kiev as their capital and their kingdom consequently becoming known as Kievan Rus. Orthodox Christianity was introduced into the country under their successors, the Rurik princes. The first ruler to be baptized was Svyatoslav.

The Eastern Roman or Orthodox church is one of a number of different branches of the Christian church. For geographical reasons, it has more in common with the old religion practised by the early Christian communities in Judea than with Western Roman Christianity. It differs from Catholicism in that it does not recognize one central spiritual leader. There are several autonomous patriarchates, the most important of which was for a long time based in Constantinople (now Istanbul).

Icons as devotional images

The Orthodox Church has its own rites, canon, and distinctive religious art. Part of its aesthetic ethos is that a given theme has no need for change but should be reproduced more or less faithfully, with perhaps just occasional, slight deviations. This same concept can be seen in icons, formal devotional images which always feature the same elements in their basic design. Although iconic art originated in the Byzantine Empire, it is Russia that is most famed for this art form. The same is also true of its sacred buildings.

As a rule, the ground plan of an Orthodox church is in the shape of a Greek cross, with the altar in the exact center situated beneath what is usually a shallow dome. This simple church design is still commonly found in many Orthodox areas of the southern Balkans. The church dignitaries and secular rulers, however, felt that such simplicity did not adequately reflect their status. They planned their cathedrals on a much grander scale, modeling them on Hagia Sophia in Constantinople, the largest and most magnificent church in Orthodox Christendom.

Hagia Sophia was also the model for St. Sophia's cathedral in Kiev. Its design, in turn, became the blueprint for other major churches in the eastern Slavic states. From the cathedral of Elijah the Prophet in Yaroslavl to the great cathedral churches of Moscow, they all owe their design to Kiev's version of Hagia Sophia.

It was built in the eleventh century, with construction work beginning in 1037. The ruler of Kiev at that time was a grand prince of the Ruric dynasty, known as Yaroslav the Wise. Under his influence, Kiev became a city of outstanding architecture. He also founded schools and introduced a code of law called the 'Russkaya Pravda.' His empire disintegrated in the hands of his successors and Kiev's importance also began to wane.

The year 1223 saw the start of the Mongol invasions, under Genghis Khan. In 1240, the Mongols attacked Kiev. Like many other towns in their path, it too was overrun and destroyed. St. Sophia's cathedral was also badly damaged and not rebuilt until centuries later. By then, the Mongols had long since been overthrown, thanks to the endeavors of the grand princes of Moscow, particularly those of the future tsar, Ivan the Terrible. Thus, a new Slavic empire was born.

Glittering gold

The renovation of the cathedral of St. Sophia was based largely on the old ground plan of a cruciform church with five aisles. This initially envisaged twelve domes, grouped around a thirteenth larger one, representing Christ and the apostles. The new church included an additional eight domes and a portico. The resulting edifice has come to be the classic model for all major Russian Orthodox churches, featuring an extremely compact main building which is topped with a veritable cluster of towers and domes.

The domes in Kiev are relatively shallow and, at most, hemispherical

in shape. There is no sign of the traditional, onion-shaped domes characteristic of other Russian Orthodox churches. Another notable feature of the cathedral is its large number of semicircular apses, built in close proximity to one another and each generally ending in a half dome, or concha.

St. Sophia's cathedral is situated in the Upper Town, one of the three most historic parts of Kiev above the right bank of the Dnepr River. Another important ecclesiastical monument, built around the same time as St. Sophia's cathedral, is the Monastery of Caves, situated in the Pechersk district of Kiev. The cathedral is beautifully maintained, with its dazzling colors and gleaming, gold decor. The almost Classical-style ornamentation around the entrance portico also features the double-headed eagle, once the emblem of the tsars and now re-adopted as the national insignia of Russia, although not that of the Ukraine. Under the Soviets, the interior of the church was turned into a museum and the Ukrainian government is content to keep it that way.

The 11th-century mosaic lining the dome depicts Christ as Lord of the World (above, left)

To the right of this, the splendid mosaic of the Virgin Mary in one of the apses also dates from the eleventh century

The bell tower of St. Sophia's cathedral stands apart from the main building (below, left)

The cathedral's numerous domes, clustered closely together (below, right)

Kizhi •
Baltic Sea
RUSSIA

Karelia's marvel in wood

The wooden churches on **KIZHI** are a unique legacy of the past

GETTING THERE:
From St. Petersburg via main roads to Petrozavodsk. From there by hydrofoil to Kizhi. Cruises from Moscow to St. Petersburg with stopovers at Kizhi island

OPENING TIMES:
Information available from your travel agent or the tourist information center in St. Petersburg

SPECIAL INTEREST:
The old cemetery near the churches

View of the two wooden churches on Kizhi, with the bell tower between them (main picture)

The domes of the Transfiguration church (below, left)

The iconostasis inside the church, with its 'doorway of the czars' (below, center)

Some legends are just so captivating that they bear relating over and over again. So it is with the story of Nestor the Carpenter who, after finishing the Transfiguration church on Kizhi, threw his axe into the middle of Lake Onega, saying: "There never was and there never will be another church like this."

The cathedral was built by Nestor and his team of 80 carpenters between 1707 and 1714. Today, it ranks as one of the finest examples of the 'multi-domed' church and the most fascinating example of old, Russian wooden architecture to be found anywhere in the country. It was built without the aid of nails or ironwork and using particularly large axes so as not to interrupt the flow of preservative resin. The building team had no design to work from, nor any type of measuring device at its disposal, but created this masterpiece in wood purely 'by eye.'

Domes of shimmering silver

The island of Kizhi is only accessible by hydrofoil from Petrozavodsk when the waterways are free of ice. The best time to visit is during the long days of June, when the aspen leaves shimmer like sterling silver among gardens filled with a profusion of marguerite daisies and phlox and the lake is calm and blue. Lake Onega in the heart of Karelia is the second largest freshwater lake in Europe.

The Transfiguration church, built for summer use, and the smaller, heatable, winter church of the Virgin's Intercession are one unit, a spectacular landmark towering above the lake. Originally planned as a large, central church serving the numerous islands

and villages in the area, the Transfiguration church is now no more than the center of a very small community. Economic and political factors have caused the population to shrink.

Kizhi owes its fame not only to the two churches but also to the large, open-air museum of Russian wooden architecture consisting of around 60 exhibits, including mills, chapels, granaries, and courtyards. Many of the farmhouses in northern Russia, whose owners were driven out during the Revolution, were saved from collapse and rebuilt on Kizhi island – in the shadow of a church which has astonished the world for more than 300 years.

The church of Christ's Transfiguration is perfectly proportioned and its fairytale appearance can easily divert attention from the fact that its construction was the culmination of a carefully thought-out plan.

The basic ground-plan of the central building is octagonal in shape. The church has 22 domes, arranged in tiers and soaring 88ft (27m) in height to a central cupola. The entire Kizhi ensemble of eaves, gargoyles, onion domes, and ornate gables also doubles as a clever system of water drainage, without which the church would never have survived for so long. In a country where winter begins in October, historic wooden buildings are constantly under threat from the elements: rain, melt-water, and damp. The additional sections of the building form an harmonious entity with the rest of the building, including the trapezoidal apse incorporated in the eastern end of the cathedral which provides more room for the altar.

The church as a living room

The interior of the church is bright and flooded with light. The height of the building is spectacular. The 16 painted and vaulted ribs, all rising and converging in the center of the ceiling, are representative of heaven itself and underline the almost homely character of the cathedral. The ceiling was protected from the upheavals of the war by being sent to Finland for safekeeping along with other treasures, including the four-tiered gilt iconostasis which dominates the congregation's section. This masterpiece, which consists of 102 icons, is thought to have been created around 1759. Its gilded carvings of foliage and flowers, together with the pillared Tsar's door, constitute an interesting example of Russian Baroque.

As unique as the use of decorative materials is the sensitivity with which the two churches have been absorbed into the landscape. The buildings are linked by a bell tower in octagonal form which was built in the second half of the nineteenth century to replace a previous construction. It now forms a remarkable ensemble with the two churches.

In 1990, UNESCO placed Kizhi Pogost, the island in Lake Onega with its amazing wooden churches, on its list of cultural heritage sites. In so doing, it vindicated Nestor, the carpenter, who threw his axe into the lake for ever.

The cupolas of Novgorod

The cathedral of Hagia Sophia bears witness to the city's former wealth

GETTING THERE:
Flights to St. Petersburg international airport, then about 119 miles (190km) south-east by car on the E 105 highway

OPENING TIMES:
These vary depending on the time of year. No admission to tourists during services

SPECIAL INTEREST:
The tomb of Archbishop Maturi in the southern gallery

St. Sophia's cathedral from the outside, with view of the cupolas and one of the side aisles (main picture)

The iconostasis within the church, separating the sanctuary from the nave (below, right)

Procession through the town to mark the cathedral's 950th anniversary in 1995 (below, left)

Novgorod is situated in north-west Russia in the vicinity of Karelia, in a landscape of lakes and marshes. Novgorod means 'new town', although there is no record of a Stargorod, or old town, except in legend. A woman by the name of Slovena is said to have founded the first town here, calling it Slovensk after herself. She bore two children, Volchov and Ilmen, who, in turn, had two lakes named after them. Eventually, the Varangians arrived on the scene and established a new town, calling it Novgorod.

There is no point trying to find Slovensk on any maps of Russia. It is a fact of history, however, that Novgorod has existed since the fifth century, and consequently claims to be one of Russia's oldest towns. Occupied by the Varangians at the same time as Kiev, Novgorod, on the Volkhov river, became part of Kievan Rus. Despite trying hard to free itself from its overlords, it did not achieve this until 1136. It adopted its own constitution, the 'posadnichestvo', something quite extraordinary for Russia of that time. It convened a national assembly under the chairmanship of the archbishop, which in turn elected the town's leader, the posadnik, from the ranks of the Boyars, the lesser nobility.

Plundered by Moscow

Novgorod's most famous political leader was Alexander Nevsky. His nickname was bestowed on him after defending the city successfully against a Swedish assault at Neva. His victory over the invading Teutonic Knights on the frozen Lake Peipus in 1242 is even more famous. Alexander came to a political arrangement with the Mongols, who held power in Russia at that time, which ensured immunity

for Novgorod against Mongol attacks and allowed it to grow extremely powerful. The brutal backlash occurred two centuries later when Ivan III and Ivan IV conquered Novgorod, plundered it, and slaughtered the administrative leaders. The city never recovered from this blow.

Its former power and republican order went hand in hand with economic efficiency. Novgorod was a wealthy commercial center and a member of the Hanseatic League. Furs destined for western European markets were traded here. Novgorod also has some important architectural treasures.

Kiev as a model

There is a fortress, or kremlin, called Detinez and there is also a cathedral. Its name is not its only link with the Hagia Sophia in Kiev: its design is also very similar. It was commissioned by Vladimir, son of Yaroslavl the Wise, of the Varangian dynasty of Rurik princes. Construction work did not get underway until 1045, making it only five years younger than its predecessor in Kiev.

Like its younger sister, the Hagia Sophia is a cupola church with five aisles, all about the same width. Three of them end in apses. Their length, including the apses, is roughly equal to the overall breadth of the nave and aisles, so that the ground plan approximates to the shape of a square.

Above the central nave is the main cupola with its awesome ceiling, soaring to a great height beneath the dome. The cupola itself is golden. Instead of the usual 12 towers, as in Kiev, St. Sophia's is restricted to 4 additional towers, symbolizing the Four Apostles. The sixth, cupola-crowned tower, which rounds off the belfry wall, is an afterthought. These secondary towers are all finished in silver and built in the traditional, Russian, onion-dome shape. Its smooth outer walls are a dazzling white. This was not always the case: according to old chronicles, the walls were originally built of huge squares of roughly hewn sand- and limestone, no doubt a very impressive sight.

Inside the cathedral, there are two galleries, one above the other. There are several lovely frescoes on the walls. Only fragments of the oldest remain, dating from 1100. The drum inside the central cupola depicts the Byzantine Emperor Constantine and his

mother Helena. The iconostasis, the screen of icons behind the altar, is a collection of works by 16th-century Novgorod artists.

The bronze portal at the main entrance is magnificent. It is known as the Magdeburg Gate and was built in that city between 1152 and 1154. It depicts a number of East Franconian church princes, including Magdeburg's Archbishop Wichman. The gate consists of altogether 26 panels, each one of these portraying scenes from the Bible.

The doors were originally intended for the cathedral in Plock on the Vistula river, west of Warsaw. No

one knows how they got to Novgorod – presumably along the Hanseatic trade route, which was also used to transport works of art.

An ensemble of domes

The monastery of **ZAGORSK** has reverted to its original name of Sergeyev Posad

GETTING THERE:
Flights to Moscow's international airport. Then, ideally, by organized coach trip

OPENING TIMES:
Usually 8:00 A.M. – 8:00 P.M. daily. No admission to tourists during services

SPECIAL INTEREST:
The grave of St. Sergius, covered by a canopy

View of the Uspensky cathedral with its four blue domes around a central golden one. On the left is the campanile (main picture)

16th-century icon depicting Abraham and the three angels (below, left)

The following quote is attributed to Alexander Pushkin, Russian national poet: "It is thanks to the monks that we have a history, and consequently a culture." Although Pushkin was, of course, referring specifically to Russia, the statement is nevertheless true of all of medieval Europe.

Many faiths practise different forms of monasticism, ranging from a total renunciation of all worldly values to a radical form of piety. It can be practised in individual or collective isolation, although Christian religions seem to have favoured seclusion as the original form.

Sergey Radonezhky was a Russian hermit. Born in 1314, Barfolomey Kirillovich, as he was then known, was the son of a Rostov nobleman from Veliky. At the age of 23, he and his brother Stepan went into the Radonezh forest, north of Moscow, and established a hermit retreat there, where they were subsequently joined by other hermits. This marked the birth of Russia's first monastic community. After being appointed abbot, Sergey went on to instigate the building of other monasteries elsewhere. By 1782, his 'Sergeyev Posad' had developed into a proper town, a mecca not only for pious pilgrims but also for the politically powerful. It became one of only four Russian monasteries to be given the worthy title of 'lavra', denoting a particularly significant monastery.

An historical site

Sergeyev Posad surrounded itself with fortified walls. It had a political role to play in the ongoing internal strife within Russia and owned vast estates, encompassing up to 2700 settlements and 108,000 serfs. In 1919, the Soviets dissolved the monastery and, in 1920, placed it under a conservation order. In 1930, it was renamed Zagorsk after a murdered Bolshevik. It has now reverted to its original name. It was reinvested with its religious status after end of the Second World War, occasionally providing residence for the archbishop of Moscow.

The Troitse-Sergiyevskiy Lavra (Trinity Monastery of St. Sergius) covers an extensive area. Still enclosed within its ancient, fortified walls, the monastic buildings include a former hospital, now a museum of art history, the czar's palace, and the arch-bishop's palace. It also comprises a further nine churches of varying sizes, including the church of the Trinity and the cathedral of the Assumption or Uspensky cathedral.

The former was built over the grave of the monastery's founder, Sergey, who died in 1392 and was beatified in 1448/49. It is the principal church in the monastery complex and was built after 1422/23, initially as a four-pillared construction with three apses, built from blocks of white stone and topped with a dome. The building is not huge, but still manages to convey an impression of monumental proportions. The walls still retain fragments of early frescoes.

Chorny and, to a greater extent, Rublyov were regarded as the two most important exponents of Russian medieval art. Andrey Rublyov was born around 1360. He was a monk and disciple of Sergey Radonezhky. Building on the original and traditional style of icon painting with its Byzantine characteristics, he added an element of early Realism. His work also included book illustrations and he is thought to have been involved in designing the architecture of the Trinity cathedral in Sergeyev Posad.

Uspensky Sobor, the other main church, was built in 1554 on the orders of Ivan the Terrible. He was the first Russian ruler to be crowned according to the rites of the Orthodox Church. He dealt a final blow to the Mongol Tatars and succeeded in uniting the deeply divided empire. He arrived in person to lay the foundation stone of the new church. The Uspensky cathedral later served as an architectural model for the Moscow Kremlin. Construction work came to a halt for a while and did not resume until 1585, aided by a financial injection from Ivan who was anxious to buy some salvation for his soul, after having beaten his own son to death in a fit of rage.

Blue and gold

The Uspensky cathedral, like many other Russian churches, is dominated by five cupolas, symbolizing Christ and the Four Apostles. The domes are onion-shaped, the central one gold and the others blue with gold stars. Its interior is famous for its magnificent frescoes, dating from around 1684 from the Yaroslavl school.

Rising behind the cathedral is the campanile, the highest and loveliest in Russia. The tower tapers upwards and consists of six sections, one on top of the other, gradually diminishing in size. Despite its height, bulk, and dark exterior, the large number of belfry windows give the tower a delicate appearance. In the words of a 17th-century traveller from Aleppo, "this monastery has no equal, either in this country of Muscovites or indeed anywhere else in the world." This view sums up the monastery's importance as an architectural masterpiece.

There are altogether nine churches within the monastery complex, all of them topped with richly colored domes (below, right)

The cathedrals of the Kremlin

Within **MOSCOW's** hilltop fortification, five churches symbolize the power of the Orthodox church

GETTING THERE:
Flights to Moscow's international airport. Good rail links from central and western Europe

OPENING TIMES:
Usually open every day

SPECIAL INTEREST:
Painting by Andrey Rublyov on the iconostasis in the cathedral of the Assumption

View of the cupolas of the Kremlin's churches, with the bell-tower known as Ivan the Great in the background (main picture)

The main entrance of the cathedral of the Assumption and some of its collection of frescoes (the pictures below and right)

The Archangel Michael cathedral with its five silver cupolas (below, center)

The word 'kremlin' means 'fortress', a stragically sited fortification found in most ancient Russian towns and similar in function to an acropolis in Classical Greece. The most famous kremlin is in Moscow and is considerably older than the town itself. The original principality was fortified in 1156 and the settlement which grew up around it did not assume the proportions of a town until 1295.

Moscow's Kremlin stands on high ground, 131ft (40m) above the northern bank of the Moskva river. It is roughly triangular in shape and surrounded by about 1.5 miles (2.5km) of wall, enclosing a collection of palaces, parks, towers, and churches. There are five principal churches, three of which are grouped around Cathedral Square. They are named after the Assumption of the Virgin Mary, the Deposition of the Robe, the Twelve Apostles, the Annunciation, and the Archangel.

Nearby stands the bell tower of Ivan Velikiy (Ivan the Great), rising to 266ft (81m) in height. It once contained the largest bell in the world, cast between 1733 and 1735 and commissioned by Czarina Anna Ivanovna, a life-size portrait of whom is painted on its outside surface. In 1737, it came crashing to the ground during a fire in the tower. The bell now rests on an octagonal base next to a fragment of the tower.

The largest church in the Kremlin is the cathedral of the Assumption, or 'Uspensky Sobor' as it is called in Russian. It was built towards the end of the fifteenth century, when Moscow was in the process of trying to unite the splintered Russian princedoms and establish itself as the focus of power. In the usual tradition of Russian Orthodox churches, the five gold cupolas of Uspensky Sobor symbolize Christ the Savior surrounded by the Four Apostles.

With its light-colored stonework and pleasantly restrained ornamentation, the façade is the work of an Italian Renaissance architect by the name of Aristotele Fioravanti. The interior contains five apses running parallel to each other, four of which contain chapels forming a roughly square-shaped ground plan. The frescoes stem from the school of the famous icon painter, Andrey Rublyov.

In the Orthodox tradition

The cathedral of the Deposition of the Robe, Tserkov Rizopolozheniya, is situated behind Uspensky cathedral. Considerably smaller in scale, the church was built during 1484/85 and boasts a single tower. The masons were from Pskov or Pleskov on Lake Peipus, a town noted for its churches which, like those of Novgorod, came to serve as a model for sacred buildings elsewhere in Russia. This relatively compact church contains frescoes similar in style to those in Uspensky Sobor.

The cathedral of the Twelve Apostles is located on the northern edge of Cathedral Square. Erected in the mid-seventeenth century as the private church adjacent to the architecturally similar Patriarch's Palace, it is distinguishable by its five, comparatively shallow-domed towers. Its arcatures are reminiscent of ancient Russian architecture. The building was commissioned by Patriarch Nikon, an extremely proud man, who wanted a representative edifice to reflect the distinctly individual national traditions of Russian Orthodoxy.

Czar Ivan's magnificent cathedral

Ivan the Terrible commissioned the construction of the cathedral of the Annunciation, Blagoveshchensky Sobor, intending it for his own use as a private church. This is evident from its nine towers, a configuration with special significance for Ivan, who regarded the number 9 as a symbolic holy number, associated with his victory over the Tatars in Kazhan. In contrast to Uspensky cathedral, Blagoveshchensky Sobor consists of

several sections and is quite ornate in parts. All the roofs and the conches over the apses, not to mention the canopies over the entrance and windows, are decorated in gold. The czar wanted to advertise his newly acquired power and accompanying riches to the world. The cathedral's intimate interior boasts a variety of frescoes, depicting scenes from the Old Testament, the Apocalypse, and the history of the Orthodox Church. One of the panels of the iconostasis was painted by the great Rublyov.

Finally, the Archangel cathedral, or Archangelsky Sobor, is situated to the east of the cathedral of the Annunciation and is on almost the same scale as the Uspensky cathedral. By way of contrast, its five towers, the central one of which clearly dominates the other four, are finished in silver.

The church was the work of Venetian architect Alevisio Novy. Like Fioravanti and Uspensky Sobor, his work was similarly based on the traditions of Byzantine-Orthodox ecclesiastical buildings. The interior of the cathedral is very gloomy. The barrel-vaulted ceiling, covered with pictures of Russian princes, is supported by six crossing pillars. The original wall paintings have virtually disappeared.

A number of czars are buried in this cathedral, including Ivan the Terrible. His son was laid to rest here before him, after Ivan had beaten him to death.

Triumphal church of the czars

St. Basil's cathedral in Red Square is one of MOSCOW's most famous landmarks

Baltic Sea · Moscow · RUSSIA

GETTING THERE:
Flights to Moscow's international airport, or by rail from western Europe

OPENING TIMES:
Usually open daily

SPECIAL INTEREST:
The cathedral's unique layout with its many passageways

The cathedral's red brick exterior is just as distinctive as its colorful cluster of decorative towers (main picture)

View of the iconostasis, the wooden screen inlaid with icons, which, in Orthodox churches, separates the altar from the nave (below, left)

Moscow's Red Square, a painting by Fyodor Yakovlevich Alekseyev, dating from 1801. The picture, which now hangs in the Tretyakov Gallery, depicts a typical 18th-century scene outside St. Basil's cathedral (below, center)

Vasily Blazhenny was one of those simple-minded vagabonds and beggars who acquired a reputation for holiness. It was Jesus, after all, who taught that "blessed are the poor in spirit." Vasily was believed to have the gift of prophecy and what he had, he shared. He hung around the shops and stalls of Moscow's marketplace, a so-called 'holy fool' who was said to be 'idiotic for Christ's sake' and around whom countless legends have been woven. When he died in 1552, he was buried with honors in the cemetery of Moscow's Trinity cathedral. A chapel was built over his grave in 1588.

The chapel was part of a much larger, sacred building which Ivan IV, grand prince of Moscow and the first to assume the title of czar, ordered to be built on the site of the Trinity cathedral. His growing distrust and brutality in later life earned him the nickname 'Ivan the Terrible.' Ivan had won a great military victory over the Tatars and captured Kazan, their final stronghold, on the ninth day of a siege. From then on, he regarded '9' as a holy number. The design of the new church to be built in Moscow included nine towers and was named to commemorate the date of his victory in Kazan, known in the Orthodox calendar as the Day of the Protective Veil of the Virgin Mary.

The many domes of St. Basil's

Construction work began in 1555. The chapel above Vasily's grave was completed in 1588 and, eventually, the entire church came to be known as the cathedral of St. Basil the Blessed.

It stands in the heart of Moscow, both the old and new Russian capital, St. Petersburg, having fulfilled this role for two hundred years. St. Basil's cathedral stands just outside the walls of the Kremlin, on the perimeter of a square called by various names throughout its history but today known as Red Square.

It is generally assumed that it was given this name by the Soviets in tribute to the color that symbolized their proletarian revolution. Its name dates back much further, however. The Russian word 'krasnoy' meaning 'red' also means 'beautiful'. The name may equally derive from the color of the red-brick walls running around the Kremlin. These too go back much further than Lenin and the October Revolution.

The monumental proportions of Red Square in no way diminish the impact of the cathedral of St. Basil. Even from a distance, its sheer size and distinctive riot of domes are an awe-inspiring sight. There are in fact nine towers which were commissioned by Ivan, plus the bell tower which was added during the seventeenth century.

The nine domes crown a complex of eight chapels, grouped around a principal, oval-shaped church in the center, the church of the Veil. The eight subsidiary chapels are arranged symmetrically. The four larger ones, namely the Trinity chapel, Christ's Entry Into Jerusalem, St. Kiprian and Ustina, and St. Nicholas the Miracle-worker, form the four corners of a square. The four smaller chapels of Alexander Svirsky, Gregory the Armenian, Varlaam Hutynsky, and the Three Patriarchs are positioned equidistantly between them, forming another square. Outside this eight-pointed star lies the Theodosius church.

The individuality of these eight encircling chapels is accentuated by the varying heights of their towers. The walls are built of brick, while the domes, far from being smooth canopies, are covered with three-dimensional, prismatic ornamenta-tion, the colorful designs of which form distinct patterns of vertical or spiraling stripes when viewed from a distance. They put one in mind, no doubt intentionally, of Islamic turbans; the Tatars, whose defeat the cathedral commemorates, were predominantly of the Muslim faith.

An all-round spectacle

The pinnacle of the central building, the cathedral of the Veil, is quite different from all the others. Although it has the highest tower, it is not capped by an onion dome but by a high spire, reminiscent of a Gothic cathedral. This feature, known in architectural terms as a tent-shaped roof, is another traditional type of spire found in Old Russian architecture. Here, in Red Square, the cathedral of the Veil echoes the design of the tower on the cathedral of Christ the Savior, which forms part of the Kremlin and whose chimes toll the hour.

Like many other sacred buildings of Old Russia, the cathedral of St. Basil the Blessed does not have a single main façade but can be appreciated equally from all sides, with each perspective offering different colors, ornamentation, and architectural details. Its open position means that its wealth and diversity of ornamental detail are on clear view all round.

The splendor of the exterior is unfortunately not echoed in the interior, a circumstance that has caused much regret despite the fact that this is entirely in keeping with the building's architectural raison d'etre. The city has an abundance of churches available for retreat, prayer, and piety. The cathedral of St. Basil the Blessed was built as a triumphal church, which is exactly the role that it fulfills.

Late Gothic from Estonia

The Domkirche St. Marien in **TALLINN** is a feature of the capital's skyline

GETTING THERE:
Good ferry connections across the Baltic. International airport close to the city

OPENING TIMES:
Usually Tues-Sun 11:00 A.M. - 5:00 P.M. Closed Monday

SPECIAL INTEREST:
St. Nicholas' church with Bernt Notke's Dance of Death

From Cathedral Hill, you can see a long way beyond the distinctive tower and spire of St. Mary's, across the sea and countryside (main picture)

View of the interior of the cathedral (below)

Estonia is the smallest of the Baltic States but, relatively speaking, it has the most successful economy. Unlike Latvian and Lithuanian, the Estonian language is not Indo-European but Finno-Ugrian. It is similar to Finnish and, even during the Soviet era, the country's geographical and cultural proximity to Finland gave the Estonians some of the advantages of a prosperous region. Finnish people often came here, partly in order to indulge in alcohol, leaving plenty of good money behind in return. In addition, the Estonians could receive and understand Finnish television, which gave them special access to information from the West.

The capital of Estonia is Tallinn, or Kolovan in Russian and Reval in German. It has spread 9.4 miles (15km) along the coast, but little more than 1.2 miles (2000m) inland. The land is flat for the most part, the exception being the steeply rising Cathedral Hill which, with the castle and two surrounding fortifications, forms the Upper City. The Lower City, that is the old civilian settlement, forms the other part of the historic center.

The Old Town of Tallinn is one of the best preserved on the entire Baltic coast, full of charm and packed with architectural gems. Among these are the Gothic town hall, the church of the Holy Spirit, and the church of St. Nicholas with its impressive Dance of Death by the great Lübeck painter and sculptor, Bernt Notke. Tallinn was founded in 1219 by King Valdemar II of Denmark, which explains why it still has Valdemar's three heraldic lions on its coat of arms. In 1227, military monks drove out the Danes and built a fortress on the Cathedral Hill.

In the name of the Teutonic Knights

The military order of Knights was an organization of nobles going back to the time of the crusades, originally existing for charitable purposes. They maintained hospitals on the route to the Holy Land, for the wounded to be healed of their injuries and the sick cured of their illnesses. Thus, the Knights of St. John and the Knights Templar came into being, and finally a third order was formed, the *Ordo domus Sanctae Mariae Theutonicorum*, otherwise known as the Order of Teutonic Knights.

All these communities lived according to monastic laws. Their charitable aim was soon forgotten, however, and the orders turned into militant, elitist companies of sons of the nobility who had no property. Even the connection with the Holy Land was lost after the failure of the crusades. The Teutonic Knights moved their headquarters to the Baltic area, where they became involved in the Germanization policy of German princes. Hated by the Slavic and Baltic peoples they had so bloodily subjugated, they were arrogant rulers. The regional order of military monks capitulated to, and merged with, them.

For a long time after that, the Teutonic Knights determined events in the Baltic area, but in the end they had to admit defeat by the Poles and some of their possessions were handed over to the Hohenzollerns, the ruling house of Brandenburg. Then the area came under threat from Sweden and from Russia.

In Tallinn, the Teutonic Knights had their headquarters in the citadel on Cathedral Hill. The civilian part of the city, a member of the Hanseatic League, built its own fortification and preferred to rely on merchant shipping and port activities rather than militancy. It could not, however, escape the continual conflicts. It was also affected by the Great Northern War between Sweden and Russia and by Napoleon's imperialist policies. After the Congress of Vienna, the Baltic area was handed over to the czar of Russia.

The great fire of 1684

Anyone who is aware of the tangled history that has continued right up to the present time will be astonished that the Old Town of Tallinn, including the diocesan church of St. Mary on the cathedral rock, has survived intact. Work on the building began under the Danes at the beginning of the thirteenth century, and suffered several interruptions and changes. The original hall church was transformed into a Late Gothic basilica in the fifteenth century. The ground plan is almost square but, as with the cathedrals of Vilnius and Riga, there is no transept. In 1684, it completely burned down, but all was restored after just two years. In 1778/79, the Baroque spire was finally placed on top of the west tower.

The interior is quite gloomy. It contains several objects of artistic worth, such as the Baroque pulpits and the high altar, the work of Christian Ackermann. Then there are the coats of arms of the great noble families of the Baltic region, some of whom were of Swedish or German origin, who were held in particularly high regard at the court of the czar in St. Petersburg and developed an arrogance to match. There are also memorials and tombs by the sculptors Arent Passer, Hans von Aken, and Nicolaes Millich.

Unlike the cathedrals in most of the Hanseatic cities, that in Tallinn is built not of brick but of sandstone. The white walls and tower with its pierced spire can be seen from far and wide, looming over the city.

Riga
LATVIA
*Baltic
Sea*

The model for the Baltic states

The Marien-Dom in the Latvian capital of **RIGA** was built in the thirteenth century

GETTING THERE:
Via the city's international airport. Ferry connections from Germany. International rail connections from Berlin and St. Petersburg

OPENING TIMES:
Usually 10:00 A.M. - 6:00 P.M. Changes possible at short notice

SPECIAL INTEREST:
Chapter house and cloisters of the nearby monastery

The center of Riga is famous for its Jugendstil houses. There are few cities in Europe which can boast as many architectural mementos of Art Nouveau as Riga, which lies at the mouth of the Duna (or Dvina). The city's architects were, without exception, Latvians and included Michail Eisenstein, father of the famous Soviet Russian film director, Sergei Eisenstein. The latter not only made the *Battleship Potemkin* but also *Alexander Nevsky*, a film portrait of the prince of Novgorod who beat the army of the Teutonic Knights on the ice of Lake Peipus (also known as Lake Chud) in 1242.

The Eisensteins were a Jewish family. They spoke Russian, which was the language of officialdom and education in Riga at that time. Their name sounded German, and many of the mementos of civilization in Riga that had associations for them were German. The city itself had been founded by Germans, and in the nineteenth century half the population was still made up of Germans, though both the city and the surrounding countryside were part of czarist Russia. The native Latvians were ranked right at the bottom of the social ladder, below the Germans and the Russians, and they provided the farm laborers and servants.

As a reaction against this loss of status, a movement for national autonomy developed in the course of the nineteenth century, drawing its strength from the recollection of a cultural tradition and the use of the Latvian language. The ethnologist Krisjanis Barons collected six fat volumes of Latvian folk-song texts, known as Dainas. He published them together with Wissendorf, a scientist of German origin, and in so doing he was, of course, following the ideas of another German, the theologian Johann Gottfried Herder, who was to become a friend of Goethe. Herder was born in Riga and from 1764 was a preacher in his home town. There is a monument to him in the Cathedral Square in Riga.

Founded by merchants

Since then, the proportion of German-speaking inhabitants has dwindled to zero. Riga can certainly still be considered a multiethnic city, but by far the biggest non-Latvian group in the population here, as in the rest of the country, is Russian. This is the result of many decades of Soviet Russification policy. Until 1991, the Russians were the undisputed ruling class. Since then, they have felt themselves to be inferior citizens, as in present-day Latvia only those who have mastered the very complicated national language may claim full rights of citizenship.

The development of the city of Riga began with a settlement of German merchants. In 1201, the bishop of Bremen, Albert von Buxhoeveden, arrived to subject and convert the Baltic tribes living in the area. He had the trading post fortified. It was founded at the time of the crusades and the order of the Teutonic Knights, a military religious order who conquered the surrounding territory. Bishop Albert made sure of the military support of the Danes, among others. Riga became an archbishopric in 1253 and joined the Hanseatic League in 1282.

The diocesan church of the city was the Marien-Dom (St. Mary's cathedral), the biggest ecclesiastical building in all the Baltic States. Bishop Albert of Buxhoeveden was responsible for its building, and work began in 1215. It was modeled on the great Romanesque churches of central and southern Europe. The choir

and transept of this early period have been preserved. The nearby monastery, whose chapter house, cloisters, and garden have likewise been preserved, also dates from those early years.

Nave with side aisles

St. Mary's was started in 1215 as a three-nave basilica. In the 1230s, a typical Westphalian hall church was preferred, until the basilica form found favor again at the end of the thirteenth century and the traditional ground plan of the great Catholic churches, whose form was that of a

St. Mary's cathedral
with its Baroque tower
dominates the
Old Town
(main picture)

View of the altar area.
The windows are
nineteenth century
(below, left)

The organ screen of
1601 is one of the
jewels of the church.
The 7000 pipes were
newly installed in 1884
(below, right)

Latin cross, was completely abandoned. In this respect, St. Mary's became the model for all ecclesiastical buildings in the Baltic States. The same is true of the Gothic superstructure; in this case, the otherwise usual buttresses are missing.

With the Gothic superstructure came the present-day nave with its two side aisles. The chapels were built last. The most recent detail is the Mannerist tower cap with its Baroque spire. Almost nothing of the once rich medieval decoration has been preserved, as it fell victim to the iconoclasts during the Reformation, though there are still one or two historic memorial stones.

Apart from these, the finely carved Baroque pulpit and a fragment of the seating remain. The stained glass windows with their historical scenes are a 19th-century addition. The organ screen by Jacob Raabs dates from as long ago as 1601. The organ itself is much more recent. It was built in Ludwigsburg in Swabia and is widely renowned for its beautiful sound.

Magnificent temple

St. Stanislav's cathedral in **VILNIUS** is a monument of European Classicism

The relationship between Lithuania and Poland is close and goes back a long way. *Pan Tadeusz*, Poland's national epic by Adam Mickiewicz, is set in Lithuania. There was a political union between the two countries from 1385, which only came to an end with the Division of Poland. Grand Duke Jogaila of Lithuania married the Polish Queen Jadwiga, and thus acceded to the

throne in Kraków. He was the first ruler of the Polish Jagiellon dynasty. The high noble family of Radziwill, which played an important part in Polish history, is also of Lithuanian origin so it should come as no surprise that Poles are still the biggest national minority in Vilnius, ahead of the Russians.

Vilnius, the seat of the Lithuanian government, is situated at the

confluence of the rivers Neris and Vilnia, far from the Baltic coast and therefore close to the border with White Russia (Belarus). The city is famous for its almost southern Italian atmosphere, created in part by buildings of the Renaissance, Baroque, and Classical periods, most of which were designed by Italian architects.

St. Stanislav's cathedral stands on the Katedros aiksté (Cathedral Square) on the left bank of the Neris, on what was once the site of one of two castles. The founding of Vilnius goes back to the High Middle Ages. The first written record dates from the year 1323, when the area was still heathen. Grand Duke Jogaila, who was later to marry Jadwiga of Poland, was the first ruler of Lithuania to be

religion of the ancients. Nevertheless, Vilnius possesses something the temples of antiquity lacked (because, unlike Christian churches, they had no need of it) – a bell tower. At a height of 187ft (57m) high, it stands some distance from the cathedral and was converted for the purpose from a fortified tower that once formed part of the castle defenses. Two rows of gun embrasures can clearly be seen on the lower part. The octagonal upper stories were only added in the sixteenth century to contain the bells, ten in number. They are only rung on Feast Days.

Old Gothic ground plan

The cathedral has a portico supported by columns, with colonnades at the sides. Only on closer inspection is it apparent that the high relief on the tympanum does not originate from antiquity. It is actually an Old Testament scene of Noah offering thanks after God had saved him from the Flood. Beneath it, things become more obviously Christian. The Baroque statues by the Italian Tomasso Righi in the niches on the front are of Abraham, Moses, and the Four Evangelists, and there are figures of saints at the corners of the two colonnades, though there are also statues of Lithuanian princes.

The old Gothic ground plan can be clearly seen in the interior – a broad central nave with two narrow side aisles and a row of chapels on each side. As with the cathedrals in Riga and Tallinn, there is no transept. The most noteworthy of the chapels is that of St. Casimir, with its magnificent, Early Baroque ornamentation. Casimir was one of the Jagiellon kings of Poland and a Grand Duke of Lithuania, so he was a powerful man. In 1451, he suddenly renounced the crown in order to devote himself entirely to his faith. He died of consumption in 1484. His body was taken to Vilnius and interred in the cathedral. The Lithuanians made him their national saint.

Baltic **Vilnius**
Sea
LITHUANIA

St. Stanislav's cathedral with its white columns stands on an historic site. The bell tower was once part of the fortifications (main picture)

View of the organ screen (below)

baptized, and he then had a cathedral built near one of the castles.

Separate bell tower

The spot was chosen with care. Until then, it had been the site of a shrine to the Baltic deities Dievas, Perkunas, and Saule. Jogaila's cathedral, as far as can be ascertained from the excavations, was an extensive brick building, which was burned to the ground in 1419. Grand Duke Vytautas, who held power in Vilnius at the time, gave orders for a new cathedral.

A High Gothic cathedral with two towers resulted, which in 1600 was transformed into a Renaissance-style building by two Roman architects, Zannobia da Gianotti and Cini. It was rebuilt in the Baroque manner after a further fire in 1610.

The cathedral took on its final form in the years from 1777 to 1801. This was the work of the renowned Lithuanian architect, Laurynas Stuoka-Gucevicius. He retained the dimensions of the previous building and left the interior largely untouched. By contrast, he made radical changes to the exterior in the then fashionable style of Central European Classicism.

Vilnius cathedral is a shining white temple on the ancient Greek model. There are few Christian churches like it. Neither St. Hedwig's in Berlin nor the Madeleine in Paris, both of which make great play with elements taken from antiquity, come as close to the heathen, polytheistic

Poland's biggest Gothic church

The restorer's art has enabled the Marienkirche in **GDANSK** to rise again

Baltic
Sea
Gdansk
POLAND

GETTING THERE:
Via the city airport.
Easily reached by car
or train from Warsaw

OPENING TIMES:
Usually 8:00 A.M. –
7:00 P.M. daily. Closed
to tourists during Mass

SPECIAL INTEREST:
The St. Adrian altar in
the chapel of the
Holy Cross

The preservation of historical monuments has long been a Polish speciality. It is a flourishing industry which includes general restoration and reconstruction activities as well as many skills that have fallen into decline, such as stuccoing and silk weaving. In Torun, you can even take a degree in the subject. Highly qualified Polish restorers are now working all over the world, having already taken care of the historic, city centers in their own country.

One of these centers of activity was Gdansk (German, Danzig), which is close to Torun. The two versions of the city's name tell a story of frequent changes of nationality. First, there was a Slavic settlement at the confluence of the Motlawa and a backwater of the Vistula, which was christianized by St. Adalbert, known to the Poles by his original name of Wojciech. The earliest mention of the town of Gdansk is in the writings of St. Adalbert.

The city was ruled by the princes of Pommerellen and the kings of Poland, and later by the Teutonic knights and the kingdom of Prussia. German merchants settled there in the twelfth century. Until 1939, Gdansk had the status of a free city under the protection of the League of Nations, with a population that was part Polish, part German. Hitler began the war by attacking the Polish post office in Gdansk and bombarding the Westernplatte, a Polish fortification in the Bay of Gdansk.

After six years, the city was almost completely destroyed and the victorious Allies decided it should belong to Poland. Twenty years later, the most important historic buildings – the High Gate, the Golden Gate, Long

the same name in Lübeck, center of the Hanseatic League, which it certainly outstrips, at least in size. The brick building at the end of Mariacka Street (German, Frauengasse) was begun in 1334 and went through several phases of growth until 1502, when it attained its present, incomplete form. The main tower, no doubt intended to be a different height, has no spire but only a shallow, hipped roof. St. Mary's is a Late Gothic hallenkirche or hall church, which means that the aisles are the same height as the nave. There are three naves in all.

The beautiful Madonna
A special architectural feature of the church is that the buttresses supporting the exterior walls – usually erected on the outside where they could be covered with sculptures or other decorations – are on the inside, where they divide up the aisles and create spaces for chapels. In this church, the pinnacles in which the buttresses usually end are at the same height as the eaves and grow out of the smooth walls around the choir in the form of narrow towers, with pointed, copper spires reaching almost to the height of the main tower.

During World War II, the art treasures of St. Mary's church in Gdansk were moved away to escape destruction. Many of them are now to be found in the collections of Polish museums, while others have been returned to their place of origin. Among these were the 15th-century altar of St. Martin in the north aisle chapel of the Trinity and, in the neighboring St. Anne's chapel, the so-called Schöne Madonna (beautiful Madonna), dating from around 1410.

Memling's *Last Judgment*
St. Mary's has an elaborate astronomical clock made by Hans Düringer, a master clockmaker from Torun. Among the many memorials, the tomb of Simon and Judith Bahr, the work of the Dutchman Abraham van den Blocke, is particularly striking.

The huge influx of art and artists was due to the lively communication between the Hanseatic ports on the North Sea and the Baltic. Another work from the Low Countries, in this case from Antwerp, is the altar of St. Adrian in the chapel of the Holy Cross, dating from the beginning of the sixteenth century. The high altar is the work of the master craftsman Michael of Augsburg, and the crucifixion group in the triumphal arch is by Master Paul.

In the Rheinhold chapel immediately to the left of the entrance, you can see what is probably the most famous work of art in St. Mary's Gdansk, Hans Memling's triptych of the Last Judgment. Memling was born in Aschaffenburg and made his home in Bruges in Flanders. His Gdansk altarpiece is one of his most important works. Though St. Mary's

Market, Arthur's Court, and the Marienkirche (church of St. Mary) – had already been rebuilt by Polish restorers.

Old Hanseatic city
All these buildings are to be found in the quarter known in German as the Rechtstadt and in Polish as Glówne Miasto (Main Town) which is one of several districts that were once autonomous. Gdansk was a member of the Hanseatic League. The rich patrician houses and huge storehouses provide evidence of its outstanding success, which created exceptional private and public wealth. St. Mary's church – Kosciól Mariacki in Polish – is evidence of this.

It is one of the biggest Gothic cathedrals in Europe and can hold around 25,000 people. As in the case of other Hanseatic cities, its architecture was modeled on the church of

View of the mighty, brick body of St. Mary's church. The tower remains unfinished (above, left)

The nave with the crucifixion group on the triumphal arch (above, right)

Part of Hans Memling's altarpiece depicting the Last Judgment, painted 1471–73. This scene shows the souls of the damned (below, right)

only has a copy now, as the original is in the Gdansk museum, the delicate depiction of the archangel in armor, serenely weighing the souls of the dead, is emphasized by the backdrop of this church. The copy is more powerful than the original.

Poland's royal cathedral

The cathedral of St. Stanislas and Wenceslas on the Wawel in **KRAKÓW** houses the tombs of the kings of Poland

Kraków is certainly one of the most beautiful cities in the world. It is situated on the upper reaches of the Vistula, and is vaguely reminiscent of Prague. The Old Town, with the Wawel Hill and castle, Town Hall Square, Cloth Hall, St. Mary's church, palaces, and fortifications, is architecturally one of the most precious urban areas north of the Alps.

For a long time, Kraków was the seat of the kings of Poland and some of the country's greatest rulers had their palaces here. During the time of the Division, South Poland was part of the Austro-Hungarian Empire, whose regime – unlike that of Prussia and Russia, the other ruling powers – proved comparatively mild, not from any predetermined policy of tolerance but from sheer laxity.

This led to Kraków being reproached by the rest of Poland for its lack of long-term devotion to the national cause, despite the fact that the uprising against foreign rule led by Tadeusz Kosciuszko began in the marketplace in Kraków. His reward was a monument on the Wawel. The general view in Poland is that Kraków – the eternal rival of Warsaw in matters of intellect, beauty, education, and good taste – is currently the capital of conflicts and catastrophes.

The first written mention of Kraków is in the works of Ibrahim ibn Jakub, a traveling merchant from Moorish-Spanish Cordoba. The diocese was founded around the year 1000 and, at about the same time, the first cathedral was built on the Wawel. Later, the castle rock would be covered with other buildings, both spiritual and secular. There would be extensions and alterations. The throne of the kings was here until 1596, when Warsaw was chosen as the capital of Poland.

The first saint

The Austrian authorities later demoted the Wawel to a parade ground and barracks and, when the German occupation began in 1939, the Nazi governor Frank chose the military installation for his residence. The memory of this dreadful time of occupation still remains, not least because of the nearby former concentration and extermination camp of Auschwitz.

Kraków cathedral is named after St. Stanislas and St. Wenceslas. The tomb of St. Stanislas is to be found in the nave. Son of a noble family from Masovia, he lived from 1550 to 1568 and was a devout Jesuit. He died in Italy and is the second Polish Catholic

saint after Queen Hedwig, who died in 1399. However, Hedwig only became a saint under Pope John Paul II, whereas Stanislas had been canonized a quarter of a century earlier.

Thirty-seven coronations

The present building is the third to stand on this site and was completed in the fourteenth century, a stately Gothic basilica with three naves and three towers. The most famous of these is the Sigismund tower.

Inside the cathedral, besides the silver sarcophagus of St. Stanislas, made during 1669-71 by the goldsmith Peter von der Rennen of Gdansk and covered with a variety of scenes of the saint's life and miracles, the Baroque high altar is also very impressive. The kings knelt before it, or at the place where it stands, on the occasion of their enthronement. The cathedral has witnessed 37 coronations in all.

Around the choir and along the aisles there are more than a dozen magnificent chapels – some Gothic, some Baroque in origin. One such is the chapel of the Holy Cross containing the tomb of King Kasimir IV of the Jagiello dynasty. The sarcophagus dating from the year 1492 is the work of the sculptor Veit Stoss. Another important dynasty was that of the Wasa, who actually came from Sweden. Three of their members are buried in the chapel that bears their name. In St. Mary's chapel is the tomb of Stefan Batory, who was elected king in the sixteenth century but actually

came from Hungary and waged a successful war against Russia. Nearby, there is a Baroque memorial to King Jan III Sobieski, who broke the Turkish siege of Vienna in the battle of Kahlenberg in 1683.

Honor for Pilsudski

In Kraków cathedral, you can walk past almost the entire history of Poland. In the crypt are sarcophagi containing the bones of other rulers, including Augustus the Strong, King of Poland and Elector of Saxony. Leading Polish artists are buried here, as is Józef Pilsudski, the successful general who beat the advancing Red Army of Leon Trotsky in the battle known as the 'Miracle on the Vistula' and later became an authoritarian president of the first republic.

Polish schoolchildren, who are shown round the cathedral in large numbers and reverent silence in order to strengthen their national consciousness, leave little notes (school tokens) on the tombs of those they most admire. Most messages are left on the tomb of St. Hedwig, and almost as many on Józef Pilsudski's.

GETTING THERE:
International airport close to the city. Rail connections from Warsaw and via Katowice and Wroclaw. Motorway connections to the west via Wroclaw/Katowice

OPENING TIMES:
Usually 9:00 A.M. - 5:00 P.M. daily. No entry for tourists during Mass

SPECIAL INTEREST:
The sarcophagus of King Kasimir IV by Veit Stoss in the chapel of the Holy Cross

The Wawel (Castle Hill) in Kraków was for centuries the seat of the kings of Poland. The huge cannons in front of the cathedral are a reminder of those times (main picture)

View of the cathedral nave. Many Polish princes are entombed in the side chapels (right)

Baltic Sea

POLAND
Krakow

Veit Stoss's second home

Stoss carved his famous altar for the Marienkirche in **KRAKÓW**

GETTING THERE:
International airport close to the city. Rail connections from Warsaw and via Katowice and Wroclaw. Motorway connections via Wroclaw/Katowice

OPENING TIMES:
Usually 8:00 A.M. - 8:00 P.M. daily. The church is closed to tourists during Mass

SPECIAL INTEREST:
Altar by Veit Stoss with carvings of Biblical scenes

Different spires make it appear that the towers of St. Mary's are of different heights. The market square outside its door is every Krakówer's favorite place (main picture)

The trumpeter still replaces the chiming of bells (below, left)

The most famous work of art in Kraków is the altar of the Virgin Mary by Veit Stoss. On weekdays, the altar panels are closed (below, center)

The South German stonemason, sculptor, painter, and engraver Veit Stoss led a wild life. In Nuremberg, where he produced most of the work he did in Germany and also the place for which he made one of his two most famous works, the *Salutation of the Angel* in St. Laurence's church, he was incarcerated in the debtor's prison and publicly branded. That meant having a red-hot branding iron pressed into his face. He lived unmolested in Kraków, where he also spent quite a long time and where his other famous piece is to be seen – the high altar in the Marienkirche or church of St. Mary. He even assumed a Polish name: Wit Stwosz.

His move from Franconia to southern Poland did not come about by chance. In those days, Nuremberg was the leading German community in invention, commerce, and culture, and maintained a connection with the prosperous city of Kraków on the Vistula, which also had a not inconsiderable German colony and had been a member of the Hanseatic League since 1430.

Towers of different heights
Among the countless churches in the city, St. Mary's, or the basilica of the Assumption of the Virgin Mary – in Polish Kosciól Mariacki – is next in importance to the cathedral on the Wawel. It is a three-nave, Gothic basil-

ica and has an extra-long choir instead of a transept, which joins the apse housing the Veit Stoss altar. The choir and apse together are almost as long as the nave plus the vestibule.

The two towers are of different heights because of their spires. From the higher one, topped by a slender Gothic structure, the time is sounded every hour on the hour, though not by means of bells as in other churches but by a trumpet call that suddenly breaks off in the middle of a phrase. This series of notes, known as the Hejnal Mariacki, is played in memory of a trumpeter who was struck by an enemy arrow as he played when the city was being besieged by the Tartars.

What is striking about the interior of St. Mary's is how colorful it is. It is painted in deep blue, with numerous gold stars, and forms a fitting background for Veit Stoss's multi-winged altar in honor of the Holy Virgin Mary. Its dimensions are extraordinary: 43ft (13m) by 36ft (11m), the central sculptures being almost 10ft (3m) high. As with almost all carved altarpieces, the wood used is lime.

The central section tells the story of Mary's death. The panels of the side wings show scenes from her life and that of her son, Jesus, and the top section of the altar shows her coronation – all very moving and expressive representations. Stoss's altar can be compared with Mathias Grünewald's

Isenheim altar and the Wiblinger altar of Tilman Riemenschneider. All three are artistic works of the highest order, originating from lands north of the Alps.

The altar has had an eventful recent history. As a great national art treasure, the Poles had it crated up at the beginning of war in 1939 and taken to nearby Sandomierz. The Nazis declared it to be a major work by a German genius and removed it from Sandomierz to Nuremberg in Franconia, where it was found when the city was captured by American troops. It was subsequently thoroughly restored and returned to its place of origin in 1957.

The marketplace as art
There is one more work by Veit Stoss in St. Mary's, a stone crucifix which has been integrated into the Baroque marble altar of the Holy Sacrament, sculpted by the Italian Gian Maria Padovano. The wall paintings in the church were designed by Jan Matejko, a native of Kraków and a prominent representative of the Polish National Romantic Movement. He died in 1893, leaving his pupils to carry out the painting.

It would be unfair to St. Mary Kraków not to mention its site – the marketplace or Rynek, one of Europe's more spacious city areas, lined by extraordinary façades facing the arcades of the Cloth Hall. It is the haunt of tourists, street traders, and pigeons. Nowhere else, apart from the marketplace in Venice, are there as many pigeons fluttering around.

The Black Madonna

The pilgrim's chapel in **CZESTOCHOWA** has become a legendary place through the miracle of Jasna Góra

Baltic Sea

POLAND
Czestochowa

GETTING THERE:
By rail from Warsaw and Katowice.
By road via the E 40 and E 67/75

OPENING TIMES:
Usually open all day

SPECIAL INTEREST:
The entire monastery complex

View down the main nave (main picture) and a panoramic view of the church (below, left)

At prayer before the picture of the Black Madonna (below, right)

It began on 21 July 1655, when Swedish troops invaded Poland, quickly overrunning Warsaw, Poznan, and Kraków. By 18 November, they had reached Jasna Góra (literally, Bright Mountain), a hill outside Czestochowa with its modest complex of monastic buildings, including a chapel to the Virgin Mary, the chapel of the Miraculous Picture. The Swedish invaders demanded its surrender. The invading army numbered 3000 troops, while the defenders totalled just 190 armed men and 70 monks. A hopeless situation!

Prior Kordecki refused to capitulate, however, and the siege of the monastery, known in Sweden as the 'hen-house', began. It lasted 40 days and ended in victory for the 'Knights of the Virgin Mary' and retreat on the part of the invading army – a development which must have seemed akin to a miracle.

The fortress of the Virgin Mary

Sweden's defeat was not attributed to those defending the fortress, but to the protective intercession of the Virgin Mary, whose portrait as the Black Madonna is kept within the mighty walls of the monastery. To combat frequent attacks by bands of robbers and soldiers sent by the Bohemian king, had begun in 1620 on the construction of a defensive wall. The monastery of Jasna Góra soon became known as the Fortress of the Virgin Mary (fortalitium marianum).

Since that time, Jasna Góra has retained an unique place in the hearts of the Polish people and attracts some of the largest pilgrimages in the world, with many miracles being attributed to the mysterious painting of the Black Madonna.

It all began with the arrival of the Paulite Order in 1382. Prince Ladislaus of Opole had summoned the monks from Hungary to Czestochowa, where they founded a monastery on top of the hill known as Jasna Góra and mounted the picture of the Black Madonna in their church. The prince had brought the painting to Czestochowa and it soon began to attract inexplicably large numbers of believers. They arrived from all corners of the world and Jasna Góra was soon receiving more pilgrims than the small church could accommodate. This led to the construction of the Gothic chapel. A wrought-iron grille, manufactured in Danzig in 1644, screens off the presbytery with its Baroque altar of precious wood dating from 1650 and the Black Madonna, whose silver cover leaves only her face and hands free.

Between 1642 and 1644, a Baroque section featuring three aisles was added to the Gothic chapel. This was Polish architecture typical of the transition period from Mannerism to Baroque and was attributed to Lublin. The chapel contains a total of five altars dedicated to the Virgin Mary: Entering the Tabernacle, the Virgin Mary's Visitation, the Annunciation, her Birth, and the Crucifixion altar with its particularly memorable, 15th-century crucifix. The chapel walls are covered with numerous votive plaques, the expressions of gratitude for miracles attributed to the Madonna. This is also true of the third section of the chapel built in 1929, the pillars and walls of which are decorated with votive plaques placed there by Polish soldiers, who witnessed many miracles during their struggle for Polish independence.

The reference to 'miracle', however, refers mainly to the unsuccessful siege of Jasna Góra centuries ago, which culminated in a Polish uprising and Poland's subsequent triumph over the Swedish invaders. This was reason enough for King John Kasimir of Poland to place his kingdom under the protection of the Virgin Mary in Lemberg cathedral, in 1656. Since then, she has figured as the country's regent, a symbol of religious and political freedom.

The Virgin Mary, Queen of Poland

After the coronation of the Madonna in 1717 and the Polish episcopate's 1920 proclamation making her Queen of Poland, the image has become an object of pilgrimage, attracting around four million pilgrims a year from all over the world. There is some disagreement regarding the origins of the picture. A handwritten document (Translato) in the monastery archives, dating from 1774, claims that the picture, which eventually turned up in Czestochowa, was painted long ago by Luke the Apostle, seated at the Holy Family's table. Scientists, on the other hand, believe it to be of Byzantine origin, an icon of the 'Holigetria' genre ('pointing the way') and have dated it somewhere between the sixth and ninth centuries.

In addition to the chapel with its picture of the Black Madonna, the monastery, which grew considerably between the fifteenth and twentieth centuries, has other interesting treasures: the basilica and treasury, the arsenal and the 600th-Anniversary museum, the Knights' hall and the refectory, and a priceless library containing almost 40,000 books, with 8000 rare and unique volumes.

Jasna Góra is regarded as the nation's spiritual source of strength. In 1886, Poland's Nobel Prizewinner Sienkiewicz dedicated a literary tribute to the country's courage and spirit of self-sacrifice in his novel *Floodtide*.

Classical beauty

The cathedral of the Finnish capital **HELSINKI** was designed by a German architect

The architect Johann Karl Ludwig Engel was born in Berlin in 1778. He studied at the Berlin Academy, incidentally with Carl Friedrich Schinkel with whom he has much in common. In 1816 he went to Finland, to assist with the building of the capital.

Helsinki had then been the capital for just four years. The previous capital was Turku, Swedish name Åbo, which had been founded by the Swedes. Helsinki, known as Helsingfors in Swedish, was also founded by the Swedes and still has a large Swedish-speaking colony. The explanation for this lies in its history, as Finland had been ruled by its western neighbor since the time of the High Middle Ages.

In 1807, Czar Alexander I and the French emperor Napoleon agreed that the Russians should have Finland, and after two years Sweden reluctantly consented. The largely autonomous Grand Duchy of Finland continued in existence until 1917 and only became an independent state as a result of Lenin's October Revolution.

Helsinki was founded in 1550 by King Gustav Wasa of Sweden. The harbor lies on a peninsula in the Gulf of Finland, surrounded by several small offshore islands well suited to the construction of fortifications. The city suffered damage in the Russo-Swedish wars, so after 1809 plans were made to transform it into a capital worthy of the name. The man responsible was the statesman and town planner Johann Albrecht Ehrenström.

Following the example of St. Petersburg

The practicalities were in the hands of an immigrant from Germany, Johann Karl Ludwig Engel. When he arrived in Helsinki, there were 4000 people living there. A quarter of a century later, the figure was almost five times as great. Engel's artistic ideal was German Classicism, in which he agreed with his fellow student Schinkel, but he also drew inspiration from the Russian rulers. He had traveled to St. Petersburg and gathered a lot of information about architectural developments there.

The Helsinki of Ehrenström and Engel was to be a Classical city. The starting point was the harbor, immediately behind which lay the old marketplace; this was extended to become the central feature of the city. Engel's first building was the Government Palace and he later built the university opposite it. The wide Senate Square between the two buildings was closed off to the north by the cathedral. This was the first purely stone building in Helsinki. The church was to be Protestant, in line with the religious beliefs of the majority of the population. For the followers of the Orthodox faith – who were there not only as a result of Finland becoming politically a part of Russia but as a result of earlier missionary activities – Engel built his Classical church of the Holy Trinity directly behind the cathedral. It was the Russian Orthodox church for the city, until Alexander Gornostajev built the Uspenski cathedral in the Katajanokka district in 1868. This is still the biggest Orthodox church outside Russia and is based on many historical models.

Monumental stone steps

The Protestant cathedral dominates the Senate Square. It is raised up on a broad terrace, with a monumental flight of stone steps leading up to it. The ground plan is a Greek cross, somewhat similar to the form preferred by the Orthodox church. The central dome rests on a tambour, which is extended to the height of a tower and features windows and imitation columns. The ends of the four arms of the cross are decorated in the manner of the ancient Greeks, with Corinthian columns supporting a flat, triangular pediment with statues.

The exterior of the cathedral is shining white, as are Engel's other buildings. They have earned Helsinki the name 'White City of the North'. The architect wanted to simulate marble, the material used to build the great temples of antiquity; as the real thing was not available to him, he had to make do with bricks and wood.

His earliest designs date from 1818, but building did not start until 1830. Originally, it was called St. Nicholas, probably in homage to the reigning czar in St. Petersburg who was also Grand Duke of Finland. The name was officially changed later on. The church was consecrated in 1852, 12 years after Engel's death. The work was continued by his assistants, which resulted in a number of changes to the original plans. The four smaller domes, a further reference to Russian Orthodox church buildings, were the work of the architect Ernst Bernhard Lohrmann.

Concerts, exhibitions, and lectures are held in the crypt, which was converted into a function room in the 1970s. The interior of the church strikes visitors as being extremely spacious, severe, and cold. There are statues of the Reformers Martin Luther, Philipp Melanchthon, and Mikael Agricola. The latter introduced Protestantism into Finland and was responsible for the first Finnish translation of the Bible. He stayed for a time with Luther in Wittenberg, and died on his way home from a journey to Moscow.

GETTING THERE:
Vis Helsinki international airport. Ferry connections from Sweden and Germany

OPENING TIMES:
Usually Mon-Sat 9:00 A.M. - 6:00 P.M. No sightseeing allowed during services

SPECIAL INTEREST:
The Senate Square in front of the cathedral

The front of the cathedral, with its dome and main door with pillared portico (main picture)

View of the altar, looking up into the great dome (below)

St. Erik's cathedral

The archbishop's brick-built cathedral in UPPSALA is the finest example of Gothic architecture in Sweden

Sweden's national patron saint is St. Erik. He was a medieval king, the ninth of that name, who came from a wealthy noble family in Västergötland and dedicated himself to spreading the Christian faith. He was killed in the summer of 1160 by the Danes. He was venerated as a Christian martyr and later became the figurehead of a religious following. A few decades later he was canonized as a saint.

He was buried in Uppsala, which had been his center of government and the old capital of his kingdom. This is not the present-day town of Uppsala, but Gamla Uppsala (Old Uppsala), situated approximately four and a half miles (seven kilometers) away. This is now an archaeological site, where the remains of various excavations can be viewed. The small stone church which still stands there was formerly the cathedral of Uppsala. Pope John Paul II once celebrated a Mass there during a visit.

Gamla Uppsala was the precursor of present-day Uppsala and its stone church was the predecessor of St. Erik's cathedral. The new town of Uppsala was initially known as Östra Aros and was originally no more than a commercial center and an inland port. In 1164, however, during the reign of St. Erik, the archbishop of Gamla Uppsala decided to transfer his seat to the new town. When the ruling family also disappeared from Gamla Uppsala and made Stockholm their new capital city, the original town fell into a gradual decline, while Östra Aros gained steadily in importance until, eventually, it also usurped the old town's venerable name.

Famous library

It is certainly true to say that Uppsala was once the power center of Sweden's reigning monarchs. Many people still regard it as the intellectual heart of the country. The University of Uppsala, founded in 1477 by Archbishop Jakob Ulvsson, is Sweden's oldest. Its library contains not only the *Codex Upsaliensis*, the oldest surviving handwritten version of the *Prose Edda*, a collection of ancient Icelandic verse by Snorri Sturluson, dating from around 1300, but also the famous *Codex Argenteus*. This is the precious, handwritten version of a translation of the Bible by Bishop Ulfilas, which stems from the fourth century and was probably undertaken in Ravenna on the initiative of Theoderic, King of the Ostrogoths. It is now stored here in the original homeland of the Germanic tribes who emigrated during the population migrations. The Ulfilas Bible is the oldest extant manuscript in a Germanic language.

Uppsala University is situated near the old castle, the building of which was begun by King Gustav Vasa. Although he later decided to transfer the royal residence to Stockholm, he returned to Uppsala on his death to be buried in the cathedral. St. Erik is likewise entombed here. Uppsala is second only to Stockholm's Riddarholm church as a burial site for Swedish aristocracy and contains the tombs of King John III and Queen Katharina Beata. Members of two of Sweden's highest-ranking noble families, the Oxenstierna and Stenbock families, are also buried here. Bengt Oxenstierna directed Sweden's foreign policy from 1680 and, prior to this, had administered the extensive territories acquired by Sweden during the Thirty Years' War in Pomerania and in Mecklenburg.

The overwhelming impression of Uppsala cathedral is one of height and space. It is 387ft (118m) long, 148ft (45m) wide, and is situated on the sloping right bank of the Fyrisån river. It was constructed of brick and followed the late Gothic style of architecture. It was modeled on the great English cathedrals until the end of the thirteenth century, when a French architect, Etienne de Bonneuil, took charge of building work. He had previously worked on the cathedral of Notre-Dame de Paris and his designs, as might be expected, were influenced by the experience and aesthetic ideas he had gained there.

New pinnacles for the towers

The cathedral was destroyed by fire on several occasions and had to be rebuilt. Radical changes occurred during the Baroque period when the two west towers were redesigned and capped with new pinnacles. Further alterations were introduced around 1880 reflecting the trends towards Historicism, but these have since been removed. People had been obliged to acknowledge that genuine medieval architecture not only looked more authentic but was also aesthetically more attractive.

Among the famous names buried in Uppsala cathedral are Carolus Linnaeus, the biologist who invented the binary system for the classification of animals and plants; he also created the Botanical Gardens at Uppsala University and died nearby. The church also contains the tomb of Emanuel Swedenborg, philosopher, natural scientist, mathematician, theologian, and mystic, who speculated not only on the possibility of building a submarine but also on the forthcoming end of the world. The former has meanwhile become a reality while the second, fortunately, has not yet come to pass.

The cathedral's decorative façade with its twin towers (main picture)

View down the vast central nave to the apse (below, center)

As usual, the pulpit is built onto one of the mighty pillars (below, left)

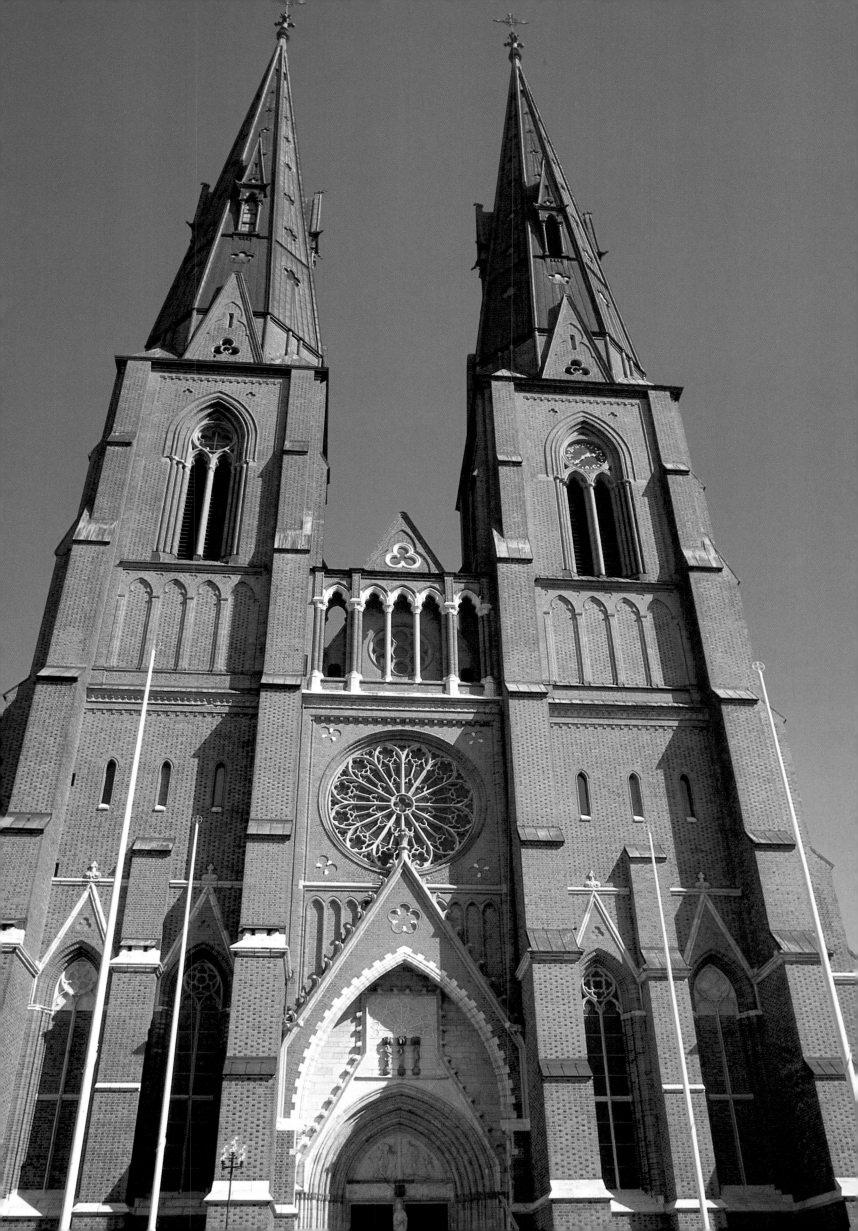

A monument to Sweden's kings

Riddarholms Kyrkan in **STOCKHOLM** is the burial place of Swedish kings

GETTING THERE:
Flights to Arlanda international airport

OPENING TIMES:
May-Aug, usually Mon-Fri 10:00 A.M. – 4:00 P.M., Sat/Sun 12:00 P.M. – 3:00 P.M. Closed Oct-April

SPECIAL INTEREST:
The tombs of all Sweden's kings

Stockholm, Sweden's capital city, is situated on Scandinavia's east coast, where Lake Mälaren empties into the Baltic. The city of around three quarters of a million people is built on a group of islands. King Gustav I Vasa made Stockholm his seat of government and, under his successors, Sweden rapidly developed into a dominant Baltic power during the seventeenth and eighteenth centuries. Two of its most celebrated rulers were King Gustavus Adolphus and King Charles X.

Both kings are buried in Riddarholms Kyrkan. Riddarholmen is one of Stockholm's islands which, together with Stadsholmen and Helgeandsholmen, comprise the city's Gamla Stan or Old Town. This charmingly picturesque part of town is dotted with old houses and dimly lit bars, a far prettier district than some of Stockholm's younger districts with their somewhat sterile architectural style. The city's many canals and bridges and the unexpected vistas which can suddenly open up across the inner harbor waters of Riddarfjärden, Strömmen, and Saltsjön make Stockholm one of Europe's most beautiful capital cities.

The Old Town boasts two other famous churches in addition to Riddarholms Kyrkan: namely, the Storkyrkan and St. Gertrude's Church. The latter is better known as Tyska Kyrkan, or German church, so-called because it was the church of the German merchants' guild during the

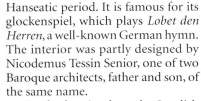

Hanseatic period. It is famous for its glockenspiel, which plays *Lobet den Herren*, a well-known German hymn. The interior was partly designed by Nicodemus Tessin Senior, one of two Baroque architects, father and son, of the same name.

Storkyrkan is where the Swedish royal family celebrate marriages and coronations. It is a brick building with many Baroque features, famous for its unusual style of ribbed vaulting and its Renaissance-style black and silver altar, created by Ostarius Erdmueller. The famous figure of St. George in the northern transept was carved by Bernt Notke, one of the greatest sculptors and painters of the Late Middle Ages, who was born in Pomerania and lived in Lübeck. The Storkyrkan, or Great church, is positioned next to the royal palace which

dominates all other buildings on the island of Stadholmen and is the largest royal palace on the continent. It is a colossal construction of five hundred rooms.

Bulwark against the Finns

Riddarholmen, meaning Island of Knights, is the second largest island of Stockholm's Old Town. It contains several palaces belonging to Swedish noble families, as well as a statue, mounted on top of a huge column, of Birger Jarl, a powerful, thirteenth regent who did much to make the country safe from attackers. It was he who built Stockholm as a stronghold against the aggressive incursions of the Finns. He also attracted German merchants to the country and took Stockholm into the Hanseatic League.

Riddarholms church is the city's best-known and is regarded as Gamla Stan's most famous landmark. It was once a Franciscan monastery. The abbey was later expanded until it reached its present-day proportions. It is essentially a brick-built, Gothic structure, with later additions and ornamentation in the Baroque style. Its extremely narrow and delicate open-fretwork spire, surrounded by four slim pinnacles, makes it easily distinguishable. The church consists of a central nave and two aisles. The one on the left is considerably wider than the one on the right. Both culminate in chapels, used predominantly as burial sites. As previously mentioned, Riddarholms Kyrkan is the principal burial church for all Swedish monarchs and is conveniently located adjacent to the palace.

The tomb of Gustavus Adolphus

It has served as a mausoleum since 1807 and is rarely used for services. Visitors tend to want to view the sarcophagi of the dead kings. A more general look around, however, will reveal shields bearing the coat-of-arms of the Seraphim Order. This association of knights, founded in 1748, evolved from earlier Orders, whose origins can be traced right back to 1336.

The high altar dates from the Late Baroque period and immediately in front of it are the monumental graves of Magnus Ladulås and Karl Knutson Bonde. The former was a medieval king, who died in 1290. He protected the common man against exploitation by the aristocracy and also established Sweden's mining industry around 1280 in Falun, recruiting miners from the Harz mountain region of central Germany. The latter ruled as King Karl VIII during a time of serious internal unrest in the fifteenth century. It was a period characterized by rival claims to the throne, which were eventually resolved by King Gustav Vasa.

The church contains the green marble sarcophagus of King Gustavus Adolphus, resting next to his wife Eleonora of Brandenburg. The contemporary ruling Bernadotte family has a chapel of its own and several important military generals are also entombed here. "It was ever thus and will ever remain so," wrote Gunnar Eklöf, the Swedish lyricist, "until the last person dreams of fire and all is over."

View of Riddarholm island with Riddarholms Kyrkan and part of Stockholm's Old Town. The church is easily identifiable by its pointed, grey tower (main picture)

A concert taking place in Riddarholms Kyrkan (below, left)

Norwegian stave churches

BORGUND near the Sognefjord is home to the most famous wooden church in the country

Norwegian
Sea

NORWAY

Borgund

North
Sea

Baltic
Sea

In 1886, the Danish painter and poet Holger Drachmann wrote: "The whim of a brilliant child, a woodland beetle carved by a simple-minded giant with his sheath knife ... the interior like a smoking room dedicated to a mystical cult, in which the darkness of the saga overwhelms the dimly burning candles of Catholicism, whose flickering light falls on the axes of peasants in armor and the flowing beards of Viking kings. An eerie experience." He is describing a Norwegian church at Borgund in Laerdal, which is a branch of the Sognefjord, the longest and deepest inlet in the much indented west coast of the country.

Borgund is a stave church. This kind of religious building, so typical of Norway and so unusual in the rest of the world, results from the combination of a barren landscape, a heathen Viking tradition, and probably also from contact with the world of Slavic and Byzantine Christianity.

Elaborate construction

Borgund is not the only stave church to be built according to a central plan, in the way the Byzantines in particular used to do it. The assumption is that the Norman connections with Byzantium and the time spent in Russia by the Norwegian kings have found expression here.

Stave churches are built of wood. The name comes from the method of construction. The four balks of timber forming the base are laid out in the form of a rectangle, on a stone foundation in order to protect them from the damp. On top of these stand the posts or masts known as 'staves'. Halfway up, the staves are strengthened by a kind of brace, using a strip made up of a series of diagonal crosses. The roof beams, which meet at a steep angle, are laid on top of the crossbeams.

Sacred darkness

By way of further support, a covered gallery known as the 'svalgang' runs round the outside at ground level. From the center of the steep roof rises a tower built on four posts, which may be one or more stories high and is also topped by a steep saddle roof.

The individual beams and timbers are held together not by nails but by mortise and tenon, the same technique as was used in the building of Viking ships, which ensures maximum elasticity and robustness. The roofs, and sometimes also the exterior walls, are completely covered with wooden shingles.

As a rule, it is dark inside. The windows, if any, are small. The main source of light is the candles on the altar, which is slightly raised and attracts everyone's attention. Visitors have to stand; a bench is provided only for the elderly and infirm. The interior beams are ornamented with carvings or runic inscriptions. The decorations reveal pre-Christian, heathen origins. Occasionally the walls are painted with representations of Biblical motifs, sometimes in a naive, rustic manner, sometimes with real artistry.

Protection from evil spirits

The svalgang is where people congregate prior to religious services. There are no openings in the walls to give a view of the actual interior of the church. Pilgrimages and processions also start in the svalgang. Right up to the towers, the pointed roof gables end in carved dragons' heads, reminiscent of the stone gargoyles on Gothic churches. In both cases, the mythical intention is the same: evil spirits must be warded off or scared away. The carvings on the bows of Viking ships clearly served as models and their heathen origin is evident.

The golden age of the stave church was the High Middle Ages, when Gothic was dominant in other parts of Europe. Distant echoes of this style can be seen in many stave churches. Of the 900 stave churches that once existed in Norway only 29 remain, most of them in the valleys between Bergen and Oslo. They are all protected as historical monuments and are among the most important architectural evidence of Scandinavian history.

Alongside Heddal in Telemark north of Oslo, Borgund is the biggest and most typical building of this type in the country. It was built around 1050. Twelve posts or staves encompass a church with three naves and there are a number of entrances, all richly decorated with carving.

Inside, it is cool and dark and smells of smoke and wood tar. The pulpit was added at the time of the Reformation. The altar table was set up later still, around 1650. In 1870, the church underwent a thorough renovation, during which the windows, which had been added later, were removed again. Nowadays, the stave church in Borgund is rarely used for services.

GETTING THERE:
Best reached from Oslo, using one of the ferry connections, or via Oslo's international airport. By car from Oslo, about 194 miles (310km) to the north-west on the E 16, direct to Borgund

OPENING TIMES:
May and September daily 10:00 A.M. - 5:00 P.M.; June, July, August, daily 8:00 A.M. - 7:00 P.M. Closed the rest of the year. Changes possible

SPECIAL INTEREST:
Carvings on the west door of artistic dragons and animal figures

A Christian monument from the High Middle Ages, the stave church in Borgund gives us a very clear reminder of its Viking origins (main picture)

The pointed roof gables are ornamented with carvings reminiscent of heathen motifs (below, right)

The resting place of royalty

The brick cathedral of ROSKILDE is still Scandinavia's largest church

A total of 38 kings and queens all under one roof: from Harald Bluetooth, the first Christian King of Denmark, to Frederik IX, most of Denmark's rulers are buried in Roskilde cathedral – in sumptuous chapels, alabaster tombs, or elaborately decorated, iron coffins. For many visitors to Roskilde, the experience proves a powerful and somber lesson in Danish history.

The Vikings were the first to establish a harbor in Roskilde Fjord, using it as a base from which to launch their raiding parties. Harald Bluetooth himself, (935-985), while fleeing from his own son, took refuge in this sheltered spot and around 960 built a church here. More buildings followed, but it was not until 1158, when Valdemar the Great installed his friend Absalon as bishop in Roskilde, that construction began on a mighty cathedral, this time not of limestone but of locally produced bricks.

Around 1400, architectural trends began to lean more towards French Gothic. A fine tracery construction replaced the Early Romanesque-style basilica. The main transepts were abandoned and the number of windows in the two-story choir gallery increased from one to three, enabling light to flood into the 279ft (85m)-long and 79ft (24m)-high central nave. The cathedral was for the most part completed by the mid-thirteenth century – representing a center of monarchical power and a stronghold of the powerful Catholic church. During the Middle Ages, Roskilde boasted a population of some 10,000, with 12 churches and 6 monasteries, making it one of the largest and richest towns in northern Europe.

Destroyed in the aftermath of the Reformation

The sale of indulgences flourished in Roskilde, as it did in many other places, and no less than 75 chapels were incorporated within the cathedral. By 1536, when the Reformation was sweeping through Denmark, all of these chapels were demolished and most of the art works destroyed. To exacerbate matters, the Royal Court had moved from Roskilde to Copenhagen in 1443 with the bishop following suit, leaving this once splendid town, mockingly referred to by Hans Christian Andersen as a "large village," to fall into desuetude. The street once frequented by kings and bishops was eventually named after the town's shoemakers.

Roskilde could not, however, be stripped of its special status as a burial place for Danish monarchs, a role it had fulfilled since Margarethe I (1375-1412) was buried here with considerable pomp and circumstance a year after her death. 'Black Gret', reputedly a daring horsewoman who succeeded in uniting Denmark, Sweden, and Norway under one throne, lies entombed in a Gothic-style sarcophagus behind the high altar.

The diversity of architectural styles to be seen in the cathedral is primarily due to the addition of a number of different burial chapels over the centuries.

Impressive burial chapels

The three-story chapel of the Three Kings, built by Christian I, dates from the Gothic period. Decorated with frescoes in 1480, it represents one of the finest examples of Danish chapel interiors from the Middle Ages. The chapel of Christian IV, enclosed by an elaborate wrought-iron grille dating from 1620, is typical of Dutch Renaissance architecture.

By way of contrast, the splendid, Neo-Classical Frederick V chapel is one of the finest examples of this style of architecture in Denmark. A strong sense of history also surrounds the chapel in which the kings of the house of Glücksburg and their spouses were buried from 1926 onwards. The tradition of Danish monarchs being buried in Roskilde was perpetuated by Frederik IX, who died in 1972 and was buried in a simple brick rotunda outside the cathedral.

The attraction of Roskilde cathedral lies not just in its royal tombs and the overwhelming sense of space experienced in the central nave but in its equally impressive altarpiece, fashioned in 1560 in Antwerp, not to mention the elaborately decorated choir stall, royal throne, and the Baroque pulpit dating from 1609, made of marble, alabaster, and sandstone. The organ is likewise entirely Baroque in style, although the organ loft actually dates from 1425. One of the cathedral's treasures is a mechanical clock dating from the end of the fifteenth century, with sculpted figures. A figure of St. George marks the hour by slaying a dragon, whose death throes are accompanied by a great deal of noise.

Despite its many additions, the exterior of the cathedral remains a uniform construction of red brick. The delicacy of its twin spires merely highlights the massiveness of the building. The view from the cathedral square looks out over the fjord, which once witnessed the arrival of the Vikings. Five reconstructed Viking ships, sunk off Roskilde, are on display in a Viking museum. Like the cathedral, these too are potent reminders of the town's history. The unique nature of this Scandinavian church has been recognized by UNESCO and, in 1995, the cathedral was listed as one of the world's cultural heritage sites.

The Renaissance-style burial chapel of Christian IV, who died in 1648 (far left)

The massive main façade is lifted somewhat by the slim spires on the twin towers. View along the Skolegade (below, center)

The decorative painting on the pillars and arches has been painstakingly restored (below, right)

DENMARK

Ribe •

North
Sea

Baltic
Sea

Of splendid brick

RIBE cathedral is the finest Romanesque church in Denmark

GETTING THERE:
By motorway from Copenhagen to the Esbjerg turn-off. Ribe lies about 19 miles (30km) further south by main road. Esbjerg has its own local airport. Good rail links

OPENING TIMES:
Normally 10:00 A.M. - 5:00 P.M. in summer, 12 noon - 5:00 P.M. on Sun, and 11:00 A.M. - 4:00 P.M. in winter

SPECIAL INTEREST:
Frescoes on the pillars dating from the Middle Ages

The two mighty towers of Ribe cathedral are visible from afar, a prominent landmark in the flat-lying countryside (main picture)

Fresco on a pillar in the long nave, depicting the apostles Bartholomew and Andrew (below, left)

The organ gallery built by Jens Olufsen between 1633 and 1636. The two unusual pedal towers were added in 1653 (below, center)

The font dates from pre-Reformation days (below, right)

How ironic that 17th-century medieval Ribe, after forging such strong trade links with the Netherlands and even espousing Dutch art and architecture, should find its role as a flourishing trade center and its importance as a town declining when the river connecting Ribe with the sea silted up. A similar fate had also overtaken Brugge in Flanders when the Zwijn silted up in the same way.

Some good did come out of these misfortunes, however. The two towns managed to preserve their medieval appearance, if only because there was simply no money available to spend on demolishing or reconstructing the old buildings. While Brugge is noted for its extensive market hall and belfry, Ribe is dominated by one single architectural feature: the cathedral rises up so dramatically from amidst the surrounding half-timbered houses that the impact is quite sensational, a forceful reminder of the power and might of the church, a stone giant in the vast marshland.

Rhenish tufa as a building material

In 850, St. Ansgar built the first church in Ribe. In 1150, Ribe's bishop, Elias, initiated the building of a mighty cathedral. It was largely built of tufa, shipped north from the Rhineland along the Rhine and across the North Sea, as well as granite from Jutland. By 1175, the apse, choir, and transept had been completed, followed by the long nave with its beamed ceiling. Above the side aisles are Romanesque-style, vaulted arches. The cathedral's most unusual feature, however, is situated above the crossing, namely the large dome crafted of tufa stone.

During the reign of King Valdemar (1202-1241), additions to the interior of the church included some Gothic features, such as a vaulted ceiling all the way through, modeled on churches in Rhineland-Westphalia. Despite these few modifications in style, however, Ribe still ranks as the finest surviving example of a Romanesque cathedral in Scandinavia. The Reformation movement which swept across Denmark was born in Ribe and, between 1542 and 1561, Hans Tavsen, Ribe's bishop and leading cleric, as well as a pupil of Martin Luther, turned the city into an important mecca for scholars, theologians, and artists.

It was during this time that the cathedral's image changed. The king seized the valuable church treasures. The side altars were removed. All that remains today is a group of figures with St. George, dating from before the Reformation, a bronze font, a triumphal cross, and a mighty, five-branched candelabra, dating from the end of the fifteenth century. The choir stalls were donated by Ivar Munch, Ribe's last Catholic bishop, whose burial place is regarded as one of the most sumptuous of all Danish medieval tombs.

Under Christian IV (1588-1648), the church underwent considerable alterations. The altar was replaced by one in Renaissance style. A Baroque-style pulpit and organ were introduced and even the paintings reflected the new genre.

Merchants and those members of the nobility wealthy enough to afford it commissioned epitaphs and tombstones with which they hoped to secure themselves a place in heaven. Ribe's residents enjoyed the candlelit atmosphere and allowed themselves to be transported by the music of the cathedral organist. Candles also illuminated the many portraits, which even today lend an almost homely feel to the cathedral.

Special role for the main tower

No matter how impressive the view along the Romanesque aisles, the massive proportions of the building can only be fully appreciated from outside. It is capped by three individual towers, the most important of which is the square tower. In 1283, the northern tower collapsed. It was not rebuilt in its old form but replaced by an imposing brick tower, aimed at protecting the town's inhabitants.

In 1594, there was fresh disaster when the spire of the new tower collapsed during building work, after which a square balustrade was built around the top of the tower. In 1599, the great storm bell was finally rehung. It rang out in 1634 to warn the townsfolk of imminent floods, when the waters of the North Sea surged into the cathedral.

From the top of the cathedral tower, there is a spectacular view of the surrounding marshland stretching all the way to the sea, unimpeded by pillars or walls, like the view from one of those high, look-out towers in Tuscany. A little touch of the south in northern Denmark.

The royal cathedral of Edinburgh

St. Giles is the High Kirk of **EDINBURGH**, where John Knox once preached

GETTING THERE:
Edinburgh has an international airport

OPENING TIMES:
Usually May-Sept Mon-Fri 9:00 A.M. - 7:00 P.M., Sat 9:00 A.M. - 5:00 P.M., Sun 1:00 P.M. - 5:00 P.M.
Oct-April Mon-Sat 9:00 A.M. - 5:00 P.M., Sun 1:00 P.M. - 5:00 P.M.

SPECIAL INTEREST:
The window by Edward Burne-Jones showing the crossing of the Jordan

The crown on the tower silhouetted against the evening light (main picture)

View of the apse with the main altar (below, right)

General view of the cathedral (below, left)

A Scottish speciality: angels playing the bagpipes (below, margin)

The Scottish capital, Edinburgh, stands on seven volcanic hills. One of them is Castle Hill, on which the castle stands. From there, a succession of streets known as the Royal Mile runs down to the Palace of Holyrood House, the official residence of the British queen in Scotland. A large number of the sights of Edinburgh Old Town, including St. Giles' cathedral and John Knox's house, are gathered together along the Royal Mile.

Edinburgh succeeded Perth as the capital of Scotland in 1437. Various other churches preceded St. Giles, the oldest in the ninth century. In 1120, there was a Norman church here, which was destroyed in 1385 by Richard II. This king, who has become famous thanks mainly to Shakespeare, set out to overcome the Gaelic regions but in the end was defeated by his rival for the crown of England, Henry Bolingbroke, and abdicated in his favor.

Mysterious twilight

Four octagonal columns from the Norman church in Edinburgh have been preserved. They bear the weight of the tower. Everything else was newly built between 1387 and 1495, finishing with the tower. Seen from outside, St. Giles is a massive building in the Gothic style; inside, the stained glass windows create a mysterious twilight.

They are comparatively recent, dating from the nineteenth century.

One, which shows the crossing of the Jordan and various Old Testament figures, was designed by the Pre-Raphaelite Edward Burne-Jones, a leading representative of Art Nouveau in Britain. He had originally studied theology and with this background was familiar with religious subjects.

Parliament and fire station

Other work continued on St. Giles.' The building needed it. Many things had happened to it over the previous 300 years. There had been rebellions, for instance in 1637, when Archbishop Laud wanted to introduce a new liturgy, and a woman called Jenny Geddes protested against it. She shouted out in protest and threw things at one of the deans. St. Giles' has been used, *inter alia*, as a parliament building, a police station, a fire station, and a coal store. The Scottish guillotine (the 'Maiden') was set up here and one corner was used as a prison for 'harlots and whores'.

This kind of thing happened after the Reformation, which in Scotland did not take the comparatively moderate form of Anglicanism but followed Calvinist ideals. Calvinism made a particularly sharp break with the Catholic attachment to the material forms of religious life. It is comparatively indifferent to the building in which its services are held and concentrates above all on spirituality and the Word.

The man who carried this through in Scotland was John Knox. He was born near Edinburgh in 1513, studied theology, and became a priest. He came into contact with Protestantism and, when his teacher Widhart was executed for heresy, he converted.

At first, the Anglican Church took him in, but the breach came when he organized a Scottish rebellion. In the conflict between the Catholic Mary Stuart and Elizabeth I, he again sided with the English queen, who for her part made the victory of Protestantism in Scotland possible. Knox became a preacher at St. Giles and wrote a number of books. He is considered an important figure by the Scottish independence movement and was ceremonially buried in the cathedral.

Chapel of the Knights of the Thistle

St. Giles is now the High Kirk of Edinburgh, making it the principal church in Scotland. The 50 altars that were to be found here before the Reformation were removed. The only new addition has been the chapel of the Order of the Thistle. This is an exclusively Scottish organization and membership is considered a particular honor. In addition to the clan chiefs, the current list of Knights of the Thistle includes Prince Charles, the heir to the British throne, and his sister Anne.

The building of this chapel, designed by the architect Robert Lorimer, was completed in 1911. It contains a wealth of religious and heraldic objects, notably stone angels with puffed-out cheeks, playing the bagpipes.

Half church, half castle

For hundreds of years, the Norman cathedral of **DURHAM** was a bastion against the Scots

A medieval image in Durham cathedral shows, among other things, a particularly repulsive representation of pigs. It is not, however, a question of hunting or stock-rearing in this case, but of defamation in the form of a pictorial allegory. It is the people of Scotland who are being disparaged through the pigs, and the reason the Celtic race was depicted in this way was that Durham is not far from the border with Scotland. The many wars between England and Scotland usually affected Durham, too, and so it was in 1346 with the battle of Neville's Cross. In 1380, a special altar of Normandy sandstone was set up in the cathedral to commemorate this event.

Durham is a city of 81,000 souls. Its name is derived from Dunholm, which means 'hill on an island'. The water surrounding that island is the river Wear and, on top of the hill, there is a castle as well as the cathedral. Both are of Norman origin. The castle was built by William the Conqueror in 1072. The cathedral was begun 21 years later under the influential Bishop Carileph. Since then, the church has become the most important Norman building in the whole of England.

Massive pillars

William's Normans were a hardy and warlike people. While they were living south of the English Channel, they had adopted the French language, but otherwise kept to their robust ways. This is visible in their buildings. In comparison with Romanesque buildings in more southerly regions, they appear massive. The interior columns are solid and remarkably thick. The patterns with which they are decorated – engraved lines sometimes in spirals and sometimes zigzags – do little to soften this effect.

Work continued on the cathedral until the middle of the thirteenth century, with the central tower of the three being completed in 1490. The last phase of building took place in the Gothic period, as can be seen from the exterior; the interior was unaffected. It is a matter of pride that almost no alterations or overbuilding followed and that the original has been preserved to such a great extent. Only the destruction resulting from the Reformation, when more than 30 altars were destroyed, has left its mark. In 1640, the building was used as a barracks by the victorious Scottish army. Ten years later, after the battle of Dunbar, Oliver Cromwell held three thousand Scottish prisoners of war captive in the cathedral.

The whole of the choir was later destroyed by fire.

Resting place of two saints

What remained of the previous furnishings was stable and made of stone – for instance, the tomb of the Nevilles, one of the most respected and powerful noble families in England in the Middle Ages. One member of the family, Ralph, the Fourth Baron Neville, defeated the invasion led by the Scottish King David II in 1346. Now he lies buried in the cathedral, together with his wife Alice, in an alabaster coffin.

Durham was the last resting-place of two saints, Bede and Cuthbert. Both are buried in magnificent tombs. The Venerable Bede was born in 672 in the village of Monkton in Northumbria. He became a Benedictine monk. As one of the most significant theologians of the early Middle Ages, he wrote a history of the English Church, as well as commentaries, sermons, and hymns, and also treatises on mathematics, astronomy, and music. His mortal remains were taken to Durham in 1093. He was canonized in 1899.

Cuthbert, a contemporary of Bede, also came from Northumbria. He distinguished himself by his exceptional piety and capacity for self-examination. First a monk and then an abbot, he later became a hermit. He was appointed a bishop, but returned to his hermitage where he died in 687. His bones were brought to Durham in 1104. Cuthbert soon became one of the most popular saints in the British Isles.

On the outside of the north door hangs a metal knocker. Fugitives from the law could use it to gain admission and a maximum of 37 days' stay. Within this time, they had to decide whether they wished to choose to go before the court or into voluntary exile. In the latter case they were taken to the nearest harbor, carrying a wooden cross on their shoulders, and left the country on the next ship to anchor there.

Sir Walter Scott as principal witness

The place where such fugitives stayed was the monastery, which stood adjacent to the cathedral. It was dissolved in 1540, the cloisters being a nineteenth century copy.

"Grey towers of Durham/Yet well I love thy mixed and massive piles/Half church of God, half castle 'gainst the Scot/And long to roam these venerable aisles/With records stored of deeds long since forgot."

Verses by Sir Walter Scott of Edinburgh, the poet and pioneer of the historical novel. Since he wrote these literary declarations of love, the bloody strife between Scotland and Durham appears to have been settled.

GETTING THERE:
From Newcastle, about 12 miles (20km) south on the motorway. Ferry connections to Newcastle from the continent

WHEN TO GO:
Summer, also the best time to visit Scotland

OPENING TIMES:
Usually 10:00 A.M. – 5:00 P.M. daily. No admission to tourists during services

SPECIAL INTEREST:
The tombs of St. Bede and St. Cuthbert

The heavy Norman arches are as characteristic of Durham cathedral as its monumental pillars. The decorations are not enough to offset their massiveness. The nave was built between 1093 and 1130 (left)

This view (below) of the cathedral, built 1093-1278 on a hill above the city, shows the stylistic unity of the building

A church of Gothic splendor

YORK minster in the north of England is famous for its diversity of styles

GETTING THERE:
Via Manchester international airport and road from Leeds on the motorway M1, about 12 miles (20km) on good main routes. By rail to York station

OPENING TIMES:
Usually 10:00 A.M. - 6:00 P.M. daily. No entry for tourists during services

SPECIAL INTEREST:
The statues in the chapter house, dating from the time of the first Norman bishops

The name of York is known to educated people everywhere because of the Wars of the Roses and the historical plays of William Shakespeare. The last ruler of the house of York, which had the white rose as its emblem, was Richard, Duke of Gloucester – the youngest son of the Duke of York, Richard Plantagenet – who became King Richard III of England. After his defeat and death at the battle of Bosworth Field in 1485, power passed to the Tudors. Richard III is generally considered to be the most impressive villain in world literature, although in reality he was not nearly as bad as Shakespeare claims; on the contrary, there is evidence to suggest that he was quite a reasonable and successful ruler.

There are a number of reminders of him in York. The city, situated in the north of England, has a well-preserved medieval center and its defensive walls are still intact. The most famous of its churches is the minster, the biggest cathedral in England and the largest Gothic building in Northern Europe, which receives two million visitors a year.

York's wealth was founded on the wool trade. The city developed from a Roman military camp called Eboracum. It first came into contact with Christianity as long ago as 306, and eight years later it had a bishop. The Christian community subsequently went into decline but later recovered. King Edwin of Northumbria was baptized on Easter Day 627 in a church that was the forerunner of the minster – a small, hastily erected, wooden building, which was soon destroyed by fire. It was rebuilt and finally, after the Norman invasion, converted into an extensive building whose fame has spread far beyond the shores of the British Isles.

250 years to build

The radical rebuilding in the newly fashionable Gothic style began in the thirteenth century, and was to take around 250 years. When Richard III knelt before the altar, the building had already acquired its present form.

The façade and entrance are at the west end. The portal is richly decorated with statues. One of these is of St. Peter, the patron saint of the cathedral with the keys in his hand. The conversion began with the south transept in 1230-1241, the foundation stone of the nave was laid in 1291, and the chapter house was finally completed in 1345.

The cathedral is famous for exhibiting three different styles of English Gothic architecture, which it harmoniously integrates. First, there is Early English, which looks towards Early Gothic in France from where several of the master builders came. A characteristic of this style is the way columns are used in the vaulting. Here, in York, they are made of dark marble from the isle of Purbeck in the south of England. The transepts are also in the Early English style.

Before the statues of the kings

By contrast, the Decorated style predominates in the nave and chapter house. This style can be recognized by particularly rich tracery on the windows and blind arcading on the outer walls, with the foil pattern as a favorite, and also by the decorative stone ribs forming a dense network on the vaults and interior walls.

Finally, there is the Perpendicular style, the English version of Late Gothic. Blind arcading has become refined and luxuriant, with particular accentuation of the verticals. As

with Late Gothic in other places, the purpose is to place extreme emphasis on all vertical lines and to draw the gaze up towards heaven. In York, the Perpendicular style is evident in the choir and the towers.

The minster has a large number of windows containing medieval stained glass. They are considered to be the best in Britain. Among the most notable are the lofty, pointed west window, the great east window, and the windows in the north transept known as the 'five sisters'. The window showing St. Nicholas of Myrna in Asia Minor has become famous. Among other things, he is the protector of those who have been robbed, and he is seen here riding his horse over a villain who has stolen money from a moneylender. As mentioned, York was a city of wealthy merchants.

The minster is extremely rich in sculptures. This applies not only to the west front but also to the interior. The life-size statues of English kings

in the ambulatory of the choir are very impressive. They include William I (William the Conqueror), who seized England in 1066 at the battle of Hastings, and Henry VI, the last king of the house of Lancaster, whose reign saw the start of the Wars of the Roses. The completion of the rose window located in the south transept coincided with the end of the Wars of the Roses and the fall of the house of York.

When 'Great Peter' booms out
A few of the medieval bishops' graves have survived, as has the crypt of the Norman cathedral in which the remains of an earlier, 8th-century church are also to be seen. The chapter house, the octagonal meeting-room for the highest cathedral clergy, opens off the north transept, which also houses the astronomical clock. Here, too, the windows are magnificent and there are valuable sculptures. The statues date from the time of

York's first Norman bishop, Thomas of Bayeux. The south transept was seriously damaged by fire in 1984, but has now been repaired. At midday every day, the bell 'Great Peter' rings out from the north-west tower. This

famous and tuneful bell weighs 197cwt (10ton) – everything about York minster is eminent and impressive.

The old center of York is dominated by the nave and tower of the Gothic minster (main picture)

View of the main door, with its two flanking towers (below, left)

One of the chapels with its beautiful stained glass windows (below, right)

The house of Etheldreda

ELY cathedral is an outstanding example of Norman Gothic

GETTING THERE:
Motorway from London to Cambridge, then continue by A10 to Ely, situated about 12 miles (20km) further north. Good rail and bus links

OPENING TIMES:
Normally open daily from 9:00 A.M. - 6:00 P.M. No admission to tourists during services

SPECIAL INTEREST:
King's School near the cathedral

View of the northern transept with tower crossing (main picture)

Its famous octagonal dome on the main tower is an unusual architectural feature (below, left)

The central nave is 249ft (76m) long and was built between 1106-1189 (below, right)

Ely, with a population of over 60,000, is situated to the north of London, halfway between Cambridge and Norwich. The surrounding land is flat and mainly devoted to agriculture. The River Ouse flows through Ely, affording the opportunity for pleasure cruises. There is also a small fishing harbor. The city is a popular destination for Londoners.

The cathedral itself is visible from miles away, thanks to its west tower which rises 216ft (66m) above the roofs of the town. The lower two-thirds of it date from the twelfth century, but it was not finally completed for another two hundred years. Its exterior perfectly mirrors the development of Gothic architecture in England. The cathedral has rightly earned its reputation as an outstanding example of English Gothic.

Romanesque ground-plan

The origins of Ely cathedral go back a long way, as the Romanesque ground plan suggests. However, its roots go back even further than this, namely to the seventh century, before the invasion of William the Conqueror to a time when East England was still firmly under Saxon rule. Etheldreda, the daughter of a Saxon king, founded a convent here.

It is virtually impossible to separate historical fact from fiction on the subject of Etheldreda. Born in 630 in Exning, near Newmarket, she discovered her religious vocation at an early age, despite which she was twice married, each time for reasons of political expediency. Nevertheless, she retained her virginity. Her first husband bequeathed her the Isle of Ely, while the second released her from her marriage vows. From then on, she lived on Ely and in 673 founded twin religious communities there, one for Benedictine monks and one for nuns.

Destroyed by the Danes

The abbey was situated on the very same spot that the cathedral occupies today. Etheldreda died in 679 of a throat tumour and was buried in the grounds of the convent. Six years later, her grave was reopened in order to transfer her remains into the church. Her body was found to be "uncorrupt" and the cancerous tumour had miraculously disappeared. At least, this is the version of events related by the Venerable Bede in his *Ecclesiastical history of the English people.*

The convent founded by Etheldreda survived for over two centuries until the invasion by the Danes, who eventually occupied large parts of east and central England. It was during this period that the convent at Ely was destroyed. It was re-founded in 970. The shrine to Etheldreda came to be a place of pilgrimage and remained so for centuries to come. More and more pilgrims visited the shrine, with 23 June and 17 October, the respective dates of her birth and death, being specially commemorated holidays in the cathedral's calendar.

Work on the present building began in the eleventh century under Abbot Simeon and the see was established in 1109. The Reformation put an end to the activities of the monastery. Its very last prior, Robert Steward, became the first Anglican deacon. Reconstruction work was carried out in the eighteenth and nineteenth centuries, with the latest restoration work taking place between 1986 and 2000.

The main entrance is via the west front through the Galilee Porch. Ahead is the impressive vista of the long nave, extending to 249ft (76m), with its painted, boarded ceiling which, it has to be said, is entirely a product of the Victorian era. This feature apart, the interior remains virtually unchanged and is an impressive example of Norman architecture, i.e. the style of Early Gothic architecture popular at the time in Northern France and imported to England by William the Conqueror, featuring ribbed vaults and the emerging buttress system.

The octagonal tower

In 1322, the old central tower collapsed. The cathedral's sacristan, Alan of Walsington, experienced, in his own words, "an extraordinary inspired vision," and, on his initiative, a decision was made to replace the conventional square tower above the crossing with an octagonal construction. At the time and even to this day, this was considered a very innovative undertaking. The tower took six years of extremely complicated building work to complete. The roof took 14 years to finish, the master carpenter in charge being William Hurley, who was also architect to King Edward III. The Octagon has remained unchanged to this day, a consummate example of medieval technology.

The choir, situated beneath the Octagon, was restored at roughly the same time. The choir stalls are richly endowed with carvings, some of which date from the fourteenth century. The shrine of St. Etheldreda stood in the presbytery until its destruction. Since 1973, it has been commemorated by a memorial plaque. At the north end of the transept is the Lady chapel, built during the first half of the fourteenth century, originally decorated with elaborate murals, stained-glass windows, and many statues, most of which were destroyed during the Reformation.

A number of medieval buildings recall the cathedral's monastic history. These are now the administrative headquarters of the see and include an academic establishment, King's School. The people of Ely set great store by the fact that this is one of the oldest established public schools in the world.

The glories of Wells cathedral

The front of this cathedral in the southwest of England is a masterpiece of Early English stonework, adorned with 297 statues

North Sea

GREAT BRITAIN

Wells

ATLANTIC OCEAN · English Channel

GETTING THERE:
By car from London, about 81 miles (130km) west on the M4 to Bristol, south 12 miles (20km) to Wells

WHEN TO GO:
May/June and late summer. Large numbers of tourists in July and August

OPENING TIMES:
Usually 9:00 A.M. – 7:00 P.M. daily, except during services

SPECIAL INTEREST:
The west front with its 297 statues

The city of Wells in the southwest of England is so named because it is sited close to a number of wells or springs. One still bubbles up in the garden of the bishop's palace; another runs under the cathedral cloisters. Towards the end of the Middle Ages, a local church dignitary, Bishop Bekynton, had a comprehensive water system constructed to enable the whole city to be supplied with water from these springs.

Wells is small and has fewer than ten thousand inhabitants. Lying at the foot of the Mendip Hills in the county of Somerset, on the road from Bristol to Cornwall, it has managed to preserve its medieval structure almost unchanged, with venerable gateways, old inns, numerous historic houses, and, right at the heart, the cathedral and the bishop's palace.

Church dating back to 766

There have always been settlements in the area. Excavations in the nineteenth and twentieth centuries uncovered Stone Age tools, Roman pottery, and early Christian burials. There have been numerous finds from early Saxon times, including an interesting group of silver coins from Friedland.

In Anglo-Saxon times, Britain was divided into several kingdoms, most of which were at war with one another. Wells was in Wessex. Work on the first church on this site began in 764, probably on the orders of the local ruler. The buildings must have been extensive and fairly impressive, according to the chronicles and the remains revealed by excavation. The first church was on the site of the present-day cloisters. It is clear that not only the cathedral but also the rest of the settlement was laid out according to a well thought-out plan.

The Norman Conquest

This early cathedral was dedicated to St. Andrew, one of Jesus' twelve disciples, a fisherman from Bethsaida and the brother of Simon Peter. The last Saxon bishop was Gizo (1061-1088). Afterwards, the seat of the diocese was for a time relocated in the neighbor-

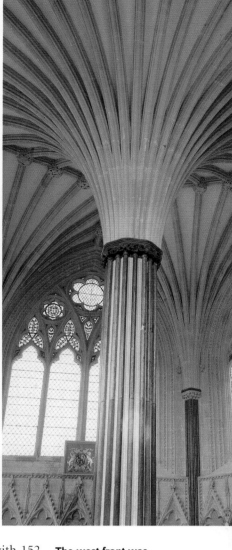

ing city of Bath, and Wells fell into disrepair.

The building of a completely new cathedral on the present site did not begin until more than a century after the Norman Conquest. The Saxon minster was demolished and much of the material from it used in the new building. It was first commissioned by Reginald, a church dignitary of Norman extraction.

Andrew, the patron saint

Other things taken from the abandoned Saxon minster were the name of St. Andrew; a font which is a particularly fine piece of stone carving, its sides decorated with Norman pillars; and the bones of the Saxon bishops, including those of Bishop Gizo, which were transferred from the old minster and reburied here.

The bulk of construction took place in the twelfth and thirteenth centuries, although the towers were not built until two hundred years later. The most important of the bishops responsible for the work were

Jocelyne, John Drokensford, Ralph of Shrewsbury, and Harewell. The most significant of all the bishops of Wells was Bekynton, a highly educated man with a talent for diplomacy. He was tutor to Henry VII, the first Tudor king, and later his Secretary of State. He supervised many colleges in Oxford and Cambridge and arranged for much of the building work in Wells.

Early Gothic art

Many of the architects of Wells are known by name, which is unusual for a time when such people mostly remained anonymous. They include Thomas of Whitney and William Wynford. The latter was quite a famous man, with historical evidence of his involvement with many English churches.

Wynford was responsible for the decoration of parts of the interior in the Early English style that was prevalent at the time; for example, the wonderful ribbed vaulting supporting the towers, the richly decorated capitals, and the impressive triforium. Like many English cathedrals, Wells has a Lady chapel, built before 1326. A staircase leads up to the chapter house, which is in the High Gothic style known as Decorated. It is considered the finest example of its kind.

Colored statues

The most striking and precious part of the cathedral, however, is to be found outside. This is the west front, which was finished in 1239. It is in the Early English style, with many subdivisions, and has row upon row of

stone statues, 297 in total with 152 being life-size.

Such a collection is unique, both in England and abroad. In addition, the statues must be thought of as colored, as they were originally painted in bright red, blue, and gold.

Also worthy of note is the astronomical clock in the north cloister. This was installed in 1392 at the instigation of Bishop Ralph Erghum, who came to Wells from Salisbury cathedral where he had also had such a clock installed. Apparently, he brought his clockmaker with him. The dial and hands show the Ptolemaic planetary system accepted at that time, with the earth at the center and the sun and stars revolving round it. When the clock strikes each quarter hour, jousting knights circle round above it. Clocks of this kind were extremely popular during the High and Late Middle Ages, and can be found from Prague to Roskilde in Denmark.

The west front was completed in 1239. It is a masterpiece of Early English architecture, decorated with no less than 297 statues, some life-size. This splendid, monumental façade has a special place in the history of art (main picture)

Inside the church, the effect is just as striking. View along the nave to the organ (center)

The chapter house, formerly the preserve of the monks, with its decorated supporting pillars (right)

Church of the royal family

Westminster Abbey in **LONDON** is full of history and is the resting-place of the rulers of England

GETTING THERE:
London has several international airports. By train via Eurostar from Paris or Brussels. Ferry connections via Dover and many other ports

OPENING TIMES:
Usually Mon-Fri 9:30 A.M. - 3:45 P.M. Sat 9:30 A.M. - 1:45 P.M. Closed to tourists on Sundays

SPECIAL INTEREST:
The tombs of the kings of England

The west front of the abbey, with its two towers completed in the eighteenth century (main picture)

The coronation of Queen Elizabeth II on 2 June 1953 (below, left)

For overseas visitors to London, what cause of regret might there be for not having been born in England? For many people, there is only one place where such feelings creep up, and that is Westminster Abbey, for nowhere else is there a greater awareness of English history, traditions, and pride than in this great church, which is over a thousand years old. If you attend Sung Eucharist here, you will be personally guided to your seat in the lofty, Neo-Gothic choir stalls, with the service seeming like a huge pageant presenting the unchanging traditions of British life. The Gloria rings out, sung by choirboys in red and white surplices, and Communion is celebrated according to the Anglican rite.

First media coronation

Ever since William the Conqueror took the crown and placed it on his own head in 1066, almost all British monarchs – 37 in total – have been crowned in Westminster Abbey. When Elizabeth II was enthroned in 1953, the ceremony lasted four hours, and it was the first time a coronation had been treated as a media event that could be seen all over the world. Most funeral services for members of the royal family also take place in Westminster Abbey although, since 1760, monarchs have not been buried in the Abbey but at Windsor. Traditionally, the Collegiate Church of St. Peter of Westminster – as the church is officially known – is subject not to the bishop but to the royal house.

The first church, which was part of a monastery, was dedicated to St. Peter. Edward the Confessor, the last Anglo-Saxon king, replaced it with a Romanesque building in 1050, and this in turn was replaced by a Norman church. In 1245, Henry III started an expensive building project – a cathedral in the Gothic style. The choir, the transepts, the crossing, and part of the arches of the nave were built first, in the same style as the cathedrals of Reims and Amiens, though the soft, pale stone from the county of Surrey had its own special radiance.

For a whole century, the Gothic choir remained as an addition to the Norman nave. In 1375, Richard II had this section pulled down, and began the building of a mighty nave. Important changes were brought about in the years between 1503 and 1519 by the addition of the chapels, which were built during the reign of Henry VII and his successors.

Chapels for the kings

Where do you start when visiting this masterpiece, whose filigree west front has already left you stunned and amazed before even entering the building? Inside, once recovered from the first impression of infinity and having allowed your gaze to keep wandering upwards to the flying buttresses, the chapels will beckon. That of Henry VII has a special place among them, as this mausoleum with its lace-like, filigree fan vaulting and high, light windows exudes a great sense of comfort and seems to remove all fear of death. In another of the chapels is the shrine of Edward the Confessor.

At the tomb of Mary Stuart

The tomb in which Elizabeth I (1533-1603) and her half-sister Mary I lie buried – "partners both on the throne and in the grave" as the Latin inscription says – is a particularly impressive work of art. Mary Stuart, the queen of Scotland beheaded under Elizabeth I, also found her last resting-place in Westminster Abbey. Her son James I of England and VI of Scotland had a tomb built for her that was even more splendid than that of her cousin Elizabeth I.

United in death and honored by a memorial tablet in Poets' Corner are many of the writers whose works have carried England's fame around the world. Edmund Spenser, William Shakespeare, Charles Dickens, T. S. Eliot, and Henry James are some of the great names to be found there. And while Poets' Corner is in the south transept, a number of statesmen have their tombs in the north transept. Politicians from Viscount Palmerston to William Ewart Gladstone and Benjamin Disraeli, whose ideas have shaped the history of the world, are gathered together within the abbey.

Westminster Abbey is more than just an open book of English history. With its high, wide nave, stained glass windows, and colorful banners, it is also a house of God, where people come to pray every day – perhaps because they feel just a little bit closer to heaven in this Gothic masterpiece than anywhere else.

View of the nave with its 19th-century choir stalls (right)

The British St. Peter's

St. Paul's cathedral in **LONDON** was modeled on the basilica di San Pietro in Rome

View down the nave of St. Paul's cathedral from the dome end (main picture)

The west façade with its twin Baroque towers and main portal (below, right)

The fountain outside the main entrance is a monument to Queen Anne (below, left)

Even while Sir Christopher Wren was still alive, people were keen to build a monument in his honor, but the architect of St. Paul's cathedral rejected the idea. His son's inscription on a memorial plaque beneath St. Paul's world-famous dome pays tribute to him posthumously, proclaiming: *Lector, Si Monumentum Requiris, Circumspice* (Reader, if you seek his monument, look about you).

What a monument to an architect! And what a monument, too, for the City of London! Not only is the cathedral the bishop's church, but it

also serves as the equivalent of a parish church for the whole Commonwealth. St. Paul's cathedral, England's only example of a Baroque church, dominates the London skyline with charm and grandeur. An exotic beauty blooming in Britain's island kingdom.

The history of St. Paul's dates back to 604, when a church stood on the hill above the present City of London dedicated to London's patron saint, Paul the Apostle. Several buildings replaced the original one, but it was not until 1300, when the new, Gothic-

style cathedral was consecrated, that it began to evolve properly into one of the loveliest and largest churches in existence at that time. Over the centuries, however, even this magnificent church was allowed to fall into a state of disrepair and it was not until the early seventeenth century that a major program of restoration was begun. Work ceased again in 1649 with the advent of the 'Age of the Commonwealth' which followed the beheading of Charles I, and the cathedral was turned into a market and stables. Charles II put the situation right by

engaging Christopher Wren to mastermind the restoration program.

Wren was regarded by his contemporaries as a veritable star in the architectural world. His designs were accepted, only to be totally thwarted by the Great Fire of London in 1666, which destroyed 13,200 homes and 81 parish churches. In view of the serious damage suffered by the cathedral, it was no longer simply a question of restoration, but of complete rebuilding. Once again, Wren was placed in charge of the building works.

He was strongly influenced by the architectural style of the Christian church of Rome. St. Paul's, the only church in England to be crowned with a cupola, is clearly modeled on St. Peter's basilica in Rome.

In 1711, the cathedral was finally consecrated after taking 35 years to build. It measures 558ft (170m) in length and its dome rises to a height of 354ft (108m) above the ground. It is one of England's greatest architectural masterpieces, providing a truly imposing setting for historic events: it was here that the funerals of the Duke of Wellington, Lord Nelson, and of Winston Churchill were held. The end of the Napoleonic Wars was celebrated in St. Paul's, as was the end of World War II.

While Westminster Abbey is the traditional venue for coronations and royal funerals, the royal family prefers St. Paul's cathedral for happier occasions: Queen Victoria celebrated her Diamond Jubilee here and Prince Charles and Lady Diana Spencer were married in 'Britain's own version of St. Peter's basilica', watched by an estimated television audience of 750 million.

Corinthian pillars

The two Baroque towers alone, which flank the main entrance in the west façade, are enough to inspire awe in the visitor, but even more breathtaking is the view that extends down the nave, beneath the great cupola to the choir stalls. There is nothing to impede the sense of vastness, and the 19th-century, Byzantine-style mosaics only serve to intensify the religious atmosphere. The choir is dominated by an altar, added in 1959, which is also a memorial to the 335,451 Commonwealth dead of two world wars. The ceiling frescoes above the choir were redone after their destruction during World War II. The choir also contains the organ which Georg Friedrich Händel used to play until all hours of the night.

It is worth taking the time to sit in the crossing and look up to where the Corinthian pillars, a continuation of eight massive columns, rise up into the cupola. To ensure that the building did not end up resembling a dark funnel, a lower inner cone was inserted beneath the outer dome, creating an usual architectural effect. Inside, the double walls created the so-called Whispering Gallery, whereby the sound of a person whispering is carried right round to the opposite side of the dome.

View across the rooftops

St. Paul's is more than just an architectural treasure, however. Its artistic monuments bear witness to English history. The crypt, the cathedral's burial place, is filled with the tombs of artists, scientists, composers, and even some national heroes such as Lord Nelson, Wellington, and Washington. Florence Nightingale was also buried in the crypt.

For many visitors, the principal attraction is climbing to the top of the dome, even if this means negotiating 530 steps in the process. Passing the Whispering and Stone Galleries, you reach the Golden Gallery, above which rises the delicate lantern. Looking over the rooftops from St. Paul's cathedral at the seething city below will serve to corroborate Christopher Wren's words: "Architecture aims at eternity."

GETTING THERE:
London has several international airports. By car from the continent via Eurostar or one of the frequent ferry links. Rail links from Paris and Brussels

OPENING TIMES:
Mon-Sat 8:30 A.M. – 4:00 P.M., closed Sun. Opening times can change at short notice

SPECIAL INTEREST:
Climbing to the top of the dome is well worth the effort

Where Thomas à Becket died

CANTERBURY was the seat of the Anglo-Saxon kings

On 29 December 1170, the Archbishop of Canterbury, Thomas à Becket, was murdered during Vespers by four knights. This put an end to the yearlong conflict between King Henry II of England and his highest church official. Yet the two men had worked closely together for some time. Becket had previously been Henry's chancellor and his appointment as archbishop was made on the authority of the king. It was generally thought that Henry had ordered the killing. This rumor caused lasting damage to his reputation, even though he was one of the most skillful men to have ruled England in the Middle Ages and many of his governmental measures should indeed be considered exemplary.

The murder of Becket took place in Canterbury cathedral and has provided material for a number of literary writers, notably Jean Anouilh and T. S. Eliot. The setting for the events was the most important church in the kingdom of England, and remained so even after a later monarch, Henry VIII, broke away from the Papacy in Rome because of his complicated marriage negotiations and founded a separate denomination. Canterbury cathedral became the mother church of Anglicanism, and the archbishop in office there became Primate of All England, with a seat in the House of Lords.

Remains dating back to 597

The medieval heart of Canterbury, dominated by the cathedral, is preserved almost intact. The city is ancient, going back to a Roman settlement. Ethelbert, one of the Anglo-Saxon kings, had his royal seat there. In 597, Augustine, a Benedictine monk from Rome later canonized as a saint, who had been sent to England as a missionary by Pope Gregory the Great, founded an abbey at a place then known as Cantwarabrig. The

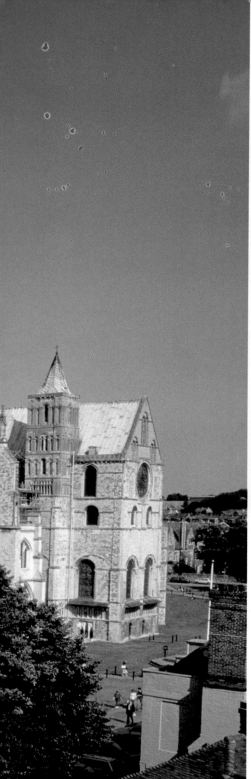

GETTING THERE:
By car from Dover about 12 miles (20 km) along the A2/M2 towards London. Good rail and coach connections from London

WHEN TO GO:
Spring, May/June, and late summer, August/ September. Large crowds of tourists in high summer

OPENING TIMES:
Usually 9:00 A.M. – 6:30 P.M. daily. October-Easter 9:00 A.M. – 5:00 P.M. No admission to tourists during services and prayers

SPECIAL INTEREST:
The tomb of the 'Black Prince'

abbey church formed the embryo of the later cathedral.

The cathedral has burned down and been rebuilt three times in the course of its history. It acquired its present form in the fifteenth century, but the crypt and the choir date from the end of the twelfth century. There are also a large number of other buildings belonging to the cathedral: the archive, a school, a hospital, and, most notably, the offices of the archbishop.

The cathedral's three towers, each one crowned by four spires, rise above them all. The church is 574ft (175m) long, 88ft (27m) wide, and 88ft (27m) high. The nave is an outstanding example of the Perpendicular style, the English version of Late Gothic, which is characterized by closely interwoven fan vaulting. Canterbury cathedral has several special features that set it apart from other sacred buildings in the British Isles; for example, the striking use of round

arches, the work of a French architect. Then there are two staircases leading from the nave to the choir and from the choir to one of the chapels dedicated to the Holy Trinity.

The French were also responsible for some of the windows, including those in the west and south of the building. The stained glass depicts Old Testament prophets, scenes from the life of Christ, and the Blessed Virgin. It is sometimes referred to as 'a Bible for the Poor' (Biblia pauperum).

Where Thomas à Becket died

The marble throne of St. Augustine stands in the Corona chapel at the eastern end of the cathedral, where all the bishops have been enthroned since the thirteenth century. The succession remains unbroken since St. Augustine, despite the change of denomination. A number of important clergymen have held this office, including Odo, Alphege, and Edmund, all three of whom have been canonized. The present primate, Rowan Williams, is number 104.

Becket is still the most famous of them all. The place where he was stabbed to death is now the Martyrs' chapel in front of the northwest transept. Here, there was once a magnificent tomb for him, but Henry VIII had it removed. Other monuments have been preserved, including that of King Henry IV, made famous by Shakespeare's three-part play, who lies buried here with his second wife Joanna of Navarre, and, most notably, the tomb of Edward the Black Prince, eldest son of Edward III. He was one of the outstanding military leaders in the Hundred Years' War, winning the battles of Crécy and Poitiers, but he

died in 1376 before being able to succeed to the throne. His tomb is considered one of the most outstanding creations of medieval art.

The same goes for the crypt, which is generally agreed to be the biggest and most beautiful underground Norman church in England. It extends under the entire surface beneath the choir, has five naves, and is famous for the capitals of its pillars.

The view of the nave with its traditional choir stalls gives an idea of its enormous size. The nave is 574ft (175m) long and rises to a height of 88ft (27m) (above, right)

Thomas à Becket was murdered in Canterbury cathedral by four knights in 1170. This 14th-century Flemish miniature shows the moment of the attack (below, right)

In the sign of the Cross of Lorraine

SALISBURY cathedral boasts the highest church spire in England

GETTING THERE:
Situated about 62 miles (100km) southwest of London, Salisbury has excellent bus and rail links with the capital

OPENING TIMES:
Normal opening hours: 7:15 A.M. to 6:15 P.M. daily (June to August, Mon-Sat until 8:00 P.M.). No admission to tourists during services

SPECIAL INTEREST:
The cathedral library contains one of the original copies of the Magna Carta

This overall view shows the cathedral's distinctive layout with its two pairs of transepts and the tower with its high, pointed spire (main picture)

Its ornate statuary is a special feature of the cathedral, as seen on the west front (below, right)

View of the nave and pillared gallery (below, left)

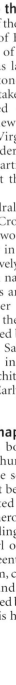

Most English cathedrals dating from the Middle Ages have flat-topped towers, ornamented with nothing more than small Gothic pinnacles at each of the four corners. Westminster, Canterbury, and York all echo this pattern. Salisbury cathedral, however, departs from this design. It has one single tower rising to a great height and tapering to a point, the very epitome of the type of Gothic cathedral church seen in Chartres or Strassburg. The spire gives the impression of a giant finger pointing skyward to where God the Father and the kingdom of heaven await.

The spire of Salisbury cathedral was completed one hundred years after the foundation stone was laid. Rising to a lofty 404ft (123m), it is still the highest church tower and spire in England. The rest of the work on the cathedral took a mere 38 years, an astonishingly short time for such a building project in the Middle Ages. Furthermore, the fact that no fundamental architectural changes or additions were introduced at a later date has resulted in a uniformity and harmony of style that cannot be found elsewhere.

Salisbury is situated in the county of Wiltshire in southern England, to the west of London and halfway between Bristol and Southampton, at the confluence of three rivers: the Avon, Bourne, and Nadder. The landscape which surrounds the city is dominated by water meadows and marsh land.

The history of the town is somewhat complicated: it began as a Roman military camp, then became first a Saxon, then a Norman fortified settlement, known as Old Sarum, During the eleventh century, it had its own bishop. Then, in 1220, for reasons not altogether clear, the town and bishopric were moved down into the valley a little way and work began on the cathedral. All that remains of Old Sarum today are a few ruins, which are open to visitors. From the settlement of New Sarum sprang modern-day Salisbury.

Dedicated to the Virgin Mary

The building of the new cathedral was in the charge of Bishop Osmond, a direct nephew of William the Conqueror. He was later made a saint. Some of the stones used in its construction were taken from the ruins of the abandoned cathedral at Old Sarum. This new church was dedicated to the Virgin Mary and the project got underway with the construction of a particularly sumptuous Lady chapel at the east end of the nave.

The cathedral is designed in the shape of the Cross of Lorraine, in other words, two pairs of transepts with the choir in between. The two aisles are relatively narrow, separated from the main nave by a row of pillars: it features an impressive triforium, or upper gallery of pillars, reminiscent of the type seen in similar Gothic sacred buildings in France and Germany. Salisbury cathedral's architect did, in fact, come from France. The architectural style is English-Norman Early Gothic, known as Early English.

Octagonal chapter house

The cathedral boasts a number of memorable church windows, for example in the southern side aisle. The best is just behind the high altar and was created by Gabriel Loire. There are numerous medieval tombstones, including that of William Longspee, Earl of Salisbury, dating from the thirteenth century. There is an effigy of him, complete with chain mail helmet and shield, lying on a shrine supported by pillars and round arches, with his head turned slightly to one side.

Salisbury differs from most other cathedrals in England in that it did not evolve from an abbey. There was and is no monastery in its immediate vicinity. Adjoining the south aisle is a large cloister, which also leads to the octagonal chapter house; this is acknowledged as being the largest and loveliest in England. It was not built for the monks, however, but for the canons of the cathedral, who enjoyed a very secular lifestyle. Each of them was entitled to his own plot of land within the cathedral precincts, on which he could then build a house. Some of these buildings are to this day occupied by members of the cathedral clergy.

The cathedral has always enjoyed a very open location. The water

meadows extend across the valley like a vast green carpet, allowing an uninterrupted view of this mighty edifice. It is an impressive and breathtaking panorama. John Constable, one of the first and finest in a long line of British landscape painters, immortalized the scene in one of his paintings.

Treasures in the library

Along the east side of the cloister is the library, housing an important and valuable collection of books as well as written documents and illuminated Bibles dating from Anglo-Saxon times.

Salisbury also possesses one of the four existing copies of the original version of the Magna Carta, another being housed in Lincoln cathedral and the other two in the British Library.

The Magna Carta was an agreement concluded somewhat reluctantly in 1215 between King John of England, nicknamed Lackland, and his barons. This document laid down the relationship between the crown and the nobles, guaranteeing certain liberties primarily relating to trade. It regulated the country's system of law and established freedom under that law. From then on, no one was to be deprived of his life, freedom, or property without trial. Supplemented by additional agreements in later years, the Magna Carta established a set of laws still valid to this day and laid down the foundations for democracy in Great Britain.

Church and memorial

DUBLIN cathedral bears the name of St. Patrick - Ireland's biggest religious building is a Church of Ireland cathedral

GETTING THERE:
Many airlines fly to Dublin. By car from England via the ferry from Holyhead

OPENING TIMES:
Usually 9:00 A.M. - 6:00 P.M. daily. Nov-Feb, Sats only until 5:00 P.M. and Suns until 3:00 P.M. No entry to tourists during services

SPECIAL INTEREST:
The Guinness brewery is a must. The original Book of Kells is in the library of Trinity College, Dublin

View of the pulpit and choir stalls. Above the helmets hang swords and banners of the knightly Order of St. Patrick, founded in 1783 (below, left)

Patrick, Latin Patricius, was born in what is now England, the son of a Roman legionary and future priest. As a youth, he was captured by pirates and sold as a slave in Ireland, but managed to escape six years later. He turned to religion and went to Gaul, where he lived in various monasteries. In 432, he was sent to Ireland as a bishop in order to complete the work of his predecessor Palladius. He died in 461 in Armagh in Northern Ireland at the age of 76.

His missionary work is also said to have taken him to Dublin, where he baptized people at a bubbling spring. A wooden church was erected on the site in commemoration. In 1190, it was granted the status of cathedral under its first Anglo-Norman bishop John Comyn, and a new building was also begun which was completed in 1270. At that point, St. Patrick's took on its present form of a cathedral in the Early English style. It was, and still is, the biggest religious building in Ireland. The baptismal spring still runs underground, directly under the walls of the church. The stone that used to cover it is on display inside the cathedral.

The building was carried out in the High Middle Ages, in the reign of John Lackland, the English king who (under pressure from the barons) granted the Magna Carta. Bishop Henry of St. Patrick's was one of those who signed. The tower and a part of the west nave were destroyed by fire in 1362. Eight years later, both had been rebuilt.

Parish church for a time

The separation of the Church of England from Rome under the Tudor king Henry VIII also had an effect on St. Patrick's, where it met with some resistance. The dean, Edward Bassenet, locked his recalcitrant canons in the chapter house until they agreed to it.

The ownership and income of the cathedral were transferred to the crown, and St. Patrick's became impoverished. The images of the saints were destroyed, the building deteriorated, and the roof of the nave fell in. Under Edward VI, the last male Tudor monarch, the cathedral became an ordinary parish church, and part of it was used as a courtroom. Then restoration work began

and for a while St. Patrick's became a Roman Catholic cathedral again.

Since the time of Elizabeth I, St. Patrick's has been irrevocably Anglican. Although Ireland, especially the south, is a predominantly Catholic country, its biggest and most important religious building, officially recognized as a national cathedral, is still dedicated to Anglican Protestantism.

Huguenots – Calvinist religious refugees from France – came to Ireland and were immediately granted permission to hold services in St. Patrick's in their mother tongue. Jonathan Swift, one of the great English writers of the beginning of the age of enlightenment and famous as the author of *Gulliver's Travels*, was a theologian by profession and held the office of Dean of St. Patrick's for 32 years. He died in 1745 and was buried in the cathedral next to his friend Esther Johnson. He wrote his own epitaph, his stone proclaiming him the champion of liberty.

Sponsored by a brewer

During this time, the building continued to decay. Although the roof was renewed at one stage, the Lady chapel was in ruins when Swift was in office. In 1792, services had to be suspended because of the danger of collapse. Once again, the roof had become unsafe and the walls were considerably bowed. Lasting renovations were not begun until the nineteenth century, when they were instigated and paid for by the wealthy Guinness family, the owners of the brewery that produces the famous Irish stout. The cathedral was reopened in February 1865, while the work of restoration continued.

Today, St. Patrick's is both a national monument and a church. The Republic of Ireland is officially bilingual, so the cathedral is also known as Ard-Eaglais Naomh Pádraig. Services are held twice a day; at other times it is full of tourists. The statue of the patron saint and national hero gazes pensively upwards. His symbol is the shamrock, which is said to represent the Trinity and has long been held as the symbol of Ireland.

St. Patrick's cathedral in its present form goes back to the High Middle Ages. The Early English building was begun in 1190 and completed in 1270 (above)

Inside, the view through the choir to the high altar is one of the most impressive in the cathedral (below)

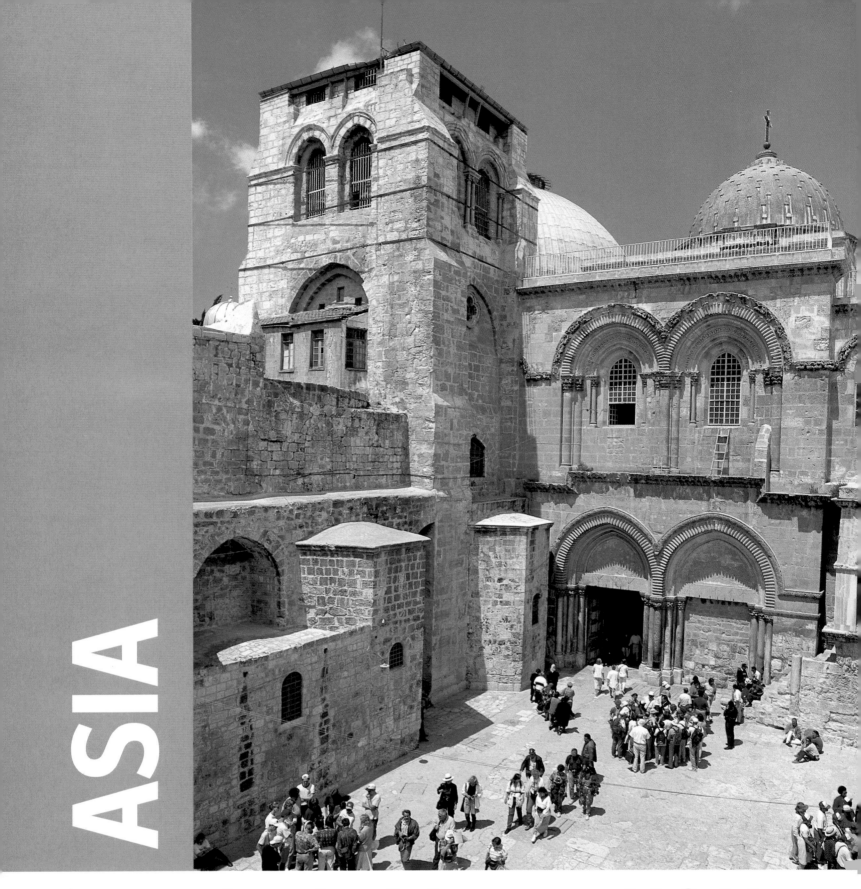

ASIA

Destination of
countless Christian
pilgrims: the entrance
to the church of
the Holy Sepulcher
(above, left)

Church of three world faiths

The church of the Holy Sepulcher in **JERUSALEM** is a holy place
for Christians, Jews, and Muslims alike

"**A**s evening approached, there came a rich man from Arimathea, named Joseph, who had himself become a disciple of Jesus. Going to Pilate, he asked for Jesus' body, and Pilate ordered that it be given to him. Joseph took the body, wrapped it in a clean linen cloth, and placed it in his own new tomb that he had cut out of the rock. He rolled a big stone in front of the entrance to the tomb and went away." This is the story as told in St. Matthew's Gospel.

Christ was sentenced, suffered, and was put to death in Jerusalem, which had been the Jewish capital since its capture by King David. It was also the place where Abraham had once been ready to sacrifice his son Isaac, and the site of King Solomon's temple. Today, it is the seat of government of the state of Israel and a scene of bitter conflict with the Palestinians, who also have a religious claim on this city in the mountains of Judaea, whose Arabic name is Al-Quds. According to tradition, it was from here that the Prophet Mohammed ascended to heaven after his death. The Dome of the Rock, the holiest place for Muslims after the Ka'ba in Mecca, stands on the Temple Mount in Jerusalem's Old Town.

GETTING THERE:
Via Jerusalem
International airport

OPENING TIMES:
Usually 5:30 A.M. –
5:30 P.M. daily

SPECIAL INTEREST:
The whole extent of the
complex and the holy
places around it

The chapel containing
the tomb of Christ, the
last station on the Via
Dolorosa (above, right)

Pilgrims at the Stone of
Unction in the church
of the Holy Sepulcher
(below, right)

The Old Town is divided into a number of districts: Jewish, Armenian, Muslim, and Christian. The Christian Quarter lies in the northwest. In this district is the church of the Holy Sepulcher, built over the tomb of Jesus, the last station on the Via Dolorosa, the Way of the Cross, the road Jesus was made to walk at the end of his earthly life.

Razed by the Romans

The garden and sepulcher of Joseph of Arimathea are a place of pilgrimage and have long been an object of veneration. After the failed Jewish rebellion of Simon Bar Kochba, the victorious Romans razed the Christian places of worship to the ground. A temple to Venus was built over Jesus' tomb. The Emperor Constantine the Great was the first to have a church built on this spot. The heathen temple was demolished, making way for a dome built on columns, adjoining an open courtyard and a basilica with a choir.

The building known as the Anastasis, or Resurrection, was consecrated in 335. It stood for almost three hundred years, until it was destroyed by the Persians in 614. It was then rebuilt but, when Caliph al-Hakim conquered Jerusalem in 1009, he had everything demolished, including the sepulcher.

A new church was consecrated in 1149. Half a century had passed between the conquest of Jerusalem during the first crusade and its completion. The church now encompassed the Hill of Calvary, where Jesus was crucified. The façade and the bell tower have survived, but there have been changes and additions and more are still being made. The Neo-Baroque shrine above the tomb was set up following a fire in 1808. The interior of the Catholic chapel dates from 1937.

Today, the church of the Holy Sepulcher is jointly administered by a total of six Christian communities. Their clergy in their various robes move with dignity amid the throng of countless pilgrims. There are Armenian and Coptic chapels, a Greek choir, and several Catholic sections.

The central point is the tomb of the Redeemer, a chapel in the center of the rotunda. Next to this is the Angel's chapel. According to the gospels, the women who mourned at Jesus' tomb, one of whom was his mother, were told by an angel that Jesus had risen from the dead. As proof, the angel rolled the stone away from the tomb and, lo and behold, the grave was empty.

Up to Golgotha

Hemmed in by other buildings of Jerusalem's Old Town, the church of the Holy Sepulcher also turns out to be a sometimes confusing mixture of very diverse styles and ways of worship. It is a basilica built on a not entirely regular ground plan, with a large number of adjacent buildings leading off it. As well as the impressive dome above the rotunda, the church has a tower. Traces of the original High Romanesque church can be seen in the tower and the façade.

The church contains the grave of Godfrey of Bouillon, the French nobleman who commanded the first crusade, and the grave in which Joseph of Arimathea was buried. Eighteen steps lead up to Golgotha, or Place of the Skull, or Calvary, where Christ was crucified; it is the seventh of the Stations of the Cross. At the eleventh station, where he was nailed to the cross, stands the Catholic chapel.

The Greek Orthodox chapel next to it marks the twelfth station. Here, Christ's cross was set in place. Here, the Redeemer died; in the words of Matthew: "When Jesus had cried out again in a loud voice, he gave up his spirit."

In the spirit of the Jesuits

MANILA cathedral is an important example of ecclesiastical building in Asia

GETTING THERE:
Manila Airport, close to the city

OPENING TIMES:
Usually from 9:00 A.M. daily. No entry to tourists during services and prayer

SPECIAL INTEREST:
The tropical surroundings of the church

The Philippine archipelago comprises seven thousand islands lying between Australia and the Chinese mainland. The population of almost 90 million originates from a variety of ethnic backgrounds. Eighty different languages and dialects are spoken there. The language most frequently used in education is English. Spanish, which was the language of the colonial power prior to their defeat in the Spanish-American war of 1898, has now been superseded.

The Philippines owe their name to the Habsburg King Philip II. The islands were actually discovered by the Portuguese explorer Fernão de Magalhães (better known as Ferdinand Magellan) who died there while in the service of the king of Spain, like the first conquistadors and missionaries who also came from Spain. As a result of this, Roman Catholicism is still the dominant religion in the islands. In the meantime, the English, Dutch, and Japanese have all cast envious eyes on the archipelago, and there are many Chinese among the immigrant population.

The capital, Manila, is named after the nilad, a mangrove plant with white flowers. 'Maynilad' simply means 'where nilad grows'. The city has one-and-a-half million inhabitants and lies on the west coast of the island of Luzon, where the Pasig flows out into Manila Bay. The Pasig river links the sea with a large stretch of inland water, the Laguna de Bay. It

constantly brings down debris and sand, so the coastline is subject to change on a continual basis.

Manila has always been an important port but has not always been the capital. From 1948 to 1976, the neighboring city of Quezon – which has a few thousand more inhabitants than Manila – fulfilled this function. Some ten million people live in the urban agglomeration surrounding the two cities, which also means more than nine million Catholics.

Symbol of the old city

Manila has a cathedral, bearing the name Iglesia de Imaculada Concepcion, whose towers are a conspicuous feature of the old town skyline. It boasts the melancholy record of having been built seven times in the course of its 400-year history.

Work began in 1581. The first church, constructed under the auspices of the Jesuits in the entourage of the conqueror, Miguel López de Legaspi, was made of wood. The building had been standing for no more than a year when it was badly damaged by a typhoon and, in 1583, a huge fire completed its destruction.

The second cathedral was built in 1592, this time of stone. This, too, was severely damaged, by a terrible earthquake in 1600.

In 1614, the construction of the third cathedral was begun. This time, it survived for 31 years. Then there was another earthquake and the cathedral was once again destroyed.

In the Baroque style

Between 1654 and 1671, Bishop Miguel Poblete had the cathedral rebuilt yet again. This time, it was an extremely simple building without any decoration, which displeased the churchfolk because the Iglesia de Imaculada Concepcion was a church built in the spirit of the Jesuits who were in the vanguard of the Counter Reformation. The building style associated with the Counter Reformation was, however, Baroque and they could never have too much dramatic statuary and sumptuous ornamentation, especially when it came to religious architecture.

So, starting in 1750, a new version of the cathedral came into being, incorporating the previous building. The result must have been very impressive and was the object of general admiration. People were truly amazed that such opulent Baroque

architecture could have been created so far from Europe.

In 1863, there was yet another violent earthquake and Manila cathedral was again in ruins. Rebuilding began in 1870, the architect being Vicente Serrano Salaverri. Internationally, it was the age of eclecticism, the unscrupulous plundering of all the European styles of the past. Gothic, in particular, was used for church buildings, which makes it all the more remarkable that Salaverri and his patrons decided in favor of the Romanesque.

Devastated by war

In the meantime, technology used in building had progressed to the extent

View of the cathedral bell tower and cupola (main picture)

The brightly lit high altar under the cupola (below, right) and an area for prayer in one of the side chapels (below, left)

that precautions could be taken against earthquakes. Nevertheless, the newly built cathedral also suffered severe damage, this time not as the result of a natural catastrophe but of war. Japan invaded the Philippines in 1941, and Manila and its cathedral suffered once again from dreadful destruction.

The latter has been restored again in the manner of Vicente Serrano Salaverri, and that is how we see it today – a basilica with a big cupola above the crossing. It is built of light sandstone. The bell tower was originally intended to be free standing but was later integrated into the façade. There are three great doors in a row, the central one being the largest.

The church is surrounded by luxuriant vegetation and the temperatures are tropical. In the midst of this atmosphere of damp and decay, the Iglesia de Imaculada Concepcion, with its borrowed Romanesque style, is surprisingly attractive.

African Anglicanism

Archbishop Desmond Tutu, the campaigner against apartheid and winner of the Nobel Peace Prize, once held office in St. George's cathedral in CAPE TOWN

SOUTH AFRICA
ATLANTIC OCEAN
Cape Town
INDIAN OCEAN

GETTING THERE:
Via Cape Town international airport

OPENING TIMES:
Usually 9:00 A.M. – 5:30 P.M. daily

SPECIAL INTEREST:
Concerts in the cathedral

J. M. Coetzee, one of the most significant South African authors of our time, described the city in which he lives as: "Cape Town – a city rich in beauty, in beauties." The latter is a reference to attractive women and makes the parasitic behavior of the hero of one of his novels clear to the reader. In another of his novels, Coetzee says it even more clearly: "The scavengers of Cape Town, whose number never diminishes. Who walk barefoot and do not feel the cold. Who sleep out and do not fall ill. Who starve but do not fade away."

It is easy to see that the person who speaks these words means the black Africans. They constitute the majority of the population of Cape Town and the rest of the country, but the white minority hold many of the key posts in industry and education. The white population itself is not eth-

nically homogenous but is divided into those of English and Dutch origins. J. M. Coetzee brings the two together in a single person, as he has ancestors from both groups.

The Dutch were the first overseas settlers. In 1652, they landed at the Cape of Good Hope, an essential stop on the sea route to the East Indies. The city became an important port and new immigrants arrived, including French Huguenots, who drove out or subjugated the indigenous Bantus.

At the beginning of the nineteenth century, British colonists arrived and brought slavery to an end, despite the opposition of the Dutch who were then known as Boers and spoke Afrikaans. Conflicts and migrations followed. The British developed a more humane social system, but their behavior was not entirely altruistic. The rich deposits of gold and

diamonds were a significant discovery and, little by little, they took over the whole of South Africa.

Christian influence

Tension between the English and the Boers continued, with the Boers playing the conservative role and the English the liberal. The black majority gradually became aware of their scandalous lack of rights and set up the organization that finally came to be known as the African National Congress. In reaction, the conservative majority of the white upper class came up with the policy of racial separation or apartheid, which brought much cruelty and injustice upon the country. The fact that it ended and Nelson Mandela's government took over relatively peacefully is one of the most remarkable wonders of modern world history.

Christianity, especially Anglicanism, played a considerable part in this. Being the English state church, it was the denomination of the British establishment in the crown colony, but also had influence and followers outside this circle. It is a mistake to assume that Anglicanism only represents an extremely moderate kind of Protestantism invented by Henry VIII and restricted to that part of Great Britain which lies between the Tweed and the English Channel.

Models from central Europe

As a legacy of the former colonial empire, today there are also Anglican communities in North America and Australia. The total membership numbers almost 75 million and, theologically speaking, they have gone far beyond the framework laid down by their founders. Worship is based on the Book of Common Prayer.

Until 1996, the Anglican archbishop of Cape Town, and consequently the head of the Anglican Church in South Africa, was Desmond Mpilo Tutu, a black African. In 1960, at the height of apartheid in South Africa, he was ordained as a priest, becoming a dea-

con in Johannesburg in 1975. This was considered an insult to government policy at the time, and Desmond Tutu only heightened this feeling by continuing to use all the power of his office to support the cause of equal rights for the black population. In 1984, he was awarded the Nobel Peace Prize for his work. With Nelson Mandela, he was the most prominent black civil rights campaigner in South Africa.

His diocesan church in Cape Town was St. George's cathedral. Situated at the intersection of Wallstraat and St. George's Mall, it is an extremely active church, culturally as well as spiritually, staging very popular concerts. It owes its great reputation to Desmond Tutu, and its moral and political significance rank far above its architectural importance.

It was built in 1862 by Herbert Baker, the English-born architect, who was very active in the colonies including India, Kenya, and Rhodesia. He was responsible for the rebuilding

of the Bank of England in London and was knighted in 1926 for his services to art. There are several buildings designed by him in South Africa. One of these, the railway station in the administrative capital Pretoria, caused him to be suspected of having Nazi sympathies because he used a swastika as decoration.

St. George's is built in the Neo-Romanesque style. It looks back not so much to Anglo-Norman as to central European sources. At first glance, it appears to be built of brick; only a closer look reveals that it is actually made of sandstone from Table Mountain, the impressive eminence on the edge of the city.

The nave of St. George's with the high altar and apse (main picture)

View of the façade of the transept (above)

The tomb of Archbishop Francis R. Phelps, d. 1938 (center)

African statue of the Madonna and Child (below)

Restoration work: the main façade with its tower encased in scaffolding (above)

An unfinished temple

Work still continues on the Neo-Gothic cathedral of St. John the Divine in **NEW YORK** after 110 years

St. John the Divine is situated in Manhattan on Amsterdam Avenue between 112th and 110th Street West. Subway lines 1 and 9 will take you right there. "You can't miss it," say the guidebooks. It is, after all, one of the largest cathedrals in the world and certainly the largest Neo-Gothic one, its size surpassing even

the Duomo in Milan which can accommodate a congregation of around 40,000.

Milan cathedral is obviously older, given that the USA is a young country and New York is a city in a continual process of regeneration. St. John, which looks back on 100 years of history, is regarded as one of the

country's most important historic monuments.

Its story began on 27 December 1892, St. John's Day, when Bishop Cosman Henry Potter laid the foundation stone. Prior to this, however, an appropriate building plot had to be bought. The area selected was an elevated piece of woodland surrounding

New York • USA

PACIFIC OCEAN

ATLANTIC OCEAN

GETTING THERE:
International flights to New York

OPENING TIMES:
Usually Mon-Sat
7:00 A.M. – 6:00 P.M.,
Sun 7:00 A.M. – 7:00 P.M.;
Sun to 6:00 P.M. only
in July and August

SPECIAL INTEREST:
The triptych by Keith Haring

an orphanage, for sale at a price of $850,000. A sponsorship program had been started in 1888, and one of the main contributors was John Pierpont Morgan, a fabulously wealthy banker and railway magnate, who donated half a million dollars.

The original plan was for a Neo-Romanesque construction in the Byzantine style, a design conceived by the architects Heins & Lafargue. By 1911, Rafael Guastavino, who was then in charge of the project, had completed the choir and apse, using brick as the building material.

Pearl Harbor brings work to a halt

Another architect then entered the scene. He was a Bostonian by the name of Ralph Adam Cram, a disciple of European Gothic. He altered the original designs accordingly, including the dimensions, increasing the size of the building by 20 percent. Newspapers added their voice to the campaign for sponsors to help finance construction work. A model of the cathedral was displayed in Grand Central Station in 1921.

World War I and economic depression hampered building progress, but did not stop it altogether. The nave was completed, with a dedica-

tion ceremony held on 30 November 1941. Precisely one week later, the Japanese attacked Pearl Harbor, precipitating the USA's entry into World War II. Building work on the cathedral of St. John the Divine came to a halt for 32 years.

In 1972, a decision was made to resurrect the project, although nothing actually happened until 1982. By this time, the USA no longer had the necessary craftsmen available and they had to be brought over from England. The two towers were tackled next. Then followed the recession of the 90s and work stopped once again. Ed Koch, New York's mayor at the time, made the comment that cathedrals in the Old Country had taken 500 years to build, so St. John's was not doing too badly at all. An international competition was held in 1988 to find a design for the Portal of Paradise; the commission was won by sculptor Simon Verity.

Two-thirds of the cathedral is now finished. It is predominantly Neo-Gothic in design, a style much favored in ecclesiastical architecture towards the end of the nineteenth century. St. John the Divine would be one of dozens of similar edifices in this respect were it not for its staggering dimensions: its size is equivalent to

that of two football pitches, and its volume equals that of Notre-Dame in Paris and Chartres cathedral put together.

Size is everything. The statues are up to six meters in height, most of them depicting familiar figures from the Bible: the Four Apostles; the Old Testament prophets Isaiah, Jeremiah, Daniel, and Ezekiel. Others represent Christopher Columbus, William Shakespeare, George Washington, and Abraham Lincoln, in honor of the secular as well as the sacred.

From the sacred to the secular

What we are seeing here is more an indication of Anglo-Saxon American identity expressing itself. Distinction is revered. The cathedral contains numerous examples of this commemoration of achievements or situations that might otherwise be considered rather more temporal in nature: for example, in the Sports chapel, where stained glass windows pay tribute to heroes of football, soccer, and baseball, and in Poets' Corner, modeled on Westminster Abbey.

In the Doctors' chapel, an altar is dedicated to people who have died of AIDS. This is particularly poignant because of what could be said to be the most interesting work of art in St. John the Divine: a triptych by New York graffiti artist Keith Haring, who later succumbed to AIDS himself.

The incumbent bishop of the cathedral is a Protestant. This does not deter him from welcoming Mormons, Catholics, Buddhists, Indians, and Jews into his church. The first Sunday in October is a really special day at St. John's: around 6000 people congregate with their assorted dogs, cats, canaries, and goldfish. In commemoration of St. Francis of Assisi, St. John the Divine holds a service to bless people's pets. Rumor has it that an elephant once turned up.

View of the main nave and altar (above)

Damaged Gobelin rescued after a fire (center)

Detail of the Portal of Paradise (below)

Surrounded by skyscrapers

St. Patrick's cathedral in New York was built in the nineteenth century and is the seat of the archbishop of **NEW YORK**

GETTING THERE:
Flights to the city's international airports. St. Patrick's cathedral is on Fifth Avenue, at the corner of 50th Street

OPENING TIMES:
Usually 7:00 A.M. - 9:00 P.M. daily, Sat 8:00 A.M. - 9:00 P.M. No admission to tourists during services

SPECIAL INTEREST:
St. Patrick's Day procession (17 March)

Raising the Stars and Stripes. View of the cathedral's main portal and twin towers (main picture)

Holy Mass at St. Patrick's. View down the main nave towards the altar (below, left)

Despite its high towers, the cathedral is almost dwarfed by the modern skyscrapers that surround it (below, right)

New York City is made up of five districts. The most famous of these is Manhattan, a spear-shaped island in the mouth of the Hudson River. Land here is obviously at a premium, and the only possible way to accommodate more apartments and business space was to build upwards, turning Manhattan into a district of skyscrapers. The city's street plan resembles the layout of a chess board. Avenues run in a north to south direction and are intersected at right angles by streets.

St. Patrick's cathedral, New York's most important Catholic church, stands on Fifth Avenue between 50th and 51st Street. It is the cathedral church of the Catholic bishop of New York. Its immediate neighbors are the Empire State Building, Saks department store, the Waldorf Astoria Hotel, and Radio City Music Hall.

When it was first built, St. Patrick's was situated on what was then open land some distance from the city center. Today, Midtown Manhattan is one of the most expensive districts in what is already a very expensive city.

Construction work on St. Patrick's began in 1859 under the direction of the incumbent Archbishop, John Hughes. Work proceeded apace until it was halted by the Civil War. The nave was completed in 1879 and the two towers were raised in 1888. The Lady chapel was not begun until 1901 and extensive renovation work was undertaken between 1927 and 1931. Many of the stained glass windows were not added until even later.

The cathedral architect was James Renwick. He was born in 1818 into an affluent New York family. Although he had begun by studying engineering, he soon made a name for himself as one of the most renowned and sought after architects in 19th-century America.

His first sacred building in New York was the Grace church built in 1843. Three years later, he submitted the design for the famous Smithsonian Institution in Washington DC. He designed buildings for Vassar College, America's expensive girls' boarding school for the rich and famous, as well as for the New York Stock Exchange. New York city library is also his work. He liked to replicate the great architectural styles of Europe, especially the medieval, and was no different, in this respect, to the majority of contemporary architects. He died, a greatly admired architect, in 1895.

Room for 2200 worshippers

St. Patrick's cathedral is regarded as Renwick's finest architectural masterpiece, executed with the help of his able assistant William Rodrique. The chapel of Our Lady was a later addition by Charles Mathews. The cathedral has the same great lofty ceilings as the medieval cathedrals of central Europe such as Reims, Amiens, and Cologne, not to mention those in England with Westminster, Exeter, and York topping the list. As a result of these influences, Renwick created a spacious basilica with five aisles, two high towers, and a rose window. The well of the cathedral can accommodate a congregation of 2200.

There are three organs and one main altar, sponsored by the firm of Louis Comfort Tiffany, the famous glassware and jewelry manufacturer. The crypt contains the tombs of New York's archbishops. In 1893, the Stations of the Cross were singled out for an award at the World Fair in Chicago. It is a source of great local pride that the Pietà is three times as big as the one by Michelangelo in St. Peter's basilica in Rome

The Irish aristocrats of New York

The cathedral is dedicated to the apostle of Ireland, St. Patrick, with the Irish population constituting the oldest of the numerous, non-Protestant ethnic groups in New York City. When planning and building work first started, the Irish enjoyed something akin to a Catholic monopoly. The situation changed somewhat during the second half of the nineteenth century in the wake of a huge influx of immigrants into New York. The town consequently acquired a large Italian community and later, during the twentieth century, a Catholic, Puerto Rican ethnic group. All of them maintained their own churches and priests who spoke their respective languages. The Irish regarded themselves as the aristocrats of this New York melting-pot, all the more since one of their key chosen professions was the police force, which also gave them a certain amount of authority.

St. Patrick's Day is a perfect opportunity to express this sense of Irishness. It is an annual event celebrated on 17 March, the Feast Day of St. Patrick. Like other major ethnic rallies in New York, it takes the form of a parade. The first one was held in 1776, organized by Civil War soldiers of Irish descent.

Today, the parade goes along Fifth Avenue, from 44th Street by St. Patrick's cathedral to 86th Street, on the far side of Central Park, with musical accompaniment provided by bagpipe players. The participants usually number around 150,000, many of them dressed in green in tribute to Ireland's reputation for being such a green island and because folk back in Ireland traditionally wear a sprig of green shamrock to mark this special day. It is supposed to be a commemoration of the Holy Trinity but, in New York at least, St. Patrick's Day has become the focus of wider celebrations.

Trinity church – Boston's pride

This Neo-Romanesque cathedral is one of the USA's finest architectural masterpieces

In 1870, the Reverend Phillips Brooks, minister of Trinity church, conceived the idea of relocating it from its position on Summer Street in the city center to Copley Square on Back Bay. Consequently, in 1872, architects were invited to take part in a competition.

Most of the plans submitted reflected the Neo-Gothic style popular at the time. The winning design, however, was for a Neo-Romanesque structure, proposed by Henry Hobson Richardson, who modeled his work on the early churches of southern France. Richardson had already gained a national reputation for himself with his design for a similar style of building in Chicago – not a church, in this case, but a department store. The store no longer exists but his distinctive architectural style became known throughout the art world as Richardson Romanesque.

Mr. Brooks' decision to build a new church proved to be a wise one for, later that year, the old Trinity church was gutted by a major fire that swept through Boston. Construction of the new church took over five years. It was built of granite from Dedham and red sandstone from Longmeadow, both in Massachusetts. The surface of the roughly-hewn granite has a light-gray sheen to it.

The great fire of 1872
The ground plan of Boston's Trinity church is in the shape of a Latin cross. It has a broad, solid tower and tiled roofs, which Richardson modeled on those he had seen in the south of France. The interior includes some evidence of Byzantine influence. The paintings are by John La Farge, who also created some of the stained glass windows. The Trinity church of Boston is reputed to be one of the most important buildings in the USA and, as such, was deservedly listed as a National Historic Landmark in 1971.

The ceremonial consecration of this new church took place on 9 February 1877 and provided a platform for commemorating the relatively long history of the community itself. Its origins go back to 1733. There were two earlier church buildings, the first dating from 1735 and the second from 1828, the latter being consumed by flames in 1872.

Trinity church is an evangelical Episcopal church, observing the theological traditions of Anglicanism. It is worth remembering that the first white settlers in North America, at least those from England, were nearly all Protestants. They brought their various evangelical religions with them to the New World and occasionally developed new ones. There are an estimated 200 different Christian churches, religious communities, and sects in the USA today.

Independence from Canterbury
Massachusetts was settled primarily by Puritans, followers of John Calvin of Geneva and John Knox from Edinburgh. Members of the established Church of England, created by Henry VIII, the Tudor king, tended to gravitate further south towards Pennsylvania.

Anglicanism has undergone many changes throughout its existence. An example of this is the Episcopal church, which was expressly sanctioned by the English king, William III of Orange. It grew steadily in influence and attracted more and more members, many of whom lived in New England. After the Declaration of Independence in 1776, it finally severed its ties with the mother country and threw off the authority of the See of Canterbury. Its representatives sat in the Philadelphia Assembly, where they declared themselves an independent religious body.

Nowadays, the Protestant Episcopal church is the most distinguished, conservative, and, in all probability, the wealthiest of all evangelical churches in the USA. The number of Trinity institutions alone, with their churches, schools, and hospitals, runs into thousands.

Boston is an appropriate location for a Trinity church. It is the acknowledged capital of New England and a focal point for the East Coast upper class known as WASPS (White, Anglo-Saxon Protestants).

Protest against slavery
Bostonians are distinguished and cultured; they have an appreciation of the arts and a strong sense of tradition. The city is also home to one of America's élite universities – Harvard. The famous Tea Party of 1773 took place in Boston harbor and represented a mass protest by the colonists against the British import tax on tea. It was one of the incidents leading directly to the War of Independence. Boston was also the first city to establish a church exclusively for black people and where, thanks to the Abolitionists, anti-slavery protests first began to assume political dimensions. One of the fundamental tenets of the Christian faith is that all men are equal in the eyes of God, a principle that is preached every Sunday in Boston's Copley Square.

GETTING THERE:
Boston's international airport has connections worldwide. By rail from New York (Amtrak Express) or by highway

OPENING TIMES:
Usually 10:00 A.M. - 8:00 P.M., closed to visitors Sunday morning

SPECIAL INTEREST:
The stained glass window within the cathedral and various details echoing Byzantine church architecture

Trinity church stands proudly cheek by jowl alongside modern glass skyscrapers in the center of Boston. Its architectural style has become known as 'Richardson Romanesque' (main picture)

Many of the services in Boston cathedral are held in the small side chapels (below)

GETTING THERE:
Via New Orleans international airport

OPENING TIMES:
Mon-Sat 9:00 A.M. – 5:00 P.M. Sun 1:30 P.M. – 5:00 P.M. Subject to change at short notice

SPECIAL INTEREST:
The hustle and bustle in Jackson Square, in front of the cathedral

Southern classicism

The cathedral of St. Louis, **NEW ORLEANS**, is a center of Catholicism in the USA

New Orleans is a magical place. It retains the degenerate splendor of the southern states that were defeated in the Civil War and whose architectural legacy is to be found in the old part of town, known as the Vieux Carré or French Quarter. Only the names are French, however. By contrast, the architecture of the houses tends more towards the Spanish colonial style. Furthermore, jazz originated in what was once the old town brothel district of Storeyville.

As its name suggests, the French founded New Orleans. The entire state of Louisiana in which it lies, including the modern administrative center of Baton Rouge, was a French colony from 1711, and to this day French is spoken here in the remote Cajun settlements. When part of Louisiana briefly became a Spanish possession, the city was ruled from Madrid. The French returned when the inhabitants rebelled; then, in 1812, Napoleon sold Louisiana to the United States. In 1815, a British attempt to capture the city failed. The American military leader was Andrew Jackson, an enthusiastic slave owner and killer of Indians, later to become the seventh President of the United States.

Hispano-French origins
The central square in New Orleans is named after Jackson. Jackson Square is laid out on a quadrangular ground plan, somewhat similar to the Place Vendôme in Paris and also the Place

Stanislas in Nancy. It lies close to the bank of the Mississippi and, for many years, provided a welcoming backdrop for those arriving at the city on one of the Mississippi paddle steamers.

Jackson Square has been used as both a parade ground and fairground. It is the site of the Cabildo, historically and architecturally the city's most important monument – a public building in the style of a classic French château and now a museum. It was once the seat of the Spanish colonial administration and, in 1803, its Sala Capitular was the scene of the ceding of Spanish Louisiana to the French, followed shortly afterwards by the transfer of French Louisiana to the USA. A few yards further on is the Presbytère, which is similar in style to the Cabildo and used to be the priests' lodgings. More recently, it has been used as a courthouse and now houses the Museum of the Mardi Gras, the New Orleans carnival.

Dedicated to St. Louis
Chartres Street, in which these two buildings stand, closes off Jackson Square to the north. Between the Cabildo and the Presbytère stands a church, the oldest in the city. It has nothing in common with the Gothic cathedral of Chartres in France, however, being built in the style of Hispano-French classicism.

It is the third religious building to stand on this site. The first was erected in 1720 as a place of prayer and the second burned down in a major fire in 1788. St. Louis, to whom the church is dedicated, was the ninth king of that name to sit on the throne of France. He took part in the second crusade, and was a patron of Christian religious communities and also of the University of Paris under its founder, Canon Robert de Sorbon.

The present cathedral of St. Louis was completed in 1794. There are unmistakable echoes of the French style of the period, although most of the money came from a Spaniard, Don Andres Almonster y Roxas, an immigrant lawyer from Andalusia who eventually became the richest man in the whole of New Orleans.

Greek revival
The cathedral is built of the white sandstone that is to be found on the façades of the Cabila and the Presbytère, with smooth, Doric columns likewise subdividing its front. This North American predilection for

The cathedral towers are most impressive when seen against the backdrop of the city skyscrapers (below)

adopting elements from ancient temples is known as 'Greek revival'. Many manor houses in the southern states are also decorated in this way.

In the case of the church, the columns are in three rows, one on top of the other. At ground level, they stand either side of the entrance; on the floor above, they flank two windows; finally, on the next one up, they frame the clock. The church has three

low towers, each surmounted by a dark-roofed steeple. Two of these towers stand on either side of the façade, while the third and highest stands above the center of the roof.

In keeping with its colonial tradition, New Orleans is an overwhelmingly Catholic city, the only one among the big cities of the USA. Catholicism can at times be seen to exhibit a certain tolerance regarding the sins of the flesh, which brings it into conflict with the puritan Protestantism of much of the remaining country. The Mardi Gras became possible, but so did prostitution. There were once 230 brothels flourishing in the Vieux Carré alone.

Nowadays, there are not so many. The whole French quarter is much more a hotbed of sightseeing. The open area in front of the cathedral is thronged with street musicians, clowns, jugglers, fortune-tellers, and pavement artists for the edification and amusement of the tourists. Immortalized in a monument on the church door, a bronze General Andrew Jackson gallops past, fighting for slavery and the fatherland.

The pale sandstone and three dark towers of the cathedral of St. Louis contrast starkly with each other. In front of the church door is the best-known square in the city (main picture)

In the French Baroque style

Notre-Dame cathedral in **QUÉBEC** is the most important church for Catholicism in Canada

CANADA
Quebec

PACIFIC
OCEAN

ATLANTIC
OCEAN

GETTING THERE:
Via Québec international airport. Good motorway connections from the USA

OPENING TIMES:
Usually October-April Mon-Fri 7:00 A.M. – 4:00 P.M., Sat 8:00 A.M. – 6:00 P.M., Sun 8:00 A.M. – 5:00 P.M. May-September 7:00 A.M. – 3:30 P.M. No admission for tourists during services

SPECIAL INTEREST:
The three church organs and crypt with the bishops' tombs

Québec means 'river narrows'. The word comes from the language of the Algonquin, a tribe of North American Indians, and the river in question is the St. Lawrence. The province of Québec in the east of Canada has its administrative center in the city of the same name. The majority of the inhabitants are French-speaking, as it was once a colony ruled from Paris known as Nouvelle-France (New France).

The area was discovered by the explorer Jacques Cartier in 1534. Three-quarters of a century later, another Frenchman, Samuel de Champlain, took possession of it for his homeland. He founded a trading station, which later became the city of Québec. The first European settlers lived by fur trading and their relations with the native Indians were extremely friendly, although there was bitter feuding between the tribes themselves. The arch-politicians of French absolutism, Richelieu and Colbert, ordered the agricultural development of Québec and elevated the province to the status of a French crown colony.

It soon became coveted by the British, who allied themselves with parts of the native population. A series of military raids followed, most of which were successfully repulsed, until Québec fell to England in the Franco-British conflict of 1763. It then remained a British colony until the creation of modern Canada in 1867. Québec was one of the founding provinces. In the twentieth century, the Francophone question and the particular cultural awareness of the people of Québec led to attempts to gain independence. These were settled peacefully, but tensions persist.

The city of Québec is still an important port. It is prosperous, with a center that is very old and very French. The streets are narrow, with pretty houses and friendly taverns. There are two traditional Catholic churches, both named after the Virgin Mary. The bigger and slightly younger of the two bears the official name of Basilique-Cathédrale Notre-Dame de Québec.

Rebuilt after 1647

As long ago as 1633, Champlain, the founder of the city, decreed that a church should be built. He named it Notre-Dame-de-Recouvrance and it stood on almost exactly the same spot as the present cathedral. After seven years, it was destroyed by fire. Rebuilding began in 1647. The church was now called Notre-Dame-de-Paix and, three years later, the first High Mass was celebrated there.

In 1659, François de Laval arrived in Québec. He was the scion of a noble family, a Jesuit, and had been sent out to take office as the apostolic priest for the whole of Nouvelle-France. Notre-Dame, his diocesan church, had to be radically extended in keeping with its enhanced status.

Work began in 1674, directed by the architect Claude Baillif. By 1697, the new façade was up, with the cathedral being further extended between 1744 and 1749 under the direction of Gaspard Chaussegros de Léry.

Ten years on, the cathedral was badly damaged during the siege of Québec, in the war between the French and the British. Rebuilding began in1766 and was carried out according to the old plans. This time, the man responsible was Jean Baillairgé, a French architect who had emigrated to Canada. He and his descendants determined the architectural fate of the cathedral of Notre-Dame for the next 150 years.

The Baillairgés made the cathedral of Notre-Dame into a church in the spirit of French Baroque and Classicism. This is the impression it still gives today, although changes to the building have continued over the years as when, for example, it burned down to its foundations in 1922.

As before, old plans were kept to in rebuilding the cathedral, and it was ready for use again by 1925. Since 1966, it has enjoyed protection as a historical monument. As long ago as 1874, it was given the title of 'basilica minor', a particularly important church outside Rome.

Classical exterior

The outside of the church exhibits a noble, restrained façade in the Classical style. Of the two towers, one has remained a stump, while the other has a Baroque top. In contrast to the severe exterior, the colorful Baroque interior is a surprise, although it adheres to the French tradition in being less exuberant than Italian examples of the genre. There are a number of chapels, the most magnificent of which is dedicated to St. Louis, the king of France who took part in the sixth crusade and died in North Africa.

In the chapel of St. Louis is an organ. Including this one, the Notre-Dame-de-Québec has three such instruments of which people are very proud. The bishops of Québec are buried in the crypt, as well as governors and two of the cathedral architects – Gaspard Chaussegros de Léry and Thomas Baillairgé. That the latter two in particular have found their last resting place here is a pleasing show of respect for art.

Holy Mass is celebrated in Notre-Dame. The furnishings of the diocesan church are continually being renewed but, so far, the French Baroque ornamentation has been retained (main picture)

With its dissimilar towers, the church is a particularly impressive example of Classicism and Baroque (below)

A Jesuit cathedral

HAVANA'S largest church dates from the Late Spanish Baroque period. Columbus was once buried here

ATLANTIC
OCEAN

Gulf of
Mexico • Havana

CUBA

PACIFIC
OCEAN

GETTING THERE:
Flights to Havana's
international airport

OPENING TIMES:
Usually open all day

SPECIAL INTEREST:
Sculptures by the
Italian artist Branchini

Christopher Columbus, an Italian-born seafarer and explorer, nurtured a lifelong ambition to discover a western sea route to India, but landed in the Caribbean instead of Asia. The island where he first weighed anchor is now known as Cuba. Since Columbus' voyages were sponsored by Madrid, virtually all this newly discovered part of the globe ended up under Spanish rule; the indigenous Indian population was routed and decimated, or, as in the case of Cuba, wiped out. Slaves were shipped over from Africa in order to provide a labor force for the new plantations.

The first significant conquistador to arrive in Cuba was Diego Velásquez de Cuéllar. He built several important harbors on the island's west coast, one of which is the city known today as Havana. French, Dutch, and British invaders all cast an acquisitive eye in

Havana's direction. It was not until the Spanish-American war of 1898 that Cuba finally gained its long coveted independence. After this, the island was ruled by a series of autocratic governments until the advent of Fidel Castro, who, in contrast to his predecessors, commands a left-wing socialist regime.

Havana has been a capital city since 1552 and today is a metropolis of two million people. The Old Town, la Habana Vieja, is a labyrinth of narrow winding streets and lovely, old, Spanish colonial-style houses with elaborately decorated balconies. Although the general decline in the fortunes of socialism has inevitably left its mark, Old Havana still has an atmosphere all of its own and is well worth preserving. It is hardly surprising that it has been placed on UNESCO'S World Heritage List. Its historical architectural treasures

include the Castillo de la Real Fuerza, once the seat of Spanish governors, as well as the Palacio del Segundo Cabo, which once formed the administrative headquarters of the Spanish military. The church of San Francisco, built in 1575, now houses a post office, while the Baroque monastery of Santa Clara, younger by just 70 years, is now the Cuban Ministry of Labor.

Built between 1748 and 1777

Not all Cuba's sacred buildings have been deprived of their religious function in this way, however. One of the loveliest plazas in the Old Town is the Plaza de la Catedral, a cobbled open square which attracts a multitude of different stalls selling everything from local crafts to second-hand items and cheap bric-a-brac in return for US dollars. The square is surrounded by several magnificent examples of

status of a principal church, a rank which until then had been held by the church in the Plaza de Armas, next to the royal Castillo.

The cathedral is a relatively flat construction, boasting a richly carved Baroque façade with undulating gables and a double row of projecting pillars, one above the other. To the left and right are two towers, one of which is clearly bigger and sturdier than the other.

Splendor within

The cathedral is built of white limestone and its roof covered with red tiles. The exterior walls have a rather shabby and dilapidated appearance and it is a much simpler building than some of the Baroque churches in Spain. Its unusual style is common to the majority of sacred buildings in the former Spanish and Portuguese colonies of the New World.

What the cathedral lacks in Baroque splendor on the outside is more than compensated for on the inside. The main altar is adorned with mosaics of gold, silver, and onyx, above which stands a figure of the Virgin Mary. There are wall paintings by a French artist by the name of Vermay, while most of the sculptures were carved by the Italian, Branchini. Following the Revolution led by Fidel Castro, many of the cathedral's ecclesiastical treasures were spirited out of the country and are now stored in the Vatican.

For well over a century, Havana cathedral was also home to the tomb of Christopher Columbus. In 1898, following the overthrow of Spanish colonial rule, the explorer's bones were returned to the Old World, where they were laid to rest in Seville cathedral.

The cathedral's main façade with its asymetrical towers, as seen from the Plaza de la Catedral (main picture)

View of Vermay's frescoes in a section of the ceiling vaulting (above)

The central nave and main altar (below)

colonial palaces with their lovely balconies, one of which now houses the Colonial Museum. The plaza is dominated by the cathedral, after which it is named.

The Late Baroque catedral de la Habana was built between 1748 and 1777 by the Jesuits, who exerted a unique and extremely positive influence in Latin America. In the Old World, this Order saw itself as a spearhead of the Counter Reformation movement, and was eventually banished on account of real or imagined scheming and intriguing on the part of its members. In the New World, however, the Jesuits built up a good relationship with the indigenous population, noting their language and trying to protect their human rights, in stark contrast to the harshness and arrogance displayed by the newly settled Spanish-Portuguese ruling classes. The Order was also eventually banned in Latin America, however. The edict issued in 1773 by Pope Clemens XIV brooked no exceptions. This brought the ongoing work on Havana cathedral to a halt for quite some time.

It was not until the King of Spain's intervention in 1789 that construction work resumed. That same year, the new cathedral was awarded the

A triumph of Christianity

The cathedral in **MEXICO CITY** was built from the rubble of the Aztecs' holiest shrine

GETTING THERE:
Flights to the city's international airport

OPENING TIMES:
Usually open all day

SPECIAL INTEREST:
The superb choir stalls

With a population approaching ten million, and a further twenty million in the surrounding region, the Ciudad de México is one of the largest conurbations in the world. Situated 7349ft (2240m) above sea level, it is one of the world's highest capital cities, and certainly the oldest city in the New World. Its origins date back to pre-Columbian times.

The Aztecs founded the city of Tenochtitlán in 1326. When the Spaniards arrived, a quarter of a million people lived there. It was built on an island in the center of Lake Texcoco. At the heart of the city was their holiest shrine, a double pyramid dedicated to Huitzilopochtli and Tláloc, who are the Aztec gods of weather and war.

"This city is so vast and beautiful that it is impossible to say even half of what I could say about it. And even that is almost unbelievable, but it really is even lovelier than Granada." These words were written to the Spanish king by the man who was the first European to set foot on Mexican soil and who would stop at nothing in his determination to capture and destroy Tenochtitlán.

His name was Hernán Cortés, a Spanish conquistador in the service of Philip II. He had studied law at Salamanca University before deciding to seek his fortune in the New World. He

began by attaching himself to the conquistador Diego de Velásquez, and later become mayor of Santiago de Cuba for a time, until Velásquez invited him to lead an expedition to Mexico.

Cortés and his soldiers landed on the coast of Yucatán in March 1519. By late fall of the same year, he had reached Tenochtitlán. He conducted diplomatic negotiations with the Aztec ruler, Moctezuma, and eventually, after various clashes and bitter fighting, he managed to capture the city. He burned the buildings to the ground and inflicted a terrible bloodbath on the inhabitants. A new town was built from the ruins of the old. Stones from the rubble of the destroyed temple pyramids served as building material for the new church. The lake, which surrounded the town, was drained and is now a valley basin in the mountains.

Construction from 1525

For several centuries, Mexico City was the administrative center for all Spain's colonies in America north of Costa Rica. It was not until 1821, following eleven years of war to gain independence, that Mexico was able to free itself of Spanish colonial rule and form its own state. The Ciudad de México is the seat of the country's president and national administration. One quarter of the entire population lives in or around Mexico City.

The Catedral Metropolitana is situated in the Zócalo, also called the Plaza de la Constitución, a large, open square in the heart of the city. It is one of the largest public plazas in the world and is surrounded by impressive old colonial palaces.

The cathedral, however, eclipses all of them, by virtue of its sheer size alone. It is 328ft (100m) in length and rises to a height of 197ft (60m). It claims to be the largest colonial cathedral in the Americas, a title for which it can compete with St. John the Divine in New York City. Building began in 1525 at the instigation of Hernán Cortés.

The church was erected using stones from the rubble of the Aztec Templo Mayor. The reasons for this were not purely practical ones: it was intended as a conspicuous symbol of the Christian Trinity's triumph over pagan gods. Construction work continued until 1532, with large sections of the church being built of wood. Spiritual matters were placed in the

hands of monks of the Franciscan Order.

On shaky ground

King Philip II of Spain declared himself dissatisfied with the building plans and all work came to a halt. He felt the church was much too small, and he did not want the portal facing west. Building had to begin again from scratch. The foundation walls already in place had to be integrated into the southwest section of the atrium. It seems that work did not resume until 1573, possibly even later. By this time, Cortés

had long since been recalled home from Mexico, where he died in 1547 on his estate near Seville.

As mentioned earlier, the island on which Mexico City originally stood was marsh land. The massive weight of the cathedral caused parts of the building, together with its 14 side chapels, to sink into the soft subsoil. Measures had to be found to stabilize the building, but even these could not entirely stop the gradual settling process. Even though the ground water level is now a long way below the surface, the soil is still soft and the

cathedral threatens to continue sinking. All kinds of braces and scaffolding have been erected inside the building to slow down the subsidence. These detract somewhat from the view of the magnificent choir, designed by Juan de Rojas, and the altar de los Reyes (altar of the Kings), begun in 1737 by Jerónimo de Balbas.

Altogether, the church took two and a half centuries to complete and many different architects had a hand in its design. By the end of the seventeenth century, the basalt and sandstone façade had been completed but

the dome and the twin towers, with their collection of 18 bells, were not added until one hundred years later, by Damián Ortiz de Castro. Work was finally finished in 1813 under his successor, Tolsá, an exponent of the Classical style of architecture.

The finished cathedral is at one and the same time the last great example of colonial architecture and the first monument of an independent Mexico.

The cathedral, with its massive, square bell towers and magnificent portals, dominates the Zócala, one of the largest public plazas in the world (main picture)

Excavations around the cathedral: uncovering the remains of the Templo Mayor (below, left)

Plaza Bolivar with the cathedral in the background (main picture)

From this square, Simon Bolivar called South Americans to arms against the ruling colonial powers. A statue in the Plaza commemorates this national hero (right)

In the footsteps of the monks

The Catedral Primada in the Plaza Bolivar in **BOGOTÁ** is an outstanding example of Iberian Classicism

Gonzalez Jiménez de Quesada was one of those adventurers and conquistadors who arrived on the continent of America, newly discovered by Christopher Columbus, determined to find gold and silver, persecute the indigenous Indian population, and convert them to the Christian faith into the bargain. In 1538, he and his party reached a high plateau in the middle of the Andes.

This was home to the Muisca or Chibcha people, who boasted a culture that was as advanced in its own right as that of the Aztecs in Mexico. Their beliefs centered around a ceremony involving gold dust. The region was consequently christened El Dorado, or Land of Gold, by the Spaniards.

Quesada decided to establish a settlement here, consisting of 12 small dwellings as well as a chapel. He named

it after a place called Santafé, a name meaning 'holy faith', situated near his hometown of Granada. The Indian name for the area is Bacatá, meaning a high place, and it does indeed lie at an elevation of 8530ft (2600m) to 9186ft (2800m) above sea level in the fertile savannah of a mountain plateau. To the east rise the mighty peaks of the Andes mountains, with the mountains of Montserrat and Guadelupe beyond.

The historic center of Bogotá is La Candelaria, where one of the twelve dwellings established by Conquistador Quesada in 1538 still stands, marked by a metal plaque giving information about its history. Most of the surrounding buildings are also very old and reflect the architectural style typical of many Andalusian secular buildings built during the period of the Counter Reformation, and featuring carved wooden balconies and patios. Their exteriors are not white, however, like their Iberian counterparts, but painted in tropical reds and greens.

The rarity of Renaissance

The district derives its name from one of its churches, of which there are quite a few. One of the best known is the Clarissa monastery, a Renaissance building constructed after 1619 which is now a museum. Its interior is pure Baroque in style. It is relatively rare to find unadulterated Renaissance architecture in Latin America, the usual architectural style being that of the Iberian Counter Reformation.

During the five hundred years of its existence, Latin America has developed its own, unique cultural traditions. It was inevitable that a certain amount of influence would be assimilated from the mother countries of the colonial rulers, if for no other reason than that the architects stemmed from there and brought their design books with them. Soon, however, the different countries began to develop individual styles of their own, partly determined by the type of building materials available, the limited equipment to hand, and meanwhile influenced by the art of the Indios, whom it was planned to convert to Christianity. This influence was much stronger in the Portuguese territories than the Spanish ones.

At the time of Columbus, the Mannerist style of Late Spanish Gothic was becoming increasingly popular as an architectural trend. It is known as Isabelline, after Queen Isabella of Castile. More commonly, the style is referred to as Plateresque, although technically this is the name of the intricate ornamentation found in the Moorish goldsmith's art. This style was all the rage in Spain at the time of these voyages of discovery and exploration, and spread from there to the New World. Two hundred years later, it was the ornate Late Baroque style of the three Churriguera brothers – the painting of the *Patio de las Escolas* in Salamander is a good example of this – that was influential in developing colonial architecture in Latin America.

Heart of the Old Town

Bogotá's most prominent ecclesiastical building surviving from colonial days is the Catedral Primada in the Plaza Bolívar, which in turn is at the heart of the Old Town district of La Calendaría. The cathedral is already the fourth church to be built on this spot.

It started off with the little wooden church of Quesada the Conquistador. This was later replaced by a stone church, which collapsed in 1560 before it could be finished. Work on a new building began in 1572 and was scheduled to take 30 years, but the tower was not built until 1678. No sooner had the new church, with its nave and two aisles, been completed than it began to crumble. In 1792, a Spanish Capuchin monk called Domingo Petrés, who was also a mathematician and architect, was commissioned by the Academy in Madrid to supervise rebuilding work. Restoration work took from 1807 to 1823 and incorporated the choir and and sections of the choir stalls. Like its predecessor, the church has three aisles, a dome, and numerous side chapels. The façade is flanked by two towers and, at first glance, is quite Baroque in appearance. The Iberian style of Classicism does not have the same degree of simplicity that is characteristic of French or German architecture of the same period.

One of the most remarkable features of the cathedral is the Capilla del Sagrario, which is pure Baroque in style and was built between 1660 and 1700. It possesses Renaissance-style wooden doors, embellished with carvings of figures of archangels and all kinds of elaborate ornamentation which the wood carvers borrowed from designs of imported European copper engravings.

GETTING THERE:
Flights to the city's international airport

OPENING TIMES:
Usually open every day

SPECIAL INTEREST:
The Capilla del Sagrario with its wood carvings

Highest city in the world

Until recently, the official name of the city was Santafé de Bogotá. The old Muisca name has endured and become exclusively accepted. At the beginning of the twentieth century, Bogotá was still a small, almost idyllic little town, which suddenly mushroomed within just 50 years to become one of Latin America's largest urban conglomerations. The city currently numbers eight million inhabitants, although precise statistics are not to hand. The slum district of Ciudás de Bolívar alone is home to one million people. Bogotá ranks before Mexico City as the highest and fastest growing super city in the whole of the New World.

In the image of Seville

The cathedral in Peru's capital city, **LIMA**, is regarded as a unique, artistic masterpiece

GETTING THERE:
Flights to Lima's international airport

OPENING TIMES:
Usually open all day. No admission to tourists during services

SPECIAL INTEREST:
The Plaza de Armas in front of the cathedral

The Spanish conquistadors were a force to be reckoned with. They combined a thirst for adventure, bigotry, a lust for gold, and military strength with extreme brutality. One of their number was Francisco Pizarro, born in 1476 in Trujillo. He sailed for the Americas in 1510 and headed two expeditions exploring the west coast of South America, during which he discovered the advanced Inca civilization in the region now known as Peru. With a small army behind him, he penetrated the heartland of the high plateaux of the southern Cordillera, capturing Atahualpa, the Inca leader. He later had him executed and slaughtered his followers.

In 1535, he founded the settlement later to become known as Lima, making it the center of his administrative rule. He was murdered in 1541 during a subsequent dispute with supporters of another Spanish conquistador; a monument has been erected to him, depicting him on horseback, in the Spanish town where he was born, while his mortal remains are displayed in a glass coffin in Lima cathedral.

Lima took over the role of Peru's capital city from Cuzco, once the capital of the Inca empire and until 1826

the seat of central administration. Peru finally gained national independence in 1821 under the leadership of José de San Martin and Simon Bolívar, following a series of bloody and unsuccessful rebellions.

Bolívar, as well as Martin, were both skilled military tacticians with a charismatic presence. Each came from a wealthy family and underwent qualified training. Clearly influenced by Jean Jacques Rousseau and the ideas of the French Revolution that resonated in the Spanish-American colonies, these two generals conducted successful military campaigns which successfully drove out Spain's colonial troops and brought about the liberation and independence of Bolivia, Ecuador, Chile, Peru, Colombia, and Argentina. The two men ended up in political conflict with one another, however, and eventually both resigned.

Frequent earthquakes

Peru's continued development was punctuated by many extremely dramatic events. There were frequent internal disputes as well as external conflicts, the worst of which was the war against Chile from 1881 to 1883 over the Bolivian saltpeter reserves. The country saw a succession of military and fascist dictatorships, which have persisted until the present day.

Lima's original name was Ciudad de los Reyes (City of Kings). It stretches along the banks of the Rio Rímac, occupying a predominantly dry stretch of coastline between the Pacific and the Andes. Lima boasts the oldest university in Latin America. Earthquakes proved to be a recurrent threat, the worst of which occurred in 1746, destroying almost all the buildings. Chilean soldiers also left a trail of devastation behind them during the saltpeter war. A period of vigorous reconstruction always followed on the heels of such disasters.

The Plaza de Armas

The city and its surrounding districts are now home to around ten million people. The elegant residential districts are San Isidro and Miraflores, while the poor live in typical Latin-American slums otherwise known as 'pueblos jóvenes', or 'young towns'. People certainly do not live to a ripe old age here.

The historical heart of Lima is its main square, the Plaza de Armas, which has existed since the city was

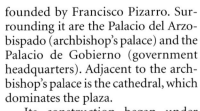

founded by Francisco Pizarro. Surrounding it are the Palacio del Arzobispado (archbishop's palace) and the Palacio de Gobierno (government headquarters). Adjacent to the archbishop's palace is the cathedral, which dominates the plaza.

Its construction began under Pizarro. This initially very modest church was then dedicated in 1540. Twenty-five years later, under Jerónimo de Alayza, it was replaced by a much larger building in what was

considered to be a more representative style of architecture. Lima had meanwhile become the seat of an archbishop. Architecturally speaking, it was modeled on Seville cathedral. Construction work progressed fairly slowly, often coming to a complete standstill. Money was in short supply and the whole project was proving too expensive. Instead of reaching completion, it kept being destroyed by earthquakes. It was not until 1775 that the cathedral finally began to

emerge in its present form and it is always reconstructed to this same design in the event of any damage.

With its majestic façade overlooking the Plaza de Armas, the church is flanked by two Baroque towers. The cathedral of Lima is regarded as a unique artistic achievement and one of the finest sacred buildings in Latin America, on a par with the magnificent cathedrals of Havana and Mexico City. One of the most beautiful features of the interior of the cathe-

dral are undoubtedly the choir stalls. The most impressive chapel is that of the Immaculada, the chapel of the Immaculate Conception, with its lavish, Late Baroque furnishings. There is a carved ivory figure of Christ, a gift from Charles V, upon whose Spanish empire the sun never set. That was all, however, a long time ago.

The main façade with its twin towers (main picture)

View into the Immaculada, the chapel of the Immaculate Conception (below, left)

Crown of Thorns

The cathedral in **BRASILIA**, Brazil's new capital city, is a modern masterpiece

GETTING THERE:
Flights to Brasília's international airport

OPENING TIMES:
Open daily. No admission to tourists during services

SPECIAL INTEREST:
The modern stained-glass panels

The mighty glass corona of this modern cathedral designed by Oscar Niemeyer rises above the city (main picture). Statues of the apostles line the way to the main entrance

The interior puts the visitor in mind of an enormous tent. The blue and white tinted glass panels create a lighting effect that is spiritual in quality (below, right)

The cathedral is also famous for its flying sculptures of angels, aluminium figures created by Alfredo Ceschiatti, Brazil's foremost modern sculptor (below, left)

Many of the more developed industrial countries are witnessing a decline in the role of the Christian church in society. Regrettable (or not) as this may be, it is nevertheless an indisputable fact of life. A diminishing role in public life will inevitably mean a decline in the church's significant role with respect to art. Throughout the entire European Middle Ages, the Church was the most important, sometimes the only, patron of the arts, commissioning works with appropriately religious themes. The Renaissance period signaled the start of a growing preference for more secular themes and sculptures, which by now almost completely dominate contemporary art. Exceptions are few and far between, notably Marc Chagall's Biblical subjects and the Christian sculptures by Ernst Barlach and Gerhard Marcks.

The most striking evidence of this ecclesiastical decline can be seen in the fact that fewer and fewer churches are being built. There are some exceptions, however, such as the justifiably renowned pilgrimage church of Notre Dame du Haut, near Ronchamps in France, built 1950-54 after a design by Le Corbusier, a Swiss-born French architect. The building, consisting of steel and concrete, his preferred material, is a highly symbolic work of abstract sculpture. Oscar Niemeyer Soares Filho, a Brazilian architect of German descent, also worked alongside Le Corbusier for a time.

Niemeyer, born in 1907, is a committed Communist. Yet, like Corbusier, he also builds churches. One of his works, São Francisco in Pampulha near Belo Horizonte, with its undulating roof, its profile resembling a series of waves, and slanting walls, provoked something of a sensation. Niemeyer's other ecclesiastical work is the cathedral in Brasília, the new capital city of Brazil.

Shaped like an aeroplane
The city of Brasília did not exist until 1956. It was inaugurated on 21 April 1960 after just three years of construction. It represents the successful realization of one of the most daring and radical projects ever to leave the drawing board: the building of a new capital city in a hitherto undeveloped part of the country. The scheme was commissioned by President Juscelino

Kubitschek, who wanted to move the government out of the overcrowded and chaotic city of Rio de Janeiro and create a new capital city, a project envisaged by the constitution as long ago as 1891.

The two famous Brazilian architects commissioned with the planning work were Lúcio Costa and Oscar Niemeyer. From above, its outline resembles an aeroplane: The 'fuselage' is the city's main axis on which all the government offices are situated, and along the 'wings' are the embassies and blocks of apartment buildings. The 'cockpit' consists of the Plaza of Three Powers with the congress and government buildings. The presidential palace stands on the shore of a man-made lake, created by damming the Paraná River which encloses the entire city on three sides.

Originally intended for 500,000 people, the population has increased to around two million inhabitants, spawning numerous suburbs includ-ing favelas or slum districts. Thanks to this massive influx of people, however, the city, described by US art critic Robert Hughes, as a "utopian horror," has lost some of its initial sterility. The largest of the city's many churches is the Catedral Metropolitana da Nossa Senhora Aparecida, situated in the government district and designed by Oscar Niemeyer. It easily bears comparison with the pilgrimage chapel attributed to Le Corbusier, his mentor, though on a much larger scale owing to the nature of the building.

Flying angels
From a distance, the cathedral resembles a giant circular tent. Its exterior walls are intersected by 16 enormous concrete struts, arching upwards and inwards towards the middle of the ceiling. They support the roof as well as the glass window panels. The structure measures approximately 233ft (71m) in diameter at its base and 39ft (12m) at its narrowest point, which

is 98ft (30m) above the ground. At this point, the arcs of these buttresses are at their nearest point to each other and enclose the roof. The concrete ribs then arch outwards again, each tapering to a point. This is intended to symbolize the crown of thorns worn by Christ. From the center of the edifice rises a filigree-style cross.

Within the cathedral, suspended under the blue and white glass panels and soaring curved ribs, is the hanging sculpture of an angel, seeming to fly. It looks quite conventional at first glance until you realize that it is made out of aluminium. It was created by Brazil's leading modern sculptor, Alfredo Ceschiatti, who died in 1989. The four giant statues of the apostles, standing sentry as you approach, are also the work of Ceschiatti.

"I did my best to make my buildings different" said Oscar Niemeyer, referring to all his designs for the new capital of Brasília. He certainly succeeded with his cathedral.

Colonial Baroque at its best

The gold of **OURO PRÊTO** financed the building of a unique collection of churches

GETTING THERE:
Flights to Belo Horizonte international airport. About 50 miles (80km) southeast of the airport by bus or car

OPENING TIMES:
Usually from 8:00 A.M. - 8:00 P.M. daily

SPECIAL INTEREST:
The different chapels around the town

Ouro Prêto means 'black gold'. Several towns in different parts of Brazil share this name, indicating that the precious metal was found nearby. Although the various invaders who came to conquer the country did so under the pretext of bringing Christianity to the Indian heathens, it was their gold that was the real magnet.

The Christian religion requires churches, of course, and these were duly built. A good supply of gold in the vicinity was reflected in the richness of a church's furnishings, as was the case in Ouro Prêto, a town situated in the Minas Gerais province, northeast of São Paolo and southeast of Belo Horizonte.

Minas Gerais means 'general mines'. The province was once an important mining region, famous for the large quantities of precious metals that were mined here – not just ouro (gold), but prato (silver) too. Gold was mainly panned from the rivers and, since black Africans were very skilled at this type of work, slave traders shipped in large numbers of slaves from West Africa, predominantly from the Portuguese colony of Angola.

Riches for England

The gold brought from Minas Gerais to Europe during the eighteenth century constituted 50 percent of the world's entire gold reserves. It was gold from Ouro Prêto that financed, among other things, the industrial revolution in England. The discovery of gold brought all the usual evils in its wake – crime, prostitution, feuding, uprisings, and excessive wealth for individuals.

It also brought churches. Ouro Prêto was regarded as a vila rica, a wealthy town. It is situated somewhat inaccessibly right in the middle of a chain of mountains, the Serra do Espinhaço, 3281ft (1000m) above sea-level. Gold was discovered here in 1698 and the town was founded in 1701. The stampede of gold-seekers was overwhelming. By the mid-1700s, Ouro Prêto's population had increased to well over 100,000.

The art of Aleijadinho

The number of inhabitants has now shrunk to barely half this number. Since 1933, when the town was declared a national monument and placed under a conservation order, the heart of the city has been carefully preserved. It contains eleven historic churches alone, the most famous of which is the Igreja São Francisco de Assis. This church was largely the work of architect and sculptor, Antônio Francisco Lisboa.

He lived from 1738 to 1804 and is regarded as one of Latin America's greatest Baroque artists, easily on a par with Gian Lorenzo Bernini or Balthasa Neumann in Europe. He was a mulatto and better known as Aleijadinho, meaning 'little cripple', a reference to his physical disabilities.

He scarcely left the Minas Gerais region and it is here that his most important masterpieces can be found; for example, the 12 figures of the prophets, carved out of soapstone, which he created for the pilgrimage church of Bom Jesus de Matozinhos in Congonhas. The route of the Passion of Christ leading to the church there is lined with 64 life size figures, which he and his assistants carved from cedarwood. The portal, altars, and pulpit in the Igreja Nossa Senhora do Carmo in Ouro Prêto are also his work. Even more important is his work in the church of St. Francis of Assisi.

In the spirit of St. Francis of Assisi

The building is a relatively simple construction, of square design with one nave and a very spacious porch. The façade is capped by two, medium-sized towers with pointed spires. The Baroque gable is crowned by a two-bar cross, while the portal is flanked by two pillars. The walls are very light, with reddish-brown hues, interspersed with small windows. The richly ornate door surround was a

speciality of Aleijadinho. It is made of steatite or soapstone, a building material he particularly favored. This mineral is easy to work and has the additional advantage of hardening when exposed to heat.

Construction work on the church began in 1766 and was commissioned by the Franciscan Order. It was designed by José Perreira dos Santos. After numerous interruptions, work was resumed under José Perreira Arouca and Aleijadinho and completed in 1794. Aleijadinho was also responsible for some of the interior: the pulpit and sculptures are his work. The Baroque paintings lining the ceiling are by Manuel da Costa Ataíde, a contemporary of Aleijadinho and arguably Brazil's most important Baroque artist. The paintings depict scenes from the life of St. Francis of Assis.

The Igreja São Francisco de Assis was built at a time when Classicism was dominating the architectural scene in Europe. Brazil was geographically isolated from such popular trends although, when compared to the Baroque architecture of Hispano America, Ouro Prêto does seem to signal some degree of change. The crippled mulatto of Minas Gerais possessed an astonishing feel for shape and form. He knew that beauty can readily be found in constraint and simplicity.

Morning mists veil the hills above Ouro Prêto. This view across the hillside shows the sprawling collection of churches (below, left)

The monastery with its richly decorated church towers rises above this former mining town (main picture)

The main entrance of São Francisco de Assis in all its Baroque splendor (below, center)

Friday procession outside one of the chapels (below, right)

Rio's cone-shaped cathedral

The Catedral Metropolitana in **RIO DE JANEIRO** is one of the few large modernist cathedral buildings

There are two famous hills in Rio de Janeiro: Sugar Loaf Mountain and, behind it, the 2310ft (704m)-high Corcovado, topped by the statue of Cristo Redentor (Christ the Redeemer). Christ is another 98ft (30m) high and weighs 984 tons (1000 tonnes). He has a full beard and has both arms outstretched, pointing to the two halves of the city, the zona norte (north zone) and the zona sul (south zone). There are many churches in both parts. The Catedral Metropolitana stands in the center, where the two halves meet.

Rio is a Catholic city. Catholicism is the legacy of European colonists from France and Portugal and this is symbolized by the figure of Christ on the Corcovado. It was originally intended as a monument to celebrate the centenary of Brazilian independence from Portugal but, at some point, the money ran out so that they had to turn to the Vatican for financial help. The sculptor of this monumental figure was the Frenchman, Paul Landowski.

Rio de Janeiro means 'January river'. Its Portuguese discoverer, Gaspar de Lemos, arrived at the bay of Guanabara in January 1502 and mistook it for a river mouth. French colonists arrived at almost the same time.

The French and Portuguese fought many bloody battles against each other, which the French lost, although this did not prevent their aristocracy from fleeing to Brazil, and to Rio in particular, during the French Revolution. When Napoleon attacked the Iberian Peninsula not long afterwards, the King of Portugal also fled to Rio de Janeiro.

Patron saint, St. Sebastian

His son Peter declared himself ruler of the newly independent Brazil in 1822. Rio became the capital and remained so until 1960. By this time, the country had long been a republic, preserving a strict separation between church and state. The Catholic church remained powerful, however, which can be seen not only from the many churches in the new capital, Brasilia, but also the many churches, old and new, in the former capital.

The earliest were built by missionaries. The oldest surviving church is the Convento de Santo António, which stands on the mountain above the Largo da Carioca. Building work began in 1607. Now beautifully restored, it is frequented mainly by local women in search of a husband. Among other things, St. Anthony is the patron saint of married couples and lovers.

Near the Convento de Santo António stands the Catedral Metropolitana, which was constructed between 1964 and 1976. Most striking, at first glance, is that it is built of concrete with colored windows made of plastic. The church is named after St. Sebastian, a Christian officer in the Roman Imperial Guard, who refused on religious grounds to sacrifice to the emperor, Diocletian. Because of this, the latter had him executed. He was tied to a tree and arrows were shot at him, until he was thought to be dead.

A memory of the Maya?

That night, Irene, the widow of a court official, came to bury the body, but she detected signs of life in Sebastian, took him away, and cared for him until he was healed. When Sebastian continued to refuse to abandon his faith, however, he was clubbed to death and thrown into the Cloaca Maxima, the main sewer of Rome. Another pious woman, Lucina Anicia, recovered the body and buried it at one of the entrances to the catacombs.

Sebastian is perfectly suited to be the city's patron saint. His repeated sufferings, the fatal attacks against him, and his sorry end in the sewer befit the sprawling slums with their smoking rubbish tips and hundreds of thousands of inhabitants.

Designed by local architect Joaquim Corréa, the Catedral Metropolitana stands in a large, open, landscaped area and is shaped like a cone that is missing its tip. Church leaders attach great importance to the idea that this shape pays artistic homage to Mayan temple buildings.

Room for 20,000 people

Mayan pyramids, however, had a square base, whereas the base of the Catedral Metropolitana is circular. The Maya lived – as they do today – in Mexico, Honduras, and Guatemala, a long way north of Brazil and Rio de Janeiro and, moreover, being mainly colonized by the Spanish, they are therefore still Spanish-speaking.

It was probably just the desire to be original, with perhaps a small gesture of reparation for the bloodbaths of the Christian conquistadors, but a suitably large church, 262ft (80m) high and 348ft (106m) in diameter, was commissioned for this city of over a million inhabitants. It covers an area of 9569 square yards (8000 square meters) and can hold 20,000 people, with seats for 5000. The altar is precisely in the middle. The various colorful figures in the four giant windows symbolize the four attributes of the one, holy Catholic and apostolic church.

The Catedral Metropolitana also runs a radio station, one of many in this city. It puts great emphasis on broadcasting spiritual programmes.

GETTING THERE:
Via the international airport

OPENING TIMES:
Usually open all day. No admission for tourists during Mass

SPECIAL INTEREST:
The figure of Christ overlooking the city

The shape of the cathedral in Rio recalls Sugar Loaf Mountain, the symbol of the city (main picture)

Inside the church, the light plays impressively through the cruciform windows (below)

The towers of the people

The cathedral of **SÃO PAULO** is a symbol of South American liberation theology

São Paulo's main shopping street is called the Avenida Paulista. It is a noisy, wide, and very busy avenue, lined with high-rise, gray, concrete buildings, accommodating banks, commercial companies, and expensive shops. Interspersed with these is an occasional, white, colonial-style villa, dating from the nineteenth century, with pillared entrances and palm trees in their gardens. These former residences of the country's coffee and sugar-cane barons are now restaurants or cultural institutions.

São Paulo owes its existence and growth to trade and wealth. In 1920, the city numbered barely half a million residents; today it is home to around 20 million people, making it Brazil's largest city, a center of trade and industry and a financial capital. One in nine of the country's total population and half the nation's industry are located here.

It was named after St. Paul the Apostle, long after it was first established. The missionary station, founded by the Jesuits in 1554, was initially called Piritinaga after the high plateau on which it is built. For two centuries, the settlement was nothing more than a village with a few clay churches. Then, in 1681, it became the center of the captaincy of São Vicente, and was renamed São Paulo in 1710. One year later, it was officially recognized as a town.

'Colonial theology'

These religious names cannot disguise the fact that conditions here were rough and profane in the extreme. Black African slaves were shipped in to work the gold mines in the region later known as Minas Gerais. The slave traders, the bandeirantes, had their headquarters in São Paolo. Even the church kept its own slaves. The statistics are fairly depressing: in 1729 the Benedictine Order had two monasteries and three hospices with altogether 144 slaves, while the Carmelites had three convents and one hospice with a total of 431 slaves. The church's attempts to justify its association with slavery were known as 'colonial theology' and its involvement was passed off as a form of missionary work.

The realization that such a situation was deeply ahorrent from a Christian point of view was very slow to dawn. A Brazilian independence movement began to gather in São Paulo. In 1822, it officially broke away from Portugal. The irredentists, who were worldly intellectuals, were also joined by Dom Mateus de Abreu Pereira, a prominent religious leader.

The church dignitaries similarly supported the abolition of slavery. There were, after all, approximately 174,000 slaves living in São Paulo around 1850. In 1853, a ban on importing any further slaves was imposed and, in 1871, parliament proclaimed that any children of enslaved mothers were henceforth free citizens. The general abolition of slavery followed in 1888.

Two front towers of 1967

São Paulo had long since had its own Sé, or cathedral. A photograph dating from 1862 shows an imposing church in the Latin-American Baroque style, with attractively undulating gables and a somewhat squat-looking tower.

The Baroque cathedral was demolished in 1911 and a bank now stands on the spot it once occupied. Construction of a new church commenced in 1913 in a different location. The foundation stone was laid by the incumbent archbishop at that time, Duarte Leopoldo e Silva.

Progress was slow and, by 1933, the floor had only just been laid. It was 1954 before the cathedral could be consecrated on the occasion of the 400th anniversary of the founding of São Paulo, and even then it was still not complete. The two front towers were not finished until 1967 and were called, somewhat poignantly, 'towers of the people'.

Was this a nod in the direction of liberation theology? This possibility cannot be excluded, given the fact that one of the most prominent leaders of the movement was the Brazilian Dom Hélder Câmara. It also included a São Paulo priest by the name of Paulo Evaristo Arns.

São Paulo cathedral is a majestic church with two tapering towers and a mighty dome over the crossing. The walls are light-colored and the architectural style is New Gothic. Why this particular style, which was waning in popularity by the end of the nineteenth century, was chosen and unwaveringly adhered to right into the mid-twentieth century remains a mystery known only to the architects. There were ample breaks in the building process, providing numerous opportunities to alter the design plans.

Nearby is the Pátio do Colegio, situated on the precise spot where the Jesuits founded their mission in 1554. The Colegio and church have been restored in the colonial style. They are on a much smaller scale than the cathedral and very beautiful.

View of the central plaza and cathedral dedicated in 1954

Cathedral for Catholics

St. Mary's in SYDNEY was founded by British clergymen

Coral
Sea

AUSTRALIA

Sydney

INDIAN
OCEAN

Tasman Sea

GETTING THERE:
Via the city's
international airport

OPENING TIMES:
Usually open all day.
No entry for tourists
during Mass

SPECIAL INTEREST:
The stained glass and
the rose window

Sydney is situated on the south-east coast of Australia and, with 3.25 million inhabitants, is its most populous city. In the eighteenth century, the British sea captain, James Cook, was the first foreigner to set foot in this area. The history of the city is in many ways identical with the development of the continent. For a long time, Australia had only a virtual existence. Early modern cartographers suspected that there was a land mass here and drew it in on their charts without having seen it.

Explorers from Spain and Portugal sailed close to it. Dutchmen made

a brief acquaintance with it. First the British, then a little later the French, took possession of the continent, but English interest lasted longer. Following the American War of Independence, they needed to find other areas to which the inmates of the overcrowded English gaols could be transported. Australia was the choice.

Sydney began as a penal colony. The first inhabitants were recruited from 759 prisoners and 211 marine infantrymen who were responsible for guarding them. Captain Arthur Phillip was in command of the colony. The 11 ships carrying them

arrived in Port Jackson on 26 January 1788. The date is commemorated as Australia Day – it might just as well be called Sydney Day – and is celebrated appropriately.

The settlement was called Sydney Cove from the then British Home Secretary, Thomas Townshend, 1st Viscount Sydney. Faced with the problem of finding sufficient food and sources of income, their first idea was wheat growing; later on, they turned to rearing livestock, especially sheep. Australian wool soon became much sought after in the Old World and provided necessary supplies for

the English spinning mills.

Foundation stone laid 1821

The majority of Australians have ancestors who came from the British Isles, not only as prisoners but also as adventurers and often driven by economic necessity. A considerable proportion were Irish Catholics. Among today's religious communities, Catholicism and Anglicanism are equally represented. The most important church in Sydney is the Catholic St. Mary's cathedral.

The first Catholic priests, John Therry and Philip Conolly, arrived in the colony in May 1820. The foundation stone for a chapel dedicated to the Mother of God, a stone church on the edge of the town, was laid the next year. In 1835, the first Catholic bishop of Sydney was appointed and St. Mary's became a cathedral. Thirty

years later, it was completely burned down.

In 1851, Sydney had 60,000 inhabitants. Archbishop Polding blessed the foundation stone of a new cathedral in 1868. The architect's name was Wardell, and the building was to be in the Neo-Gothic style, which was then in fashion for new churches across the globe. Throughout the industrialized world, fast-expanding cities were rapidly acquiring churches with point-arched windows, buttresses, and flying buttresses.

Designated a basilica minor

St. Mary's cathedral in Sydney was consecrated in 1905. It was certainly not finished at the time; in fact, a further 23 years would pass before its completion. In 1930, Pope Pius XI accorded it the rank and title of basilica minor. Pope Paul VI preached there in 1970. The Polish Pope John Paul II (Karol Wojtyla), a keen traveler, has visited it twice. The architect William Wardell, who was born in 1823, came originally from England where he had made a name for himself as an advocate of British Neo-Gothic. He emigrated to Australia in 1858 and settled in Melbourne. His first building in Sydney was St. John's College for the University, which left such a deep impression on Bishop Polding that he commissioned Wardell to build the new cathedral. Moreover, the architect had recently converted to Catholicism.

St. Mary's has features of the English style of High Gothic architecture known as Decorated. The church is built of Australian sandstone. It has a façade with double towers reaching to a height of 245ft (74.6m). The tower above the crossing is about 98ft (30m) lower and the building is 351ft (107m) long.

The interior is the usual high hall with arcaded galleries; it has mosaic floors. One of the chapels is dedicated to Irish saints. Light enters through colorful stained glass windows. The high altar is of marble and among the statues is a painted Madonna which is very elegant and charming. The Catholic bishops of Sydney are buried in the crypt.

Neo-Gothic in Australia

St. Patrick's cathedral in **MELBOURNE** is the church of those of Irish descent

GETTING THERE:
Via the city's international airport. Good road links from Sydney

OPENING TIMES:
Normally open all day

SPECIAL INTEREST:
Gargoyles in imitation of medieval church architecture

Melbourne has almost three million inhabitants and is the second biggest city in Australia after Sydney. Unlike other parts of the country, it did not originate as a penal colony. The bay at the mouth of the Yarra River was discovered in 1803 and the first voluntary immigrants arrived in 1835. It was named after a British Prime Minister, William Lamb, 2nd Viscount Melbourne. The city experienced a period of rapid growth in the middle of the nineteenth century when gold was discovered nearby.

On 9 April 1850, the Catholic bishop of Melbourne, James Goold, laid the foundation stone for the building of a new cathedral. The area, Eastern Hill, had previously been used for grazing sheep. To start with, only a comparatively modest church was envisaged, but when the city suddenly expanded a larger building was planned. The commission was awarded to William Wilkinson Wardell, the harbinger of the English Gothic Revival – the British version of Neo-Gothic – who had recently arrived as an immigrant. Wardell was also the architect of St. Mary's cathedral in Sydney, so the same man was responsible for designing the two Catholic diocesan churches in the two biggest cities of the fifth continent. They are naturally, therefore, somewhat similar.

There is a considerable difference between Medieval English Gothic and that found in France and Germany. Political relations between England and France had broken down as a result of the continual conflict over supremacy in France, ultimately resulting in the Hundred Years' War and a severance in cultural communications. Whilst the Norman upper classes in England had actually come from France, with the royal house at their head they considered themselves as a separate cultural and political entity, with unique origins and rights.

Thick wall technique

Thus English Gothic created its own artistic standards, though never denying its Norman roots. It founded its own tradition, whose hallmarks in church architecture include the chapter house, the completely rectangular shape of the choir, and the Lady chapel. The cathedrals turned out to be relatively low, with the buttresses of their aisles hidden under the roofs. The Norman technique of murs épais (thick walls) continued in use, running completely counter to Continental Gothic with its thinned-down walls. The English Gothic Revival quite naturally looked back to those kinds of elements, both at home and in the colonies.

The first section of Melbourne cathedral was consecrated in 1858, being completed in 1897 under Bishop Goold's successor, Carr. The costs, met by zealous fundraising and donations, had by this time amounted to £200,000 sterling. Later building activities, apart from restoration work, centered particularly on the spires of the two towers, which were only erected between 1937 and 1938. In 1974, Pope Paul VI conferred on the cathedral the rank of basilica minor, a particularly important church outside Italy. This rank is symbolized by the papal tiara above the crossed keys on the arms of the cathedral.

Simple façade

It is named after St. Patrick, the patron saint of Ireland, making clear that a large proportion of the Catholics in Australia, or at any rate in Melbourne, are of Irish descent. St. Patrick's prides itself on being amongst the most beautiful places of worship in the country. Pale yellow sandstone was used in its construction. The façade with its two towers crowned with spires is striking in its simplicity, without extra statuary or exaggerated ornamentation. Only a wrought bronze gate directly in front of the entrance ameliorates this impression. In addition, in direct imitation of medieval churches, there are a number of gargoyles – demonically grotesque half-figures – which serve simultaneously to channel away rainwater from the roof and frighten off evil spirits.

The interior of St. Patrick's is impressive, due to the effects of light and shade and various other details, including mosaics. One of the altars shows Isaac about to be sacrificed by his father Abraham, just prior to God's intervention. Compared with other works of this genre, it is astonishingly restrained and refined. Another, rather less subtle, mosaic shows the Holy Family during the flight into Egypt: Mary and the infant Jesus on a donkey being led by Joseph.

Another picture, a painted panel, is of St. Augustine, who was bishop of Hippo Regius in North Africa at the end of the fourth century. Today, the place is known as Annaba and is part of Muslim Algeria. Augustine, who studied theology and philosophy in Carthage, was one of the most important Christian thinkers and represented Catholics in a country from which Christians have now migrated. So it is natural that, in a country that many of them experience as immigrants, Catholics should appeal to St. Augustine.

General view of St. Patrick's, built in the English Neo-Gothic style (main picture)

View of the main altar and interior of the church (below)

PHOTO CREDITS

IMPRINT

© copyright: REBO international b.v., Lisse, The Netherlands

Published and edited by: Dr. Manfred Leier

Text: Rolf Schneider (8 - 13, 16 - 19, 24 - 51, 56 - 57, 72 - 77, 80 - 107, 112 - 115, 118 - 137, 140 - 147, 152 - 161, 166 - 207) Anne Benthues (14 - 15, 20 - 23, 52 - 55, 58 - 71, 78 - 79, 108 - 111, 116 - 117, 148 - 151, 162 - 165) Arno Rattay (138 - 139)

Graphics: BartosKersten Printmediendesign, Hamburg

Photo editing: Maria Hoffmann, photonetwork/Hamburg

Copy editing and editorial technology: Edwine Bollmann, Peter Rieprich / Hamburg

Documentation: Mathias Güntner

Production: HVK Hamburger Verlagskontor GmbH / Germany

English translation by Susan Ghanouni and Rae Walter in association with First Edition Translations Ltd., Cambridge, England

Typesetting: The Write Idea in association with First Edition Translations Ltd., Cambridge, England

Proofreading: Jarmila Peskova Skranakova, skranakova@rebo-publishers.cz